ROUTLEDGE LIBRARY EDITIONS:
FAMILY

I0127933

Volume 6

HOUSING AND YOUNG FAMILIES IN EAST LONDON

HOUSING AND YOUNG FAMILIES IN EAST LONDON

ANTHEA HOLME

Routledge
Taylor & Francis Group

LONDON AND NEW YORK

First published in 1985 by Routledge & Kegan Paul plc

This edition first published in 2023
by Routledge
4 Park Square, Milton Park, Abingdon, Oxon OX14 4RN

and by Routledge
605 Third Avenue, New York, NY 10158

Routledge is an imprint of the Taylor & Francis Group, an informa business

British Library Cataloguing in Publication Data
A catalogue record for this book is available from the British Library

ISBN: 978-1-032-51072-9 (Set)
ISBN: 978-1-032-54237-9 (Volume 6) (hbk)
ISBN: 978-1-032-54238-6 (Volume 6) (pbk)
ISBN: 978-1-003-41586-2 (Volume 6) (ebk)

DOI: 10.4324/9781003415862

Publisher's Note
The publisher has gone to great lengths to ensure the quality of this reprint but points out that some imperfections in the original copies may be apparent.

Disclaimer
The publisher has made every effort to trace copyright holders and would welcome correspondence from those they have been unable to trace.

HOUSING AND
YOUNG FAMILIES
IN EAST LONDON

Anthea Holme

with a foreword by
Michael Young

ROUTLEDGE & KEGAN PAUL
London, Boston, Melbourne and Henley

First published in 1985
by Routledge & Kegan Paul plc

14 Leicester Square, London WC2H 7PH, England

9 Park Street, Boston, Mass. 02108, USA

464 St Kilda Road, Melbourne,
Victoria 3004, Australia and

Broadway House, Newtown Road,
Henley on Thames, Oxon RG9 1EN, England

Set in Garamond, 10 on 12pt
by Input Typesetting Ltd, London
and printed in Great Britain
by Hartnoll Print, Bodmin, Cornwall

Library of Congress Cataloging in Publication Data

Holme, Anthea.
Housing and young families in east London.
(Reports of the Institute of Community Studies)
Bibliography: p.
Includes index
1. Housing—England—London. 2. Family—England—
London. 3. Housing—England—Wanstead and Woodford (Essex)
4. Family—England—Wanstead and Woodford (Essex)
5. Bethnal Green (London, England) I. Title. II. Series.
HD7334.L6H65 1985   363.5'1'094215   84–17999

British Library CIP also available

ISBN 0–7102–0362–4

For Christopher

CONTENTS

Contents

Contents

FOREWORD

If history cannot repeat itself, neither can anything else. When a willow puts forth its catkins it is legitimate to say it is doing so 'again'. The willow is always one of the first messengers of spring. But for the tree each successive spring is different. Each willow is older. Its climatic environment is different. For each person taking delight in it the burgeoning tree also seems different from the last time, depending upon what the tree is like in the spring of 1985, or 1986, or 1987, and what the observer is like at these conjunctions between tree and person. If that is true of events whose marked similarity from one year to another provides part of the seeming stability which gives order to our lives, so much the more is it true of repeats in sequence of the 'same' observations by different observers, and even more so when the observations are not intended to be as much alike as the flux of time will allow.

Anthea Holme has not focused on the same things as my colleague, Peter Willmott, and myself when we made two studies in the 1950s. One was in Bethnal Green and Greenleigh, the fictitious name we gave to the Debden estate in Essex to which Bethnal Greeners were sent down the Central Line;[1] the other in Woodford.[2] We wanted to study family life in different environments as they presented themselves to us in the 1950s. Anthea Holme wanted to study housing but against the background of family life in the 1980s. Two of the places being the same, and some of the interests, certain comparisons *can* be drawn and, from her angle, the author has when she wished referred back a quarter of a century in order to underline what she is saying about a past more recent than that.

The author has raised again a question which was already an important one in the 1950s. Have inequalities between Bethnal Green and Woodford been becoming greater or less? A difficult issue. But from my angle, which is more that of someone from the more distant looking forward to the more recent past, certain impressions do stand out.

To say that the 'standard of life' has generally risen since the 1950s is more odd than it seems. Everything people consume is packed together in that parcel labelled the 'standard of life'. This means that, over a period, like can never be compared with like; what is consumed is always changing. Moreover, the implication is that the 'rise' is also an 'improvement', and that clearly need not be so. People spend more now, even in real terms, on the rents of flats in new tower blocks than they used to on the rents of old houses on the ground. Their standard of life has on that account been regarded as having risen. But few of the tenants who have had both experiences would claim it is an improvement to be parallel, up in the air, over where they used to live, on the ground. Most of them would consider that the rise has been a fall.

But on the other counts there would, I think, be more agreement. It is an improvement to have a mobile room in the form of a Ford or an Austin; it is an improvement also to dispose of more machines inside the dwelling, and to own an array of tools and equipment for maintaining its quality. In many such respects Bethnal Green and Woodford seem to be more alike than they were. If we had in the 1950s foreseen all this clearly, we might have concluded that by the 1980s there would be less inequality than there was at the time of writing.

More homogeneity

It may be stretching the words to talk in terms of equality/inequality. But if we had known what was to happen, we would have forecast another kind of move towards greater homogeneity (to change the notion a bit). For the style of life has altered in a way which matters as much as the extra cars, TV sets, washing machines and paint-rollers.

Bethnal Green was in the 1950s most obviously different from Woodford in the extent to which there was a public life.

In Bethnal Green [we said in the Woodford book], there are noisy people everywhere, large mothers with oilskin shopping bags, young mothers in red high-heeled shoes, children playing around the stalls of the street markets, neighbours talking to each other from one door to another. The suburb is sliced by main roads, and the long-distance buses speeding to Southend and Newmarket leave only a distant hum in hundreds of empty sideroads. In Bethnal Green people are vigorously at home in the streets, their public face much the same as their private.

In one particular street in the East End

On the warm summer evening of the interview, children were playing hop-scotch or 'he' in the roadway while their parents, when not watching the television, were at their open windows. Some of the older people were sitting in upright chairs on the pavement, just in front of their doors, or in the passages leading through to the sculleries, chatting with each other and watching the children at play.

By the 1980s Bethnal Green has become more like Woodford, that is apart from the most westerly part of it which has become the home of the Bangladeshis. They are the successors of the Huguenots and Jews who settled there after earlier persecutions. The life of their men if not their women is much more communal than it is in the rest of the district. For the most part Bethnal Green and Woodford are, to use Orwell's description, both 'sleeping the deep, deep sleep of England'.

The new class division

Anthea Holme's main conclusion is, however, not that. It is that in one vital respect inequality has increased. In the 1950s Bethnal Green was still moving out of the era of private tenancies of unfurnished dwellings into the era of council housing. Owner occupation was clearly going to expand. What we did not know, and had no means of foretelling, was that the stock of council housing would, after a further growth, move into a steady decline. We did not know that once the street-people of Bethnal Green no longer engaged in street-politics, once they had been separated from each other, the political force favouring council housing would be weakened to the extent it has been.

The result has been a running down of public housing – so much so that if more is not spent on its upkeep vast numbers of further properties in the public domain are going to become slums. If they are not pulled down they will fall down. The greater the neglect the stronger the push to move into owner occupation. The combination of the push of neglect and the pull of tax incentives has been powerful, and will become more so.

If no other goal ever had to be considered we could consider the present, even if it were a long-drawn-out present, merely as a phase of transition until eventually everybody was an owner occupier. That cannot happen. Many people cannot become long-term mortgagees. The unemployed cannot. The old cannot take out 20-year loans. The single parent families cannot, nor the disabled, nor the chronically sick, nor many others who have not the entry qualifications for this housing market.

Such people are forced into a position of less eligibility from which there is no escape. Anthea Holme reports that taxi-drivers will not come to certain estates, firms will not rent TV sets and even GPs called out for home visits are said to discriminate against them. If public housing continues to deteriorate the minority of people who live in the Bethnal Greens of our inner cities will become absolutely worse off with every year that passes and in relative terms even more disadvantaged in comparison to the not-so-silent majority in the booming private sector. In the final quarter of the century, housing[3] is becoming the great sorter of people into the deprived on the one hand and the privileged on the other.

Michael Young

References

1 *Family and Kinship in East London*, Routledge & Kegan Paul, 1957 and Penguin after.
2 *Family and Class in a London Suburb*, Routledge & Kegan Paul, 1960, and the New English Library thereafter.
3 See P. Goldblatt and J. Fox, 'Household Mortality from the OPCS Longitudinal Study', *Population Trends*, No. 14, Winter 1978.

ACKNOWLEDGMENTS

This study was funded by the Leverhulme Trust Fund. I am most grateful for their generous support and the freedom they have allowed me in carrying out the work. My second great debt of gratitude is to the families who gave so freely of their time and whose experiences and opinions form the basis of this book.

There are many other people I should like to thank most warmly. There are those with whom I discussed the project in its exploratory and later phases, in particular, Bob Brett, Vere Hole, Chris Holmes, Bernard Ineichen, Valerie Karn, Linda McDowell, Janet Madge, Della Nevitt, Jan Pahl, Anne Power, Oriel Sullivan, Elizabeth Watson and Stephen Wolkind. Then there was the help and co-operation of members of the two main area health authorities – City and East London and Redbridge and Waltham Forest – which enabled me to draw my samples for the pilot and main studies. I am thinking especially in Tower Hamlets Health District of Dr Jean Richards, then Acting District Community Physician, Miss S. M. Mowatt, Divisional Nursing Officer, Mrs Christine Christophe, District Nursing Officer, the Nursing Officers and nursing staff of the London and Mile End Hospitals and the Chairman, Professor J. M. Ledingham and members of the District Ethics Committee; and in East Roding Health District of Dr A. Clay, District Community Physician, Dr Gerald McEnery, Consultant Paediatrician, Whipps Cross Hospital, Miss G. Mays, Divisional Midwifery Nursing Officer, the nursing staff of Whipps Cross Hospital, Mrs M. Warnes and Mrs E. Blundy of Redbridge and Waltham Forest Community Health Services and Dr Jennifer Webb, Senior Registrar, Community Medicine; and of Dr Bernard Lawrence, then Consultant Paediatrician, Queen Elizabeth Hospital for Children. I am also much indebted to the senior officers and staff of the housing and planning departments of the London Boroughs of

Acknowledgments

Tower Hamlets and Redbridge and the Greater London Council for their time and practical help, particularly to Mr C. Rodhouse, Mr A. Stungo, Mr M. Pettit, Mr T. Slater and Mr W. A. Tomlinson.

My task was eased by the provision of 1981 Census data hot from the press and by advice and help generally on statistical matters. In this connection I should like to mention Alfred Maizels and also Bill Armstrong of the Greater London Council Research and Intelligence Unit. I am very grateful to Peter Willmott for taking the time to read the text and for his comments.

I am greatly indebted to my colleagues at the Institute of Community Studies. It is impossible to measure my appreciation of Michael Young's advice on the design of the study and the presentation of the material. Though he must not be held responsible for the opinions expressed in this book, many of them would not have surfaced without his comment and criticism. I was especially fortunate in my interviewing team. Alistair Allender, Tessa Bain, Quita Glynn and Joan Wides had exceptional skills and were delightful to work with; Suphia Ahmed gently but firmly interpreted not only language but also cultural differences. I should also like to thank Elspeth Arnold and Sue Chisholm very much for their patience and exemplary typing. But perhaps my greatest debt of gratitude is to Wyn Tucker, the perfect colleague. Always supportive and patient, she made available her fund of experience and skill with great generosity and invariable good humour. Her name should have appeared more prominently but, with characteristic modesty, she insisted that it should not.

Finally my special thanks go to my husband, Christopher Holme, who kept me going at all stages and whose many valuable suggestions have helped to improve the text.

NOTE ON NAMES, PLACES AND TERMS

1 All the families have been given fictitious names. Occasionally, without falsifying the findings, other means have been taken to conceal their identity if renaming did not seem enough. For families from parts of the world where there are different naming systems I have given husbands and wives a common family name.

2 Housing estates in the two study areas have also been given fictitious names.

3 The comparisons are with two districts where studies were made in the 1950s. Bethnal Green was then an independent borough; so was Wanstead and Woodford. Under the London Government Act of 1963 they were each absorbed into a newly-created London Borough – Bethnal Green into Tower Hamlets, Wanstead and Woodford into Redbridge. To give a basis for comparison of the two periods, I used the original borough boundaries within which to draw the two samples.

4 The sample family for the purposes of this study stands for the two parents, or lone parent, and their child. I make it clear when I am discussing the extended or wider family.

5 Some of the mothers were single; some of the couples were not married. To keep things as simple as possible, I have nearly always referred to them as mothers and fathers. There are occasions, however, where to avoid confusion or circumlocutions I have described the couples as wives and husbands, including, with apologies, the co-habitees.

6 A 'home of your own' or a 'place of your own' is not to be confused with 'an owned home'. The reader, I am sure, does not need me to spell out the difference.

INTRODUCTION

This is a study of one small part of family life in two small parts of London. Bethnal Green is inner city; it belongs to the 'East End'.[1] Wanstead and Woodford, which I shall for convenience henceforth call 'Woodford', is an East London outer suburb. In my choice of these two places I have followed an earlier 'journey across the Hackney Marshes' made by Peter Willmott and Michael Young in the late 1950s.[2] They made the journey because they wished to compare family and community life in Bethnal Green, which they had studied earlier,[3] with a suburb containing a 'high proportion of middle-class people'. I wanted to see what changes might have occurred in both places, especially what had happened to housing and how this now affected the lives of people in the first stages of forming their families.

People in Bethnal Green had shown strong attachment to the neighbourhood, in which most of them had spent all their lives, and strong family bonds – between mothers and daughters over three generations and between the wider kinship groups. They were warm and friendly; they 'knew everyone'.[4] But things were different out on the new housing estate of Greenleigh on the Essex edge of London where so many Bethnal Green families were rehoused during the 1950s. There people were 'cut off from their relatives, suspicious of their neighbours, lonely'.[5] What my predecessors had found in Bethnal Green was possibly, they thought, 'peculiar to the working class – and in cities to the older central areas'.[6] The second of these two propositions was confirmed in Greenleigh. There the pattern of family and community life had been scarred by uprooting and separation from kin. But the new estate was still predominantly working class. The effects of social class were evident in Woodford. There, too, family life had changed, but not in all the expected ways. Kinship ties were looser;

1

the old were nevertheless cared for. Wives were more independent of their mothers in Woodford than in Bethnal Green but 'the feminine relationship was still stressed'. Both places were friendly but in different ways. The Woodford working class had to assert itself against a dominant middle class. Bethnal Green was a one-class community which gave its residents their strength.[7]

The 'inner city' and the 'outer suburb', as descriptions, precisely denote places within or on the edge of 'relatively large, dense and permanent settlements of socially heterogeneous people'.[8] They can, however, take on various shades of meaning – according, perhaps, to the tenets of a particular school of urban sociology or of the current conventional wisdom. These days, the term 'inner city' has come to mean something it did not mean a quarter of a century ago. The seat of government – Westminster – is in 'central London', like its twin city, the City of London; people living in Mayfair or Belgravia live in or near 'the centre'. It is people in Brixton or Bethnal Green who live in the 'inner city' and the implication is that they live in problem areas. Such areas these days may even lie outside the inner ring. It is the same in Liverpool and Birmingham and other great cities. We read almost daily of the interacting problems of dereliction and decay, poor housing, unemployment, population decline, inadequate services.

'Suburb', especially when converted into 'suburbia', also evokes a host of notions about ways of life and types of building. People move outwards from cities in search of space and freedom to breathe – that is part of the definition. But the places they have moved to have changed over the years and, with the changes, comment – rarely neutral[9] – has fluctuated from the panegyrical or nostalgic to the condescending or downright disparaging. Lewis Mumford, though recognising its value in 'the development of a new type of open plan and the new distribution of urban functions'[10] and giving high praise to garden cities, is generally deeply critical of the twentieth-century suburb, with its 'low-grade uniform environment'[11] and its 'bland ritual of competitive spending . . . an asylum for the preservation of illusion'.[12] But the debate continues. Three defenders have met the challenge head on in the title of their book: *Dunroamin: The Suburban Semi and Its Enemies*.[13] Popenoe, on the other hand, is concerned about the effects of suburban living on at least half of the resident populations – the women, teenagers, elderly, handicapped and, increasingly, the suburban poor.[14] These groups, in his view, suffer mainly because they are mostly without access to a car.

City populations are in a state of constant flux as new waves move in and others move out. The suburb and the inner city are not as divorced from each other as they seem. People tend to stay within the same sector or wedge. Woodford was selected in the 1950s partly because it was the place to which Bethnal Greeners had gone. In a later book this kind of migration was described as 'sectoral centrifugal movement'.[15] The movement began well before the middle of this century. Improved methods of transport have accelerated it, enabling the less well-to-do to follow their earlier richer fellow citizens along the main rail and road transport routes radiating from the centre. 'People mostly go to the nearest place with space for new houses.'[16] Ten years ago migration within the same sector over a period of ten years was found to be as high as 81 per cent of people (whose place of origin was known) moving within the Inner and Outer Metropolitan Region.[17] Coming for the moment to the present study, probably some of Mr Turner's family were of this kind. He told us that his grandfather was the first of the family to move from Bethnal Green to a district near to Woodford in 1958.

What had happened in the two neighbourhoods and to the link between them during the last twenty-five years? Universal change, notably in patterns of consumption, would have reduced differences between the two places. Would housing also have been a force for bringing them together or had it pushed them further apart? How significant was housing *tenure* in creating or reinforcing differences in the housing circumstances of young families? How much were their housing aspirations subject to social and economic influences or those of family background, over which they could have little or no control? The earlier Bethnal Green study was 'about the effect of one of the newest upon one of the oldest of our social institutions'.[18] The new was the housing estate, the old the family. The influence of housing was implicit in much of what was discovered in the Woodford study. I have chosen to study only families who had just had their first child. As well as bringing happiness, the birth can cause stress, and one cause of stress at this time may be worry about housing.

The relationship between housing and the family cycle is clearly important.[19] According to Gans, along with social class, the fact that needs differ according to stages in the family life cycle is the most important explanation for people's preferences for housing and neighbourhoods.[20] Donnison has outlined five 'housing stages', of which the third begins with the birth of the first child.[21] In an ideal world there would be housing available to correspond with the wishes and needs of individuals and families at all stages of their lives. Take simply four basic needs: shelter; adequacy of space and amenity – adequacy, that is, according to currently accepted standards; proximity to place of work and amenities appropriate to the stage of life in a particular family (schooling, for example, or support in old age). Such needs call for a condition, flexibility and distribution of the housing stock which it cannot meet today. And this leaves wishes altogether out of account – preference for neighbourhood, tenure, type of dwelling, social amenities, aesthetic qualities, and so on. The young families in my sample expressed clear preferences which arose partly from their new family circumstances and partly, as will appear, from other causes.

Social stratification by housing is no new phenomenon. In the nineteenth century the 'rich man in his castle' and the 'poor man at his gate' were descendants of similar rich and poor men and women who had dwelt in castles or cottages or had no home at all since time immemorial. Nor is there anything new in the premium set on the ownership of property – characterised in present times as a 'deep and natural desire'.[22] 'There is nothing', wrote William Blackstone in 1793, 'which so generally strikes the imagination and engages the affections of mankind, as the right of property.'[23] And on the same tack here is Mr Wace the brewer in *Felix Holt*: 'There isn't a greater pleasure than . . . improving one's buildings and investing one's money in some pretty acres of land'.[24]

What is new in Britain is the proportion of people who can nowadays indulge this 'pleasure' and also the fact that ownership of domestic property has come to hold a significance far beyond pleasure. It is now a material element in major political, economic and social issues. This century has seen an astonishing change in the tenure of its housing. Before the First World War, 'so little interest was taken in owner occupation that no contemporary figures exist about the numbers of owner occupiers',[25] though they are estimated to have been as few as 10 per cent of the total number of householders.[26] The remaining 90 per cent were mostly tenants of private landlords. In the ensuing years these proportions have gradually reversed until today over 60 per cent of households are in owner occupation and a mere 11 per cent are privately rented.[27] The other great change dating back to the First World War was brought about by local authority housing. This now stands at less than 29 per cent of the total housing stock.[28] In a spirit of social reform, or some might say social control, it was originally intended for the 'working classes', as testified in the following extract from the King's Speech to Representatives of the Local Authorities and Societies at Buckingham Palace, quoted from *The Times* of 12 April 1919 by Burnett:[29]

> While the housing of the working classes has always been a question of the greatest social importance never has it been so important as now. It is not too much to say that an adequate solution of the housing question is the foundation of all social progress . . . The first point at which the attack must be delivered is the unhealthy, ugly, overcrowded house in the mean street, which all of us know too well. If a healthy race is to be reared, it can be reared only in healthy homes; if drink and crime are to be successfully combated, decent sanitary houses must be provided; if unrest is to be converted into contentment, the provision of good houses may prove one of the most potent agents for that conversion.

Thus, publicly-subsidised housing as a welfare service was born, and the seeds of stratification by housing tenure sown. The stocks of completed dwellings grew with the attractions. Public housing provided relative security and, certainly at that time, prospects of a better-maintained property and a better-disposed landlord. At the same time private ownership became more and more a financially and socially desirable goal.

Tenure patterns are intimately bound up not only with the demand for housing but with its supply and distribution. Government intervention – or non-intervention – will affect these last two. The dual process of control through fiscal policy, for example, and the interaction of inflation and market forces contributed to the increases in home ownership and council housing. In the same way, it was a combination of private forces and government intervention in the form of legislation that accelerated the decline of private renting. Kemeny suggests that the 'key to understanding what has been happening to Britain's tenure system over the post-war period lies in the changing nature of the private rental sector'.[30] The great decline has occurred in unfurnished as opposed to furnished lettings.

It arose originally out of the post-war housing shortage – a vicious circle of desperate demand and much diminished supply leading to abuse of the landlord's role, high rents, neglect of property and murky practices with consequent exploitation of large sections of the tenant population. Though there were always good private landlords, legislative efforts to control the bad discouraged both alike. The market dwindled still more and quality further declined. There were no accompanying financial compensations, and law-based security of tenure for the occupier proved a severe discouragement for small landlords, actual or potential. Recent changes in the law under the 1980 Housing Act leave some tenants vulnerable again.

Private landlords in the old sense have not disappeared altogether. But the fact of their rapid decrease has been an additional factor in the limitations on choice and mobility for home seekers – 'the loss of private rented accommodation has reduced the flexibility of the housing market, particularly for newcomers to London and for young people establishing their first home'.[31] It is now the rich, the mobile and childless young or the elderly immobile poor who can be found in this sector. With the continuing decline, apart from the last group, it is becoming altogether more middle class.

Meanwhile another form of tenure had appeared, sometimes known as housing's 'third arm', that branch of the system promoted and funded by the Housing Corporation (a statutory body originally set up in 1964 with powers and functions much expanded under the 1974 Housing Act). I am talking of subsidised housing, not that subsidised by local authorities or new town corporations, but the various forms of renting, or even owning, effected through housing associations and housing co-operatives. There are at present some 2,500 registered housing associations,[32] and the dwellings for which they are in one way or another responsible constitute only 2 per cent of all private residential dwellings. As a tenure option for the average home seeker it still therefore ranks very low, though it has considerable potentiality for the future.

Demand for housing seems always to exceed supply. Paradoxically, this has been the case even when the housing stock was growing rapidly and the population increase was slackening, as after 1911, yet demand did not slacken in proportion. One reason lies in the continuing fragmentation of the population into smaller household units.[33] Families break up and seek separate homes, and the time it takes to build them or rehabilitate old ones means that supply will lag behind demand. There are other reasons, as Nevitt has shown, to do with the way housing markets work.[34] Then there is the question of how 'shortage' is interpreted. It is, for instance, argued that today shortage is no longer absolute. But, even if this were true,[35] the failure to match the character of housing locally available to local needs produces a similar effect. Tenure is a vital component in such failure.

Demand in the private ownership sector is more readily met than in the public sector. Central government policy during the last two decades has been increasingly designed to encourage private home-ownership. This is now matched by a deliberate rundown of public housing which, for the first time, is now declining not only in relative but in absolute terms. Such stock as there is must now more than ever be distributed, shared out, according to the suppliers' assessment of the applicants' needs. Unlike the potential purchaser, the home seeker in the public sector is not so much chooser as chosen.

I began this study at a time when the press was full of references to mounting unemployment figures:

UNEMPLOYMENT REACHES NEW POST-WAR RECORD OF 2,133,000

The total of unemployment is growing at a rate of 25,000 a week and ministers are resigned to a further sharp increase in the New Year. Mrs. Thatcher said there was no instant solution.[36]

and to the reductions that the government was proposing for public spending, most notably in the field of housing:

Savage cuts in the housing budgets of over 350 local authorities in England were announced for the next financial year by Mr. Heseltine, the Environment Secretary, last night.

They will be combined with rent rises of £3.25 a week for five million council house tenants in England and Wales, with even higher rent rises expected in Greater London.[37]

As I end it, the 'Treasury predicts unemployment will exceed 3.5 million next year.'[38] and the reductions are beginning to bite.

DISASTER COMES HOME

To judge by his presentation of the long-delayed English House Condition Survey 1981 . . . Stanley could have made the sinking of the Titanic seem no more than an upset on a boating lake.

If you bring together houses which lack amenities, unfit houses and homes in disrepair . . . then 4.33 million houses, or nearly one quarter of the housing stock, are unsatisfactory.[39]

My attempt to place the findings of this study in the context of the future has been coloured by the fact that Conservative rule is probable for some time to come. There is therefore no likelihood of a change of direction in housing policy. The direction is all too clear: the screws on public housing; promotion of private. But what is perhaps less clear is that housing will be an important part of the government's political philosophy – overt laissez-faire, hidden intervention; the prosperous should prosper, the poor should refurbish their bootstraps or go to the wall.

The sample

The sample was very small for both places – fifty families in each. In Bethnal Green there were thirty-nine couples and eleven single mothers, and in Woodford forty-nine couples and one single mother (see appendix 1, table 1.1).[40] Since the people were at a particular – relatively brief – stage in life, the study cannot speak for those at quite different stages with different family circumstances. Furthermore, a survey in two local areas obviously cannot stand for all of Britain, or even all of London. This does not mean, however, that speculations about possible change cannot be made nor that impressions of how some people live today are not worth making. It helps that the sample families do not differ too much from others in the locality in certain of their characteristics.[41] In social class and employment they are reasonably representative of Bethnal Green and Woodford residents as a whole (see chapter 2 and appendix 2); in housing tenure also, allowing for the fact that not all have yet formed their own households (see below). Most important is that they should be as representative as possible of the newly-formed families in Bethnal Green and Woodford. They were in so far as they consisted of a valid proportion of families to whom a first child was born over a given period. In Bethnal Green the response rate was 75 per cent and in Woodford 81 per cent. There were thus two mini-cohorts of first-birth mothers and their husbands or partners if any. For details of the method of sample selection and the response rate, see appendix 1.

The main interview took place when the babies were three to four months old, and that is the chief limitation. For it is possible to talk about only this one short time in their lives, though there was a very brief follow-up contact one year later with 97 of the 100 families. This gave factual information on any household moves, employment changes or second children.

In my sample only three Bethnal Green families were home-owners, compared with thirty-five in Woodford (see appendix 2, table 2.1). Council tenancies numbered twenty-seven in Bethnal Green and only nine in Woodford. Another notable contrast was in the proportions of families who, not having yet acquired a home of their own (either as tenants or by purchase), were living with relatives or friends. There were fifteen of these in Bethnal Green (only five of whom were couples) and two couples in Woodford. The remaining nine families were in various forms of private tenancies (chiefly housing association or Crown)[42, 43] or in flats over their place of work. One young Woodford couple were in council accommodation for the homeless.

Of the fifteen Bethnal Green families in shared households, fourteen were in council flats and there were twenty-seven further families actually holding council tenancies, so that altogether forty-one of the fifty families were in council homes. Of the earlier Bethnal Green sample, only 28 per cent had lived in council-owned dwellings; in 1961 council housing in Bethnal Green made up 45.6 per cent of all dwellings.[44] Today it is almost double – 80 per cent.[45, 46] Thus the forty-one families in my sample who lived in council property can be deemed reasonably representative. Private renting meanwhile has dropped from 38.5 per cent to 17 per cent. These proportions reflect those in the parent-borough of Tower Hamlets which, at 81.7 per cent, has the highest percentage of households living in local authority tenure in Inner London.[47] So Bethnal Green now has an extreme bias towards council housing. Tenure has changed dramatically since the time of the earlier study.

In Woodford, where there are so many fewer families sharing accommodation, the tenure distribution in the sample matches well with the 1981 Census overall figures. For the equivalent Redbridge wards, households in owner occupation are given at 72.5 per cent,[48] thus matching reasonably closely my thirty-five out of fifty. In Woodford generally the pattern of tenure change has been less marked than in Bethnal Green. Even so, owner occupation and local authority housing have increased since 1961 by 6.9 and 4.3 per cent respectively, both at the expense of private renting which, in twenty years, has dropped from 21 to 9 per cent.[49]

Method of work

The mothers were selected with the co-operation of the Community Health and Hospital Maternity Services and interviewed shortly after the birth of their child to ask if they would be willing to take part in the study when their child was about three months old. I began the selection and preliminary interviews at the end of March 1981. The main interviewing was begun in July and completed for all but a few stragglers by the end of November 1981. For details of the method of work, see appendix 1.

The interviews tended to be long – from one and a half to two hours, and often longer. Quite often a member of the interviewing team returned for a second or third visit. The team consisted of four part-timers and myself. We met regularly for discussion on our interviewing techniques and the content of the interviews, exchanging views and ironing out problems. I had the help of an interpreter for interviews with non-English-speaking mothers.

Who was interviewed

Since this was to be a family study, I was anxious to see fathers as well as mothers. Sometimes they were present at the preliminary mother's interview. If so, they were asked then about a second interview. Otherwise they were approached either directly or through their wife or partner when telephoning or calling for an appointment for the main interview with her. The questionnaire was devised so that the main factual information could be obtained from the mother. It was impossible, as it turned out, to have a full interview with all the fathers, though their response was better than I had expected (see appendix 1, table 1.2). In twelve of the sample families there was no resident father. In all, sixty-six fathers in the eighty-eight two-parent families were interviewed. The mother's point of view therefore predominates. Where the same questions were asked of both parents, the material has been separately analysed according to their respective replies and is usually so presented. Where the information is factual and concerns the family – irrespective of who has replied – it is presented as family information.

I also interviewed eight grandparents – three belonging to Bethnal Green families and five to Woodford – with the idea that their personal recollections would add further background. It of course does no more than that, but their flood of reminiscences brought the past vividly to light. The interviews took place at about the same time as the follow-up contacts with the mothers and fathers. The selection was arbitrary in so far as it was dependent on their willingness to be interviewed, and I naturally made no approaches if I was aware of any tensions or other kinds of problems within the family.

Scheme of the book

I have tried to arrange the material of the study so that the complexities I have briefly touched on in this introduction can be illustrated by the experiences and observations of the 100 families. First I introduce the places and the people. Chapter 1 is about the two neighbourhoods – Bethnal Green and Woodford. Chapter 2 is about the 100 families. Chapter 3 traces their housing history and their reasons for being where they are, and in chapter 4 I discuss how their family building may have influenced their quest for somewhere to live.

In chapter 5 I describe the families' present homes and give their own views. Chapter 6 is concerned with their way of life, how this relates to their housing circumstances and how it compares with that of the families of the studies in the 1950s. Chapter 7 looks at their housing aspirations and what the future may hold for them. Finally, in chapter 8, I attempt some conclusions.

1

THE NEIGHBOURHOODS

Up to the middle of the eighteenth century Bethnal Green, or Blithe Nook as some say it was then called, was little more than a rustic hamlet, though there were already signs of an increasing density of population in the district bordering Spitalfields.[1] There were then some 15,000 people housed in 1,800 dwellings – 'above eight persons to a house they being mostly of the poorer sort of manufacturers'.[2] In the space of 150 years the population increased to 129,680 – the figure for 1901. This was the highest it ever reached, and Bethnal Green was then one of the most crowded districts in London.[3] Thither as elsewhere came the immigrants of the industrial revolution, crowding into newly built houses of unbelievable squalor within and without – 'an absence of common sewers . . . undrained soil and other abominations'.[4] Behind Paradise Row, for instance, an attractive terrace of Georgian houses still standing, Hector Gavin in 1848 discovered Paradise Dairy, in which[5]

> 16 cows and 20 swine are usually kept. The animal remains and decomposing refuse were piled up to a considerable height . . . in order that a sufficiently large quantity may accumulate. Moreover, the soakage from the neighbouring privies found its way into this receptacle for manure and filth. The surface of the yard was dirty and covered in refuse.

In Meath Gardens in 1845 a cemetery was opened especially for children who had died from poverty and disease.

Hovel upon hovel was for the artisans and journeymen – silk weavers mostly. But there were also larger, even stately, homes, their gracious façades dating from previous centuries when Bethnal Green was in part a suburb for merchants from the City of London. Many of these bordered 'Poors Land'. The families residing there appointed trustees and fought to preserve this open space for their own benefit, and also, through a charity, for the benefit of 'poor persons' living in the vicinity. Hence its name. Today in public ownership – it was sold to the London County Council (LCC) in 1892 – it is enjoyed by all-comers. One large piece lost to development divides Bethnal Green Gardens and the Green. At either end of the Green stand the famous Bethnal Green museum and the elegant Soane Church.

Wanstead and Woodford were each a manor in earlier times. In 1578 that of Wanstead had been owned by Queen Elizabeth's favourite, Robert Dudley, Earl of Leicester. Woodford changed hands many times.[6] Within the parish, 'separate hamlets only tenuously linked together' grew up along the High Road and around the ford which spanned the River Roding at the point now known as Woodford Bridge. For 200 years until the middle of the nineteenth century, the history of Woodford revolved around its private mansions.[7] In 1801 dwellings in Wanstead and Woodford totalled only 442, mansions far outnumbering cottages. Taking Woodford alone, in the same year the population was 1,745. Slowly, however, through the first part of the nineteenth century the numbers increased until, with the advent of the Eastern Counties Railway in 1843 and the opening of a branch line from Stratford in 1856, the real expansion began.

As the gentry moved out, estate after estate fell to the developers; the villas of 'New Wanstead' and Woodford housed the new middle classes who had arrived not only to separate themselves physically from the evils of the town centre – the dirt, noise, disease and crime – but also, as Burnett has observed, in search of a different set of social values. They were 'drawn out of the cities by a dream or image of a different style of life'.[8]

By the beginning of this century in the inner area, hamlets under the patronage of great families living in large and handsome houses were totally engulfed by an industrial economy. A dense working-class population inhabited 'one of the most extensive congeries of slums in the metropolis'.[9] In the outer a predominantly agricultural economy and comparative remoteness from the metropolitan centre had succeeded in accommodating the influx of middle-class city immigrants to an extent that the prevailing way of life still belonged to the village rather than the town. Bethnal Green, it is true, boasted 200 or so acres of Victoria Park on its northern borders, but what was that compared with the thousands of acres of the Wanstead Flats and Epping Forest? The Forest had been saved for the nation in 1878. William Morris wrote of it in 1890, 'When I was a boy and young man I knew it yard by yard . . . In those days it had no worse foes than the gravel stealers and the rolling fence maker and was always interesting and often very beautiful.'[10]

The first half of the century

From the beginning of this century on, the character of the two places, allowing for the general improvement in urban living conditions and shifting distributions of social class, changed relatively little. Their physical appearance, however, did change.

In Bethnal Green, as well as the terraces of little two-up, two-down houses with front doors opening on the pavements, tenement blocks appeared well before the First World War, foreshadowing the massive agglomerations to come. Many of these turn-of-the-century tenements still stand, gloomy reminders of brave charitable efforts to improve conditions. Several of the sample families were living in them. One of the earliest – the Boundary Street development of 1895 – was carried out by the LCC under the responsibilities given by the Housing Act of 1890. In its imaginative design, on a radial plan with a central raised garden, it was a deliberate attempt to 'raise standards of space and amenity compared with those provided by most of the housing trusts'.[11] This area – the Jago or Nichol district – was famous, or notorious, for other reasons. Crime was rampant among the children, as we learn from the memoirs of Arthur Harding, 'the Terror of Brick Lane'.[12]

Local industry of considerable variety provided most of the jobs; private landlords provided most of the homes, though after the First World War local authority housing began to assume greater importance. Mrs Gedge, a Bethnal Green grandmother to one of the sample families, had lived for a short time in such a block:

'Brand-new, it was. I didn't like it at all, not at all. We missed all our friends, we were among strangers, although it was our territory. The people were too nosey. But we had a bathroom, though it was in the kitchen. How about that? It was luxury. And we didn't call them lounges then – to us it was just a front room and a kitchen.'

Before then, Mrs Gedge recalled, the street she had lived in was

'a nice street – poor, but nicer than Coronation Street. You could talk to the people. You knocked at the door and if you wanted to borrow a shilling you did and if you wanted a cup of tea you had one. If we needed something then they was there. It's a different life now. They're all competing with Mrs Jones. And during the summer months – everybody was like out of doors – you could go to the pub and get your pint in a jug. Where I was brought up has all been taken over by flats, blocks and blocks and blocks of them.'

Jewish immigrants escaping the pogroms of Eastern Europe continued their trek westwards to London, eastwards again to Stepney, Mile End and Bethnal Green as they had done since the seventeenth century.

Towards Woodford,[13] meanwhile, a different trek continued, including some of these same Jews able by now to make an independent choice of where to go. Some of the suburban immigrants severed their ties with their place of origin; others were forging the links between inner and outer East London which I have referred to in the Introduction. The trickle eventually became a flood, the speculative builder in the inter-war years giving rise to the first upsurge of owner occupation. There were a few council estates. Mrs Stubbs, one of the Woodford grandmothers, was now in a house which she and her husband had recently bought from the council, which was next door to the one she had lived in as a child. In contrast to Mrs Gedge in Bethnal Green, she recalled the Woodford estate as 'nice in those days'. She thought of it as 'rougher now. There are no more facilities for children now than when we were children and we could play in the road, and there were fields then too. It was so quiet. We used to be out in the road all day long, with our dolls and prams, and have the skipping rope fixed up across the road. There were no cars or anything.' In the thirties and forties corner shops, cottages and fine houses were demolished. Further transformation of the Green at Woodford occurred in 1947 with the electrification of the Underground system.

There had of course always been working-class pockets in Woodford – brickmakers and domestic servants in the eighteenth and nineteenth centuries, operators of the various new services of transport, telephone and the like. The continuing expansion still consisted chiefly of middle-class settlers. But they were not all well off. The varying dwelling types, small terraced houses and semis and larger detached houses, show that. Rather than a single social class, a tier of sub-classes stretched from bare sufficiency to extreme wealth.[14]

The 1950s

And so to the 1950s. Mrs Shaw, one of the Woodford grand-mothers, will serve well to introduce that period, for her experience spanned the inner city and the suburb. She told her story with passion and yet, in her recognition of it as the conventional history of upward and outward social and geographical mobility, with detachment. 'I mean,' she said, when she was describing their move out, 'Wanstead at that time [the early 1950s] was an East Ender's dream. It was the ultimate at that stage. You'd made it.' She was very conscious of the finer shades of social class distinctions, attributing to them the 'hell' of her early married life.

> 'They [her husband's family] were lower working class and I came from the upper working class. This made all the differ-ence in relationships and conditions. You see, there were two parts of the borough. Where I come from, the west side, was considered the respectable side; where I lived with my in-laws was a slum. You get classes within classes, don't you? My father always considered that he was a cut above and I was brought up to consider that I was too, and not to go into the other part of town.'

Her decision to marry, under age and involving a court case, caused a rift with her parents, not healed until the arrival in 1952 of her first baby. This she had had while living in cramped conditions with her parents-in-law because when she had become pregnant she and her husband had been turned out of their furnished room. And then the 'gates of heaven' had been opened for her by the fact that her parents moved to Wanstead and suggested that they could set up a joint establishment. 'And that's how my life changed. They needed help with the mortgage, so they offered us two rooms.' Though the kitchen was a converted box-room with no laid-on water, they were on their own and she did not think of it as at all 'tough'. Her trials, however, were not over. When a brother, also living in the house, got married and started a family, they were deemed overcrowded. While still in the East End they had put themselves on the council waiting list. It had been 'hopeless' at that time, but as they had not removed themselves from the list – which was later run jointly with Wanstead – they were offered a council flat. There they lived for ten years.

'I hated every minute of it and it definitely influenced my daughters against living in council property. No doubt about that. I'm pleased – I hated it. I hated the tenants' attitudes. I'm fully conversant with working-class attitudes but I've mixed a great deal with middle-class people, so I'm caught between two stools. Although I tried to escape from my background I've great sympathy with it. And when I became a council tenant I was all for the workers and said to myself that I must adjust to being a council tenant. We're the underdogs. It didn't take me long to discover that they were dreadful people. They were just at each other's throats. And if you're a bit different, everybody attacks you.'

Her childhood home had been owned by her grandmother, so this was her first experience of being a council tenant. 'You don't have any identity – no status. Any complaint you made was null and void. It wasn't your property anyway.' Her father died and her mother suggested that they return to the house so, 'in a way, her misfortune was my luck.' There they have been ever since.

What was this 'ultimate', this East Ender's dream, like at the time of the earlier studies?[15]

When we first visited Woodford it was clear that we had come to a different kind of place from Bethnal Green. East End children do not trot their ponies along forest paths wearing velvet hunting caps. East End houses do not have stone gnomes in their back-yards. There are no golf courses near the docks. How few people there seem to be in Woodford, and how many dogs! . . . People seem to be quieter [than in Bethnal Green] and more reserved in public, somehow endorsing Mumford's description of suburbs as the apotheosis of 'a collective attempt to lead a private life'.

Traditionally, Woodford has always endeavoured, says the

official guidebook, 'to keep the disadvantages of civilization at a proper distance without permitting the advantages to escape it'. The disadvantage of civilization is evidently industry, while the advantages are the cultivated trees and flowers, the garages and the Tudor half-timbering which a modern economy makes possible. In Bethnal Green homes and factories are packed tight and surrounded with asphalt whereas in Woodford the houses are spaced out at intervals and surrounded by grass. The most important physical difference is that there is relatively much more space – in 1959 Woodford had 61,000 people upon 4,842 acres, a density of 16 per acre, while Bethnal Green's 49,000 people were pressed in on 760 acres, at a density of 64 to each acre.

How do those of the sample families who lived there as children[16] remember it – Mary Clifford, Mrs Shaw's home-owning daughter, for instance? She remembers Wanstead 'as sort of villagy, sort of religious in a way, I suppose'. She could remember

'the vicar coming to visit and things like that. We were christened at the local church and all that sort of business. I don't think my parents know anyone living in their road now. Whereas before we were very friendly with all the neighbours. I can remember going and playing in their gardens and things – it really has altered to a great extent. It was always very tidy. I can remember in Wanstead the fish and chip shops were only allowed to fry once a week, and woe betide them if they did it at any other time. And now it's absolutely full of restaurants and takeaways. And there was always the local policeman in Wanstead. Now you can park your cars on the pavement. It just isn't the same place. They're all stupid little things probably, but I notice them. I never went to school in Wanstead actually but I can remember the High School and how they wore their straw boaters. Now that just doesn't happen. They just sort of trudge along in anything. I dunno whether it's declined or what. But it just isn't the same. People in this street, most of whom have lived her for 40 odd years, often go on about the changes, how things aren't the same, but I guess everybody does that. I already do!'

Mick O'Kelly now lives in a great slab block of council flats. As a child, he remembered the land as 'all marshes'.

One thing that Wanstead and Woodford did not provide at the time, nor has it done so since, was the opportunity for Bethnal Green families to move there under the 'benevolent guardianship of local councils'.[17] For this they went to brand-new estates elsewhere such as 'Greenleigh', described in the earlier Bethnal Green study, or the huge estate at Dagenham, the subject of Willmott's book, *The Evolution of a Community*.[18] Movement into Woodford, then as now, more often than not implied a change of tenure and a step up in the social scale.

There has already been a reminder earlier in this chapter that Bethnal Green and Woodford in the 1950s differed as strikingly in their physical appearance as in their daily life and activities. Moving in those years down the Central Line, back from Woodford to Bethnal Green, it would have been immediately apparent that Bethnal Green still had a mixed industrial and commercial economy.[19]

> You do not have to live there, you only have to take a bus down the main street, to notice that this is a place of many industries. You pass tailors' workshops, furniture makers, Kearley & Tonge's food warehouse, and near to Allen & Hanbury's big factory. The borough has by itself a more diversified economy than some countries. But the borough has no frontiers: it belongs to the economy which stretches down both banks of the Thames. At its heart is the largest port in the world, which lines the river for nearly twenty miles from London Bridge to Tilbury, and supports on every side a web of interconnected industries – ship-repairers and ship-suppliers, docks and lighterage, stores and depots, railways and motor transport, and the thousands of manufacturers, warehousemen, and merchants who process and pass tea and coffee, palm oil and wool, spices and hides, meat and wheat, from half the world on into the metropolis and the interior.

The people working in these various factories and workshops still for the most part lived in small cottages, nineteenth-century tenements and pre-war LCC housing blocks,[20] though Hitler's bombs had left the scars which anticipated the extensive clearance and rebuilding programmes to come. At that time, its outstanding feature, particularly in that part west of Cambridge Heath Road known as West Bethnal Green, was 'the intermingling of residential, commercial and industrial land uses',[21] a feature which had long persisted.

The predominant type of housing tenure was still private renting which, according to Mr Mitchell, one of the Bethnal Green sample fathers, allowed great mobility. He was full of tales of how in those days

> 'you could move when and where you liked. You just popped your things on a wheelbarrow and went off to another house round the corner. Now, people are *forced* to move because there's nowhere for them to live. Like my brother who was forced to go to Basildon because he only had one room with a baby. Why did they pull down all the little houses and put up those diabolical tower blocks?'

How did others of the large number of the mothers and fathers who spent their childhood in the area remember it? With affection and nostalgia, mainly, though a few found that things had changed for the better. One young mother thought that Bethnal Green Road was 'a better, more friendly shopping place now' than it had been. She was, in fact, the only one who reversed the expected then-and-now comparison of this characteristic of the neighbourhood. There were many who thought, along with Christine Smith, that people were not as friendly now. Allowance has to be made for the almost inevitable gloss cast upon childhood memories such as those, for instance, of Carol Clark.

> 'We used to have fun years ago. We used to play out on the streets in the area till late at night. We'd go out on day trips from the street. They used to hire a coach from the local pub. Most of the street would go on a day trip to Brighton or something. It used to be good fun because I was an only child you see so I enjoyed the company. I was an only child for 20 years.'

It was the same with many others. Nita Watson's husband told the interviewer that he used to live across the road from his present flat and that 'the family atmosphere had changed a lot. You'd not go borrowing sugar these days!' Rob Tooley thought there were 'a lot more people around in those days. They seemed to be more neighbourly and there were a lot more children in the street. A lot of the people went out of their way to say hello.' Pauline Gregg found that 'only the people' had changed; 'everyone's in such a hurry, people are not so friendly and yes there's definitely more mugging and violence and that!'

Many of the sample mothers and fathers were too young[22] to have experienced Bethnal Green in the 1950s. They grew up in the 1960s and early 1970s, by which time physical changes in the area, and also possibly changes in its atmosphere, had already taken hold. But for those with longer memories, other differences were observable. Here is Christine Smith again: 'It used to be really clean and people used to be right strict about how they kept the stairs and things, but they don't bother now.' And Jean Brogan, who thought it was 'much dirtier now. There used to be rows of little houses where now there's just waste ground. There used to be gardens and roses. You don't see anything like that now, do you?'

The 1980s

So what *do* you see now? Throughout the neighbourhood there is still a tattered patchwork of the famous streets and the occasional tranquil grass-centred square. Compared with some other areas of Tower Hamlets, Bethnal Green has a lot going for it.

A few of the houses display estate agents' 'For Sale' boards and a few show signs of already having been bought by young middle-class occupants, such as the Benthams, one of the sample couples. Most have been taken over and rehabilitated by housing trusts and associations. Many have exteriors in mint condition. They bravely intersperse the council housing estates.

These, of all shapes, sizes and textures now dominate the area. Thus, in West Bethnal Green, the north end of Brick Lane has been transformed. At the south end dirt and dereliction – the satellites of planning blight – infect the lane and adjoining streets. Poverty obtrudes; a sense of despondency prevails. There is nothing here for middle-class observers to romanticise, nothing to extol except the twin glories of the Lane, the seventeenth- and twentieth-century buildings of Truman's Brewery, monuments to successful capitalism.

Further north there are indications again of planning blight:

deserted cobbled streets, much corrugated iron,[23] a general air of decay broken up by pockets of council blocks and grass islands. Mr and Mrs Tomlinson live on a large mixed-period estate adjacent to the canal. Their block, dating from the early 1960s, was an addition to an estate of mainly pre-war blocks, the latter very run-down and dirty – tinned up, a bleak tarmac area where children played as cars drove around blocks, endangering their lives. There was no apparent parking control, and no area for children to play safely, a fact particularly shocking on an estate with so many young children. I shall return to this and other estates in chapter 5.

The borough planners, in one of their frank consultation reports, recognise this fearful gulf between intention and achievement. 'A number of estates suffer from being in a relatively poor environment due to lack of time and money which has been devoted to the areas surrounding the blocks and flats.'[24] Remnants of old Bethnal Green remain in the Hackney Road workshops, though many of these are now boarded up, in the quantity of pubs and in the Sunday markets. Even here, change is apparent. Columbia Street flower market, for instance, as well as the crowded stalls brimming with house-plants and nursery seedlings, pots and vases in garish colours and convoluted shapes, and the queues for cockles and winkles and prawns, now boasts a long-skirted lady selling discreet earthenware flower-pots and glazed pottery door numbers.

East Bethnal Green is essentially residential in character – again dominated by post-war housing estates. None of the sample families, as one or two were to complain, was in any of the latest crop of handsome, low-rise brick-built blocks. Groups of quite substantial Victorian terraced houses remain. All are converted into flats. Mr and Mrs Watson and their baby live in one of these, situated in a wide street lined with large plane trees. From this point of view it was easy to understand Mrs Watson's outburst – that she 'wouldn't dream of living down by Brick Lane' – if not her stated reasons, which were to do with 'the Indians'! 'They're filth. There are so many of them down there. What my sister has to clean up on the stairs, you just wouldn't believe. They're just not like us.'

This, as will appear in chapter 5, was by no means the only such reference to the latest wave of immigrants – mainly from Bangladesh – to add colour and variety to Bethnal Green and, it must be said, to cause dissension among its residents. Tower Hamlets, compared with Inner London as a whole, has a smaller proportion of the usually resident population who were born outside the UK, 19 per cent compared with 24 per cent, though very slightly more where the head of the household was born in the New Commonwealth or Pakistan.[25, 26] Four of the sample babies were born to parents who had come recently from Bangladesh. People from Asia are a new feature, hardly present in the Bethnal Green of the 1950s. It is not that immigrants are new. It is that they come from different places. Also the proportions these days are larger, at least compared with thirty years ago.

Another kind of immigrant – Michelle Bentham, mentioned above, a member of the professional classes and one of the three home owners of the Bethnal Green sample – saw the area as

'a mixture – there's a lot of council property, a lot of family and a lot of people who've been here years and years and generations and generations. It's quite a close network but there's also quite a lot of newcomers. It does go very much in areas because we don't know anybody over the way, over the other side of the main road which is a totally different type of housing. They're big old houses, these are little ones. Some of them have been done up and they've obviously been brought up to scratch recently. There are nice houses going down toward the park. And then you get Victoria Park which is a lot richer area. It's quite friendly – this street and the adjoining one are. It's friendly but very much in small units. The people within one block of flats or within one street – like it's these two streets together and we don't know the people in that block there. It's very patchy like that. There's an awful lot of old people down the street. We had Charlie [the baby] here and the neighbour next door – she's been here years and years – said she can't remember that last baby being born in the street. It is changing because a young couple have bought next door but one, and there are several that are being converted and sold up.'

Bethnal Green Road and Roman Road – 'The Roman' as it is often called – are still the main shopping streets of Bethnal Green. They still contain small shops – a popular baker who bakes on the premises, a renowned fishmonger – and Bethnal Green will continue to be Bethnal Green while it contains its market stalls.

But the inevitable supermarkets are driving out the small traders. Corner shops still exist, and not all, as in so many parts of London, and so successfully, have been taken over by Asian families. But some are no longer what they seem. Within a short distance of the Institute of Community Studies, which is housed in one of a group of seventeenth-century houses fronting the Green, are two little shops, each on the corner of one of the surviving old-style streets. In one, all the traditional groceries are sold. In the other they now sell travel – packages to Spain, along with coach tickets to Southend.

In the 1950s employment was predominantly local. By 1977 in West Bethnal Green there were 4,000 to 4,500 people employed in manufacturing in some 380 firms – approximately half the figure for the early 1950s.[27] In East Bethnal Green – always more residential in character – 4,000 jobs had gone from the manufacturing sector between 1957 and 1977.[28] It is the public sector – the council and its services – who are East Bethnal Green's big employers.

There are of course many reasons for these changes, not least the closing down of firms, 'job rationalisation', and the effect of national and local planning policies. Gans suggests that 'most urban neighbourhoods are as much dormitories as the suburbs'.[29] Certainly, very few of the sample fathers worked within the same postal district that they lived in, though marginally more, proportionately, did so than the Woodford fathers. Nevertheless, four in seven of those in Bethnal Green had relatively local jobs. But, whatever the reasons, the rate of unemployment in this part of London is extremely high (see chapter 2).

Despite the problems, the mothers and fathers found more to say in favour of Bethnal Green than against it. Where they were well disposed towards the neighbourhood its amenities – particularly public transport – were praised. But the single feature most often commented on was its friendliness. Here is a father, John Briggs. A council tenant, fairly new to the area, he found that

'some of the people in Bethnal Green are salt-of-the-earth people. For a start there are pie and mash shops. Having lived north-west of London I have found a bigger difference. Some of the people are a lot friendlier here specially the older people. But of course like most areas there's a lot of new people.'

The attachment was most marked among those who had lived in

24

the district for a long time. Thus Pauline Gregg again: 'I love it. I wouldn't move away from here. Perhaps it's because I know everybody. Then there are the pubs and the market. There's never a dull moment.' Or Janet Tate, a single mother, who had lived 'round here' all her life. 'All our friends live around. We've all grown up together so, yes, I like it here.'

Others thought it *had* been like that. Carol Clark was one:

'Well, I think the friendly neighbourly atmosphere has gone. I remember even in my mum's block in summer we'd all be sitting outside drinking cups of tea chatting. The neighbours don't seem to be as friendly as they used to be. I think people are frightened of you knowing their business. Years ago everybody just sort of – well all right there's still a lot of nosey people about, but years ago it didn't seem to matter people thinking, "I don't want them to know what I've got." Well, people have what they can afford, it's nothing to do with anybody else. I think it creates an atmosphere. That's the worst thing I think. And people just talk about the East End as if it's the slums of the earth. I mean there can be slums in whatever district you go to. You've only got to mention the East End and they immediately drop back about six paces. If I said I lived in Sutton in Surrey it'd be a bit different from Bethnal Green, E.2.'

And she further characterised the push and pull of long residence and aversion to change:

'It's a bit noisy. A couple of people who happen to like their music blaring out come hell or high water or the great flood! Quite a few coloureds in the area, which I'm afraid I think they bring . . . down a bit. We had a look this morning and the condition of the places just walking by, they're atrocious. I've seen them looking out of the window, you can tell who's living there. I'm not saying the English are all pure white and tidy, but from the outside of some of those places they're deplorable. I think they tend to put them in a block by themselves. It's a good thing in one respect and not in another. If you get one or two, a block can still look reasonably clean, but when they put them in a whole block, then it just brings the whole building down. It's only friendly because I've been

25

here all my life. The people here are reasonably friendly. We know all the people on this landing and a couple downstairs and if you meet someone downstairs you have a chat.'

Whether brought up in the neighbourhood or not, as with the favourable comment, so with the unfavourable – it was their fellow residents who came in for the most censure.

The striking changes since the 1950s in the physical appearance of the area were matched by a sharp decline in population. In 1959 it numbered 49,000; in 1981 something under 32,000,[30] which gives a density of 42 persons to each acre compared with 64 thirty years ago.

This density is still much higher than that of Woodford, with its present resident population of 58,768,[31] and density of 15 persons per acre, only slightly lower than in the 1950s. The fundamental difference remains in the sense of space. The astonishing Wanstead flats where sheep still graze; stretches of water bordering main roads; little parks and larger commons; roads edged with grass and bordered by shrubs and flowering trees and the ever-present forest, scrubby and sandy some of it, but over-spread with noble trees and criss-crossed with inviting paths going on for miles – all these are still there.

The main roads that 'sliced the suburb' in the 1950s are even more the unacceptable face of suburbia. Now it is six-lane highways, motorway approach roads, clover-leafs and large roundabouts with their insistently thundering lorries and speeding cars that leave more than 'a distant hum' in many of the side roads. But the side roads are still empty. And in other ways they have not changed much in twenty years. The new private housing estates are rapidly becoming absorbed into the general pattern. The Rosens live on such an estate – brand new, curved roads, well-spaced and well-sited houses, half-weatherboarded with steep-pitched roofs, American-style open front gardens, coach lamps and chime bells. There is an air of prosperity and quiet, plenty of parking space and good clean air. A two-year-old was running about when I called on the Rosens, and few other people were to be seen. Some of the new council estates sit uneasily in that landscape. One which housed most of the Woodford sample council tenants was made up of a clutch of ugly twelve-storey slab blocks. But in general the suburb retains its quiet, leafy, inward-turning air.

26

The area covered by the old districts of Wanstead and Woodford is five times the size of Bethnal Green and there is of course, and always has been, variety within it, representing the different eras of expansion. Houses dating from different periods have different styles. Some of the families live in semi-detached houses decorated with 'Tudor half-timbering', others in Edwardian terraced cottages, one on the first floor of a splendid decaying house dating from the end of the last century. The Greys' home was in a narrow street of Victorian two-storey terraced houses with small front gardens. The street's status was changing. The houses had probably once all been rented but were now moving into owner occupation.

In the street where the Symonds lived, some of the houses, mostly fairly small, had clearly been built in the early nineteenth century, many in the second half, and there was a good sprinkling of modern ones. They all seemed in good condition. Most had small gardens but no garages, so that the street was lined with cars. The Forest was to one side of the street and there was a further bonus of a substantial wedge of grassy bank running the length of the street. The Bells' house was in a shabby run-down little terrace with a decidedly working-class air, but it was approached from one end past a spacious brick-built estate (ex-council, now run by a housing association), some purpose-built blocks of private flats, some modern council houses and some smart 'town houses'.

A busy road runs through one corner of Woodford which, with its green, Victorian church and row of little shops, recalls the village it once was. Now it is a strange mixture – semi-countrified and semi-suburban. Monkhams Estate with its detached houses and large gardens is still 'the posh estate'. Numbers of streets are grass-verged or lined with shrubs or trees; culs de sac abound ('It's lovely living in a cul de sac. Sometimes I go outside with the baby when he's unhappy and they all want to hold him'), but pubs do not.

The shopping centres have certainly changed, as they have in twenty years almost everywhere in England. Supermarkets have superseded small shops and, as the mothers testified, shopping is more likely now to be a once-a-week, or even a once-a-month, affair than a daily trot to the local shop. For some of those, however, who have opted for the domestic round, this last does still go on – for Mary Charles, for instance, who used the row of shops at the end of her street.

So here, in the 1980s, it seems there is still what many would think of as a typical suburb, a place where the householder may have[32]

> a tangible indication of locality. He has a garden (the traditional requisite of the Englishman since Saxon times) and yet is close to a station to commute to Central London. He lives in a low density area and yet is close to the largest shopping and entertainment centres. His road is quiet and yet is close to garage repair facilities when his car breaks down and bus routes to enable his children to get to school. Perhaps the suburban dweller would prefer to live in similar comfort in the city centre but the equivalent house and quiet street in Chelsea or Kensington are beyond his financial means. Or perhaps he would ideally like to live in a country town or village but again the combined cost of a country cottage and his annual season ticket to town may be more than he can afford.

It was the same in Woodford as in Bethnal Green, only more so; more than half the mothers (and proportionately nearly as many fathers) could find nothing unfavourable to say about the place, and only nine could think of nothing favourable. Newcomers were sometimes critical. A number of these Woodford families, as to a lesser extent those in Bethnal Green, had come there from parts of London further west, south, north or east, from towns and cities in other regions of the UK and from countries overseas near and far. Some of them preferred the places of their childhood. Mick O'Kelly found that

> 'people are different in Ireland. The front door's always open – the only time you close the front door is when a funeral goes by. People are so friendly I used to get fed all over the place by different people. My grandfather, when he came over here, he couldn't make it out. Scratching his head with his old cap on the back of his head, he'd watch all the traffic go by. They're nice to them, old people, over there. Everything's free for them. I consider myself Irish – not English.'

Two perhaps more sophisticated comparisons of a more recent period – this time with the north of England – were made by Fred Dixon and Hannah Baker. Mr Dixon, a teacher, thought that Newcastle was 'more friendly; lots of houses therefore lots of space to be friendly and neighbourly. Here there's a shortage of space. And there's a difference between the cultures. In pubs for instance down here if it's small and crowded and you're close to people and touch them, they mind. In the North, if you find your arm round someone's shoulder, that's fine, they expect it.'

For Hannah Baker, the comparison was with a small town near York where she had been for four years at university. Her comments recalled an earlier Bethnal Green:

'It's a small town, one church and the people lived in the neighbourhood. That was a live country, a kind of living I haven't had since, simply because of the problems of distance. One could pop in and out of each other's homes all the time. In some ways that was more like what it used to be in the East End amongst people's natural family network. In one house, I remember, I was there for half an hour and at least six people came by. Somebody would want to borrow a chair, somebody would leave a pile of washing for a while before going to the laundrette, or could someone borrow a washing line because theirs had broken. There was a continual coming and going. That is how it should be. Anyway it's partly true of small Northern towns that there is a greater friendliness but it was certainly more marked because we went to the same church. I wonder if it's possible in London . . . whether there's just too much space. Up there they're little houses and the doors open on the street. There's no avoiding the neighbours. Here in London we have semi-detached houses, hedges between, great long gardens and if you don't want to you don't have to see your neighbours in 20 years. It's just a different approach. I mean I remember a lady who was quite insulted because I knocked on the door. I was expected just to walk in. She said, "Oh that's your Southern nature." If I knocked on the door, I wasn't a friend.'

Not all, however, took this view. Mrs Patel was one who, though missing her native India, was content with her new environment. It was 'very good. No one interferes with others. We never have any trouble between the black and white here. All is quite calm.'

Mrs Shadwell, who had moved only a short distance, had found the people next door 'exceptionally helpful' when they had first moved in, whereas before, their neighbours had 'really kept themselves to themselves'.

Hannah Baker's reference to the East End is a reminder of the special link between the two study areas created by some of the Woodford mothers and fathers who had been brought up in Bethnal Green or neighbouring districts. Mrs Winthrop found present-day Bethnal Green very different from the days of her childhood.

'It's changed even since I've left it, which was years ago. It's all flats. It was a lot better then – a different atmosphere – friendly, as it is here now. But nowadays the neighbourhood spirit has all gone. People don't notice their neighbours. There's no real private housing, nearly all council. Not that that makes any difference. But I don't think it has been modernised as it should be. The estate I lived on – in a small block – we knew our neighbours then. And there's a lot more violence in the area. Of course there was always violence but now it's frightening. My mother's been burgled several times. They just break and smash everything up and then say it's kids. Both neighbourhoods are very different now from what they were. Woodford used to be very snooty. It still is a bit, of course, but now you've got the tradesmen moving in and houses with tradesmen's van's outside. But Bethnal Green is absolutely changed. I suppose we led a rather sheltered life as children. I mean my mother used not to let us play with certain children on the estate and as I went to the grammar school the other side of the park my friends tended to come from Essex and other places like that. My brother went to boarding school because the primary school headmistress said that's where he should go. They were quite different sort of people then. I don't know what it is. Of course there was vandalism a bit in those days and pickpockets, but now I'd be frightened to go out in Bethnal Green at night and I worry about my mum. And some of the people on the estate now are terrible; disgusting rubbish and peeing in the lift. I don't understand it. I mean nobody's as poor now as they could be when we were children. The State sees to that so why do they behave like that? I suppose some of them just aren't educated. It's interesting the difference in the problems and the types of the immigrants I had to do with when I worked in Tottenham and those my husband comes across in Hackney. The kids just don't seem to know a thing when they leave school.'

When Linda Rush first moved from the East End her present neighbourhood seemed 'very, very strange', it was so quiet:

'Down there from Monday to Sunday it's always noisy, it's never quiet. Here on Sundays you hardly ever see a car on the road, you hardly hear anybody in their gardens. Ninety per cent council estates. Not that I've got anything against that, I was brought up in one. There's not the facilities for the children. Most have no gardens so when they do get out they run riot. And also, of course, it's dirtier because it's industrial.'

Linda Rush's husband, who was brought up in Stratford, shared her views:

'I do like Woodford. Very clean and quiet. People are decent. They look after what they've got. You meet people in the street you don't know from Adam and they all nod and say hello and you get talking. Just a nice general happy atmosphere. Stratford – I didn't want to move from there when I was a kid. Totally different that was. I thought the atmosphere was really great. It was lovely. You used to leave your street door unlocked, you know, it was that sort of atmosphere. And you'd know Joe Bloggs down the road, and the corner shop would be on the corner. It was very much as you'd see a . . . well, like Coronation Street, I suppose. It was good. But my Dad saw into the future and I think he was right. Now, no way would I go back there. Because it's not the same. It's not the place as I knew it. I mean I went back there when all those vandals were running riot and all the shops were boarded up and I thought, I used to live round here. It's a crying shame, really, disgusting. My dad still works there and one night when he was coming home he had to get out quick. And I thought well, to think we had 11 great years there. And, as I say, when we moved it was only five miles but I felt we were coming out into the country. It took us a long while to get accustomed to it, specially for me and my mum. My dad went back to work every day.'

And so it goes on: 'This is cleaner, more tidier, not so much rubbish about.' 'The people are different – not so many coloureds or vandals.' 'Compared to where I used to live, problems are minor here in Woodford. It's the people generally. As you move out this way, the class is improving.' For Clarise Berman also it was the social class differences:

'Accents for a start. There's a delicatessen here and not in Mile End. It's a higher-class neighbourhood here. I think I've changed with it. In my job I mixed with all sorts of people and we did things like public speaking courses. There's less people here than there. If you walk down the Mile End Road there's lots and lots of children and people. Here, there's hardly anybody. They're all terribly together-ladies. And I like that.'

Mr Turner left Bethnal Green at the age of fifteen. He did not see such a difference in the people – 'I'd say they're essentially the same people here as were there then.' He thought, nevertheless, that there was a great deal of difference in other things, 'the usual things, more space, less pressure on youngsters to be in gangs, middle-class kids to mix with. I'm not interested in this for myself but for the baby. I wouldn't want to bring up a child in a central urban area today.'

Mr Henry thought of Woodford as a neighbourhood he'd be 'quite happy' for his children to grow up in. His immediate present neighbourhood was

'full of lovely people. An older generation of very nice, respectable people. They must have lived all their lives there. Homes well cared for, services and shops are good. No fly-by-night shops. All old-established businesses. You can walk into a shop and they'll say good morning, Mr So-and-So. It seems like a village community on a larger scale. A feeling of homeliness about the neighbourhood.'

But Mr Henry had strong loyalties to the Stepney of his upbringing. For him the sentimental ties persisted long after the physical severance had occurred. He represents, furthermore, that important component of population movement into and out of the cities – the successive waves of immigrants from overseas. 'It's a funny thing,' he said, 'Stepney always was and always will be an area for the immigrant community.'

'My parents were probably among the last generation of the Jewish community that came over in the early part of this century whereas now it's the Asian community that lives there. It seems a natural progression that, since it's always been an area for people to come to; then they move out. Funnily enough a lot of Jewish people have moved either to North London or further out in East London into the Essex area. There's quite a big Jewish community in Ilford that used to live in Stepney.

A lot of famous people came out of the East End. Although they're never ashamed or forget their roots and they plough a lot of money back into it, one of their first achievements in life is to get out of the area. That's how I feel. I don't want to be there but I'd never want to forget it and when I'm asked – on holiday and that – where do you come from, I always say Stepney.'

Only for June Pratt was her place of upbringing more desirable still than Woodford. A wonderfully resilient young single mother, she had experienced tragedy in the first month or two of her baby's birth. She was a tenant of the forbidding council estate in Woodford already referred to.

'We lived over my Gran's for the first 11 years. That was lovely. Nobody ever used to shut their doors then. People were always coming and going and there was the market just underneath us and my cousin had the cucumber stall. And I remember the tin bath. We used to say are we ever going to have a bathroom, but we didn't mind. My brother and I used to bath together. It's so much cheaper up there and everyone's friendly. As I say, it's a different thing altogether. I mean we went to the doctor's yesterday and they're so unfriendly, so official. Our family doctor in the East End knew everybody from my grandparents down to my little brother.'

Mrs Turner had come from Limehouse and had very recently become a Woodford home-owner. She said she did not yet really know the place, though 'up the road is very posh – enormous houses. Chigwell is East End Mafia country. They all come from Bethnal Green and have all got Rolls Royces, though I'm sure the majority of the population would be outraged if they heard that. This part is quite a nice mix; not ethnically, which is a pity.'

When asked about the comparative feel of Woodford and Lime-house, she quoted 'the old Chinese proverb' of the gateman who, in response to questions from newcomers about what the town was like, replied by asking the questioner what the town he had come from was like, and then giving his town the equivalent label. Mrs Turner did, however, concede that there was one 'real difference' in the shops and facilities, these being much better in Woodford. And there was 'a different kind of quietness. Here there's openness and grass, there it was just quiet because the docks had closed and there was no work.'

Unfavourable comment on the area, irrespective of affinities with the past or its rejection, were spread lightly over various aspects of the suburb. To a great extent it depended on the family's particular location. Thus, Mary Clifford, who ran a string of employment agencies, had 'a lot of moans and groans' about her neighbourhood. Echoing a comment from the earlier study,[33] she said that it was

'very split. The other side of the [railway] line has a very well-maintained feel. This side is very neglected. The condition of the roads is shocking, absolutely appalling. It just does not happen over the other side. I think this is because this is a more working-class area. Generally it's very scruffy. There have been lots of committees and things. When we first came here we did go and look at some plans to make this a general improvement area, but that all got shelved. So that peeved me a lot. I feel very hard done by. This immediate bit is fine but . . . there's just this boundary and as soon as you go over there it's different. You just can't get any response from the council. That's the way it's always been. It's always been a Tory council. Very sort of tight. And that's going to be another thing when it comes to education – nursery provision and so on. I'm already thinking very hard about it, if there'll be any at all by the time Sam gets to it. All these sorts of things niggle me, but that's just because it's Redbridge Council, I suppose.'

Mrs Grey had found, with her previous home, that the road was 'friendlier and quieter, mainly because it was a cul de sac'. Jenny Steel could see no further than the confines of her council housing estate, which she found 'rough and noisy and dirty. Nobody talks to each other round here.' Furthermore, public transport, which received far more praise than censure from the majority of Woodford residents, was, in Mrs Steel's view (shared by one or two others on the estate), 'not that good really. There's only one bus and that's about every half-hour or three-quarters of an hour.'

It is, inevitably, change which comes through most strongly from the preceding pages. From the middle of the eighteenth century in their population density and in their physical characteristics the two neighbourhoods have diverged to an ever-increasing extent. Bethnal Green has changed most drastically. There have been hints of what will appear more clearly in subsequent chapters of fluctuations within this changing scene – fluctuations peculiar to Bethnal Green and the inner city. Compared with Woodford, its population increased and then declined with a greater rapidity. The effects on the 'core' community of such population shifts may be similar in different periods. The scale and nature of its primarily industrial and commercial economy has varied over the years and stands now at a crossroads. What was in the past the inner-city industrial perimeter is now the inner city.[34] 'The era of the central city dominating its hinterland is now undoubtedly over.'[35]

Woodford's economy, originally agricultural, has been slowly transformed, also with fluctuations, into one that now aims to take advantage of new technological processes and industrial and commercial decentralisation. The economic life of the city depends just as much on the Woodford as on the Bethnal Green families. Since the 1950s, the period of the earlier studies, what has perhaps most governed the general feeling of change in Bethnal Green – its type of housing – contrasts vividly with the relative stability of Woodford. Even there, it is true, a sour gesture to the spirit of the age has pointed its finger to the skies in the shape of a few of what Richard Holmes has somewhere described as 'battery sheds of the poor'. But for the most part it has been more a question of change in the style of small-scale domestic architecture and an increase in the number of dwellings, which the area seems well able to absorb.

35

It is the expansion of arterial roadways that has most affected Woodford's physical face.

For the grandmothers, Bethnal Green has changed decidedly for the worse. Nearly all of those who spoke of change, not only the grandmothers, thought it less friendly now. But, again with exceptions, they still found much to praise and some would not live anywhere else. Through the eyes of those *who used to* live there but have since left there is a greater concurrence of view. Bethnal Green and other East End neighbourhoods they have left behind are no longer what they were. Greater noise, dirt, violence are all mentioned. Racial prejudice is evident also. It is ever the case that each generation, absorbed in the impact of the current wave of immigrants, forgets how previous ones have become assimilated.

Satisfaction with their neighbourhood for the residents of Woodford, though not unanimous, was nevertheless widespread. It too had changed according to some – for the worse and for the better – but in less strident ways. One thing is clear. The link between inner city and suburb remains; the outward-bound migration continues.

2

THE FAMILIES

The one thing the families had in common was their new baby – in all cases a first child. In other respects they of course differed: in health, marital status, age, employment, income, social class, and so on.

Mothers and babies

The overwhelming impression in both areas was of friendly, responsive parents and splendid, contented babies, boys and girls alike. Since the 1950s the health of infants has improved.[1] Only one family was excluded from the sample because of the baby's serious ill-health.[2, 3] A very few were, by either the mother's or our own judgments, a bit thin, peeky or complaining, but only two seemed to be in really poor health. In one case, at the time of the interview the parents were living in one room with their under-weight ailing baby. An assortment of unwashed bottles, some half-filled with milk, were on the table. The twenty-two-year-old father had been out of work for fourteen months, but 'the crunch' had come several months before that. 'I didn't even know I was paying no stamps. It took a long while to find out.' He had been 'a biker' – a 'non-aggressive Hell's Angel' – and proudly showed the interviewer a photograph of himself in full gear – shoulder-length hair, head band, leather jacket with fancy studs. He had to change his life style completely, he said, before Betty would marry him: 'short hair and jeans now'. In the second family the baby had been prematurely induced because of the mother's high blood pressure.

Loving, you would expect the mothers to be. So many were relaxed and competent as well. Mrs Berman, already in her thirties, was 'into psychology', working, as it were, from the book but, in the interviewer's eyes, showing all the signs of 'natural' maternal affection. Ann White was back in her full-time job as a teacher, her extremely advanced baby giving every indication of an unfussed, loving upbringing. Mandy Wallace was living with her boyfriend and her parents, only sixteen years old but, as described by her interviewer, a very well balanced girl, coping well with being a mother. She seemed to have a clear view of her role in life, and at present to find it satisfactory. The baby seemed very lively and well cared for. Mrs Aslam, beautiful, seventeen years old, showed no sign of the strains of separation from her parents and native culture of Bangladesh. And May Riley, a single mother living on her own, managed her baby with ease.

The first two of these were from Woodford, the remaining three from Bethnal Green. It is not by chance that Mandy at sixteen years of age lived in Bethnal Green with her parents, nor that Clarice Berman aged thirty lived in Woodford. Nor that May Riley as a single mother belonged to Bethnal Green and that Ann White as a working mother to Woodford. These are four of the characteristics of the mothers – age, composition of the household, marital status and employment status – which show decided differences according to the area. There was also a slight difference in the mothers' and fathers' state of health.

Mothers' and fathers' health

Generally, by their own assessment, the mothers and fathers in the two areas were in remarkably good physical health.[4, 5] There had been quite a few difficult deliveries including several Caesarian sections and other complications. Not surprisingly some of these mothers had still not quite recovered by the time of the main interview. More mothers in Bethnal Green than in Woodford thought their health was 'not very good', and more in Woodford than in Bethnal Green described it as 'very good', but in both places the great majority were satisfied. Neither age nor the fact of being in paid work appeared to have any bearing.

I also thought it important to ask about their state of mind – 'Have you ever suffered from your nerves?' was the way I put it. This was after all a period in their lives when they might well be subject to depression. Some, as will appear, had quite severe housing problems. Yet nearly three-quarters of the ninety-seven mothers replying to the question said they had never suffered from any form of nervous trouble. When the few who talked of depression were asked what it was that caused it, housing was rarely mentioned. There were nevertheless occasional remarks in answers to other questions which connected poor housing and distress. Vivienne Stokes, for instance, referring to the conditions on her housing estate said, 'Sometimes I sit and cry. It's so depressing.'

A few described themselves as 'a nervous person' or said that they sometimes felt 'a bit depressed', but they had had no serious problems. Seven in Woodford and four in Bethnal Green had at some time in their lives been given 'tablets' or had sought a doctor's advice for depression. None actually talked of post-natal depression but it is of course possible that some may have been suffering from it, particularly those who spoke of feeling a bit depressed at times.

Other research concerned in more detail with the health of mothers and first babies living in Tower Hamlets has less reassuring findings.[6] For that the mothers were interviewed over a period of seven years – from early pregnancy onwards. One set of interviews took place at about the same period in their lives as the main interview for my sample and showed even then a higher proportion of mothers with symptoms of depression and stress. The picture on the whole became more serious later on.

Couples

Eight of the marriages were not the first. In two, both the husband and wife had been divorced and, in two others, the wife only. One of the differences between the 1950s and the 1980s is that now not all the couples are legally married.[7] Two partners of the nine cohabiting couples, one still under twenty-one when she was interviewed, had been married before. None of the fathers appeared to be involved in maintaining a second family.

For all the mothers the sample child was their first. Six of the fathers, however, had a child or children from a previous marriage. Tom Peters had never seen his elder daughter, but the resentment he expressed about this was clearly being rapidly dispersed by his delight in the new baby girl. In only two of the families did the new babies have step-siblings living in the same household. While the great majority of two-parent families were in their own homes at the time of the interview, only marginally fewer in Bethnal Green than in Woodford, the reverse held true for the twelve one-parent families.

Single mothers

There is evidence that one-parent families do badly in housing. They are likely to suffer a stressful history of housing instability, particularly if single and young,[8] and they form a disproportionate percentage of homeless families.[9] The little group in my sample lived mostly in poor quality housing. But so did many two-parent families. It is a matter of proportions and the sample is too small for reliable comparisons. Two had their own council flats. June Pratt, the only Woodford single mother, had been living with her parents when she became – intentionally – pregnant, but they were not prepared for her to stay on with the baby. She told me that the day she walked into the office of Redbridge Council Housing Department to register as a homeless person, 'He said he'd got a flat for me and gave me the keys.' May Riley's flat was on the fourth floor of a 1930s GLC estate. New lifts and rubbish chutes had just been installed but there were signs of neglect everywhere – broken-down walls, bent fencing, stained steps, dark and dingy stairways. She complained to the interviewer,

> 'Social security don't listen to me. They don't take no notice of me. I claimed for a wardrobe and things and I haven't got them yet. They know I've got the baby. They say I should have heard in three weeks and I never did.'

All the rest lived with their parents. Their average age makes this unsurprising. Seven had not yet reached nineteen when they were interviewed, and Tina Sydney, Kathy Garnett and Geraldine Herbert were under seventeen.[10] Only two were anxious to leave. Thirty-three-year-old Janet Tate was a long-standing Bethnal Greener.

> 'Well, I put my name down but I also went to the GLC because previously I was living with someone for many years and I had to give up the flat. I went to the GLC and they said they couldn't help me because I was classed as housed, even though I'm not living there any more because he took someone else in there to live. They don't class me as homeless. And my

name is still on the rent book and I've tried everything to get it off, but that is why the Borough says they can't help me because my name's still on the GLC list. They won't rehouse me. I've been everywhere. Social services I've tried; I've wrote to MPs, everything, though I'm entitled to be rehoused. Someone told me to go on the single parents list but this list doesn't exist. They reckoned we're not overcrowded until baby's a year old. And I went to ask about squatters' rights but they haven't got any now. They can get you out as quick as you get in.'

Carrie Nichols, more than twelve years younger, had so far been frustrated in her wish to live with her boyfriend with whom she hoped ultimately to return to Grenada.

'I had no choice but to stay with my mum, because I went to the council with my boyfriend and they said they hadn't got anywhere for me to stay. I went to them and they said they'd send us a letter which they've never done. They said after I've had the baby I should be able to get a flat but we haven't heard anything. All they said is they can't help very much and that's it and I've been on it three years now. They kept on getting me mixed up with my sister. She's been on their waiting list three years as well. We wasn't together at the time, but after we both went back they did us both together.'

Carrie was still there one year later, but Janet had just been rehoused by the council. It was difficult to be other than pessimistic about the future for many of them. They were all poor; all were on supplementary benefit. None had any educational qualifications, and job prospects were dismal. One was on probation; the baby of another had been taken into care for several weeks because his father with whom she had then been living had battered him.

All sorts of influences and pressures are at work on young girls in inner-city areas which often result in pregnancy, wanted and unwanted. There is no doubt that babies are being born to single mothers at an increasingly early age.[11] It has been suggested that one reason for this is that a baby fills the vacuum when a girl leaves school with little education behind her and little or no prospect of a job. Having a baby is an alternative to doing nothing.[12] In Britain today there are many cultures whose active traditions dictate different choices for girls and young women in the matter of pregnancy outside marriage. Such choices are inevitably less straightforward as they become subject to influences and counter-influences from outside – and within – their own culture.[13] But whether the pregnancy is a conscious or unconscious response to these cultural pressures or those of unemployment or poor education, a passport to a home of their own or a deliberate attempt to go it alone, problems and stress are likely to be a part of their lives. In my sample the problems seemed to be shared independently of skin colour.[14] And the satisfactions and the advantages too. There was evidence of much parental support for the young mothers and affection for the new babies. The support was manifested financially as well as in warmth and acceptance. Janet Tate, for instance, and Alice Richards paid no regular amounts for their keep. The remaining sums ranged from £5 to £10 per week, except for April Lang, who managed £15. When asked if they thought the amount they paid was fair, four said, 'No, it is too little.'

Age

Though the high proportion of very young single mothers accounts in part for the youthfulness of the Bethnal Green sample, it is not the whole story (see appendix 2, table 2.3).

Nearly twice as many Bethnal Green mothers were under twenty-five – those in two-parent families in a ratio of three in Bethnal Green to two in Woodford. Since the Bethnal Green fathers were also younger, it follows that there was a greater proportion of younger couples in Bethnal Green. Only Mrs Powell and Mrs Clark – both, as it happens, in Bethnal Green – were over thirty-five. The youngest mother, Geraldine Herbert, was still only fifteen when I first met her. This general discrepancy in age has important implications, which will be followed up in chapter 4.

Education

In Bethnal Green over half the mothers had left school as soon as they were able to, and only four out of the fifty got to or beyond A level. In Woodford these proportions were more or less reversed, just over half reaching A level or better. The proportion in Woodford with some kind of higher vocational or professional training or academic education was far higher than that in Bethnal Green.

As with the mothers, so with the fathers. Both in schooling and in further education the level was noticeably higher in Woodford than in Bethnal Green. It must also be said that in both areas more men than women had reached higher levels in schooling and further education. This depressing imbalance inevitably carried forward into their working lives.

Mothers' employment

What were the jobs the mothers had or had been in? Such is the structure of women's employment it comes as no surprise to find (using the Registrar-General's classification by socio-economic groups) that the largest cluster of occupations falls in the junior non-manual group. Thus, typically, 49 per cent were working – when they were employed – as shorthand typists, secretaries, clerks, hairdressers, shop assistants and the like. There was, however, a marked difference between the areas. Of those twenty-three mothers who were or had been in the higher-ranking occupations, only four belonged to Bethnal Green. The past or present jobs of the thirteen Bethnal Green and three Woodford mothers in manual occupations were nearly all semi-skilled or unskilled – machinists, cleaners and the like.

The women and girls my colleagues and I interviewed were all still enjoying the first flush of motherhood. The idea of paid work, whether at home or out of it, was with most very much for the future. Only two mothers in Bethnal Green had jobs at the time of the interviews or were about to return to them, compared with eleven in Woodford, six of whom were part time. In view of the age of the baby and the fact that it was a first child, it is not surprising that in each case these proportions are lower than the 1981 Census figures for economically-active mothers with children under five in Tower Hamlets and Redbridge,[15] though other studies show quite substantial minorities of mothers of first babies in some form of employment within the first year.[16]

The separation of home from work was originally reinforced by migration to the suburbs. This had the dual effect of giving a new kind of significance to the home and of attaching the woman more firmly to it. But it seems that suburban mothers may be changing.

The first thing to note about the Woodford group is that the jobs for nearly all who were planning a return were relatively high-ranking. Thus Mary Clifford, in a management job, said she would be glad to get her 'mind working again'. 'I've been feeling very sort of mindless at home. You obviously do have these guilt feelings but I haven't been through all that at college – using my brain and everything – just to give it all up.' And Isobel Turner, an economist, thought she might 'go a bit loopy' if she stayed in all the time. She did, however, have 'mixed feelings: I love my job but I want to be with the baby.' Predictable enough, as was also what Mrs Grainger, a self-employed physiotherapist working from home, had to say. She gave two reasons for her return.

> 'Meeting people, I quite enjoy that aspect of it. It gets you away from thinking of the baby too much. And financial, it's helping towards the bills of our house and upkeep of baby. If I wasn't working it would be very difficult to pay the bills because of the high mortgage rates and interest.'

Marion Henry, who helped a friend with the catering in a pub, thought she had got it 'just about right. Three days I'm at home, and it means at weekends I can be free. My husband working the hours he does the last thing I want to do is to be running round with the Hoover then.' Mrs Shadwell had reluctantly and only temporarily gone back to work part time as a secretary, because of her husband's unemployment. She 'couldn't imagine doing a full-time job. I'd hate to miss all that time with the baby.'

Apart from Mrs Shadwell it was the interest of the job, the desire for stimulation, that seemed to be uppermost in their minds. And in this perhaps lies one important reason for the difference between the two areas, for relatively few mothers in Bethnal Green had 'interesting' jobs to go back to. Michelle Bentham was one, and she had returned full time to her solicitor's practice. The other Bethnal Greener, Jenny Langley, also working full time, alone of the thirteen back at work, was in a manual job. Like Mrs Shadwell, she had gone back reluctantly because they 'needed the money'. And here the first surprise that more Bethnal Green mothers were not apparently feeling financial pressures acutely enough to prompt them to seek employment is tempered by the realisation that for many quite substantial sums in maternity allowance and maternity pay had tided them over the first month or so after the baby's birth.[17] And then there was the little group of mothers who had never worked outside the home (eight in Bethnal Green and two also in Woodford), either because they were too young or because they came from places overseas where it is still unusual for women to do paid work.

What of the rest? Boredom and loneliness had already afflicted a few. Mrs Briggs had ended her 'diary' of the preceding day with the comment, 'the usual boring day'.[18] Most others, it seemed, kept boredom at bay. The reasons given for not yet returning to work centred mainly on the pleasure of being with their baby or on the baby's 'need' of them. The 'first few years are the most important years of a child's life', was a typical comment. Mrs Sadler said, 'I don't want to miss all the pleasure of watching him growing up.' There were even some among them (17 per cent) who could not envisage a return to paid work at all, or not until their children were grown up. Mrs Perry 'liked being a mother too much'. 'I wouldn't want to leave my children until they're about twenty.' Mrs Reeves said that they had 'waited nine years to have him and I don't think it's right to leave him with some one else.' A small group were unsure. Like Mrs Green.

'I don't know if I will be going back or not. I don't really think I'd like to. But then I miss the company at work. Whilst I do have friends and I can get in the car and go and see them all, one actually has to make an effort to go and do that. When you were at work, there were always people around. On the odd days I can go crazy if I talk to this baby any more! It would take a lot of organisation. I haven't got any parents locally; my in-laws are in Scotland. There's not that natural set of people to fall back on. In some ways my upbringing tended towards mother staying home, and looking after the baby; but having gone out and been to college till I was 21, and got myself a good career and good salary, it is a bit of a dilemma as to what to do. It does cause you conflicts.'

Mrs Berman, even more than Mrs Green, was clearly chafing from restricted domesticity.

'It depends on money and my brains. I'd really, really like to stay at home and bring him up till he starts school. But I don't know. I even thought of doing a voluntary job with

45

handicapped children. It's just not enough to do with one baby. I need to be busy. I started to write a book when I was pregnant about the psychology of a pregnant woman – how unassertive you can become. Yes, I will go on with it. And I'm definitely going to take a swimming instructor's course.'

Mrs Green and Mrs Berman had both returned to their jobs a year later.[19]

The majority were planning to embark on the now accepted dual career at some stage in the future,[20] though four-fifths hoped that one part of the career would be part time. Some were going to have to overcome their husband's resistance. Over one-third reported that their husband wanted them to stay at home, five that their husband 'won't let' them. One of these, Mrs Black, told me that she'd like to go back – she missed 'the girls and the friendly faces'.

'I can't talk to the baby about dresses and shoes and that, can I? I've asked my husband about going back and he says no. I've got to wait a couple of years. He seems like very old-fashioned. Mother's place is at home. Baby needs me more than he needs the money coming in. He says it's not fair bunging them on to someone else to look after. He's your responsibility and he's right in a way. No, no arguments about it. No – no idea that he might take a turn at looking after the baby. He does a lot of overtime but he's at home a lot 'cos of shift work. That's good.'

In fact proportionately even more husbands than their wives had led me to expect were against their wives working outside the home. Here is Mr French:

'We've discussed that, my wife and I. She seems to want too many things at once. The main problem is, who do you give the child to and really the child should obviously be looked after by his mother, at his age anyway. Our financial situation is a bit tight at the moment but we can manage and I don't want her to go out to work, though she does because she wants to have money in her pocket. She don't want to ask me for everything she wants. I understand that but the baby's too young. The only person would be my mother-in-law but you know what that means. Like all mothers-in-law she tends to smother her daughter, and Sybil is young and she can be easily influenced.'

The remaining two-thirds were 'easy' or positively approving. Such was Mrs Clifford's husband: 'She's obviously got some ability and talent. It would be wasted if she was to stay at home. From her point of view I'd prefer her to go back.' I shall return to these husbands and wives and their attitudes and way of life in chapter 6.

Fathers' employment

Bethnal Green shares the familiar inner-city economic decline, and the disappearance of so many of the little workshops and the closing down, or removal from the area, of four major sources of employment – Kearley & Tonge's, Allen & Hanbury's, Charrington's and Allied Supplies – was reflected in the high proportion of unemployed Bethnal Green fathers. Nine were out of work, the equivalent of 23 per cent, which is even higher than the unemployment figures for all economically-active men in Bethnal Green – 17.2 per cent.[21, 22]

Only one of these nine fathers had held a non-manual job. He had given up being a pub manager because he and his wife had not wanted to bring up a child over a pub. He was training to be a bus driver when we met him. Otherwise all were in semi-skilled or unskilled manual occupations.

In Woodford also most of the seven unemployed fathers had been in manual jobs. Rob Shadwell was the exception. After six years in his first job as a computer technician he had been made redundant. Two or three months as a commercial traveller had shown him that this was not for him. When we met him he was optimistically anticipating a return to the type of work for which he had been trained, an optimism that a year later was proved unfounded.

Although the number of jobs that each of the fathers had held and the time spent in them varied, age of course being one factor, there was no marked difference between the areas. For some, like Mr Shadwell and two Bethnal Green fathers who had been in their last job for more than three years, things had previously been pretty steady. For others, less so. Nineteen-year-old Dan Sutton, for instance, had got through ten or more jobs since leaving school.[23]

Some of those in work at the time of the interview had had similar, somewhat checkered, job histories. Over one-fifth, however, had been in their present jobs for ten years or more and a similar proportion for between six and ten years. The majority were on a 40-hour week and relatively few worked overtime.

Within each occupational group there was on the whole a much greater diversity of occupation among the fathers than among the mothers. A variety of skilled trades and professions were represented. The rest ranged from an assortment of managerial, technical, public-service and agency posts to a varied collection of semi-skilled and unskilled occupations, which included a museum attendant and a butcher.

Income

None of the families had substantial capital assets except of course for their owned homes. Only the Greggs, who had a caravan on Canvey Island, and the Mitchells, who shared a family cottage in Lincolnshire, had a second home. None even lived in a detached house. Nor on the other hand were any among the poorest. None was destitute. All had a roof over their heads, even if it was some-one's else's. Of misery caused by poverty there was seemingly none or very little, but that was perhaps a measure of resilience. There were, however, families who could certainly be identified as poor whether by absolute or relative standards.[24] More would be poor according to the third currently used measure of poverty, that commonly known as 'relative deprivation'. According to this concept, money income is relevant only in so far as it provides the ability to meet needs as prescribed by the group to which a person belongs. As Peter Townsend has put it,[25]

> Individuals, families and groups in the population can be said to be in poverty when they lack the resources to obtain the type of diet, participate in the activities and have the living conditions and amenities which are customary, or are at least widely encouraged or approved in the societies to which they belong. Their resources are so seriously below those commanded by the average individual or family that they are,

in effect, excluded from ordinary living patterns, customs and activities.

It is not at all easy to find out in detail about money coming into the family. The first difficulty is that as well as cash income something should also be known about savings and other possible financial resources. Furthermore, to obtain a full picture, there must be information about expenditure, including housing costs. To get all such information would call for an enquiry devoted to just that. It certainly would have entailed more questions than there was time for. Here I am concerned mainly with cash income. Housing costs are discussed in chapter 5. The relationship between income and expenditure is touched on in chapter 6.

Another difficulty is that this is a sensitive area. Some people are entirely reluctant to talk, though in the present sample the mothers and fathers were on the whole forthcoming and responsive. A separate short money questionnaire was used. Where the mothers were single and where, among the couples, there was to be no father's interview, the mothers were asked these money questions which were all together on a short separate questionnaire. Otherwise, the choice of who should reply on matters of fact was left to them. When possible, both were asked for their assessments of need. In only two instances was there a blanket refusal to answer any questions about money, and in another the interview was terminated for other reasons before they were reached. I am not so naïve as to suppose that questions on income always picked up on the occasional gains from the 'hidden economy' – earnings from side jobs, and so on.[26] Nor that 'don't know' was not sometimes a polite substitute for 'Mind your own business.' With certain questions, particularly to do with savings, some informants were quite frank over not wishing to reply. Apart from savings, the 'don't knows' were, in fact, more likely to refer to outgoings than incomings.

Wives are traditionally ignorant of their husbands' earnings,[27] which could be a further difficulty in the way of obtaining accurate information. Where the husband was replying and his wife was not present there was, of course, no means of knowing whether she knew his earnings. In one instance where she was present, ignorance was probable, Mr Watson pointing to the written amount with a joking show of secrecy. But there were no other incidents of this kind during joint interviews, and all the wives replying on their own did so with apparent knowledge. In fact, I am reasonably confident that the great majority of the mothers knew as much about the family finances as their husbands; in some instances more so. Young and Willmott[28] saw some signs of change by the early 1970s, and it seems that the trend has accelerated in the past five years or so.[29]

My sample families were urban and of the South East. This may have influenced their attitudes as may also their relative youthfulness.[30] The most important factor was perhaps their stage of life. Their first child had only recently arrived; the great majority had both been earning before that. I can only speculate, but I suggest that, since many must still have been in the process of reorganising their family finances and adjusting to changed financial as well as other circumstances, they would have been more likely to do this on the basis of pooled rather than one-sided knowledge.[31]

It seemed sensible to go straight for the income in the 'pocket', which meant that I asked about 'take-home pay' rather than gross earnings. The amount received by those on unemployment or supplementary benefit is more complicated. Here it is a question not only of deductions from income but also of additions to it. These are the allowances, principally money for rent or rates. Whether these are called additions to income or deductions from costs is a matter of choice. But it is important for the reader to know which system has been adopted. I have, in fact, included them all – rent and rebate payments made through supplementary benefit,[32] special allowances, home-owners' subsidies and rates rebates – under income.

So how much money did the families have coming in? Three things stand out (see appendix 2, table 2.4). The first is the difference between areas, the second the position of the single mothers, and the third, tenure. Of the forty-six Bethnal Green families for whom there is information, over two-thirds had less than £80 a week coming into the home. Taking only two-parent families, the proportion on this low income was still very much higher than that of the equivalent group in Woodford. Twice as many, in fact. Again taking only two-parent families at the other end of the scale, the difference is also marked – only seven of the thirty-four in Bethnal Green had an approximate income of more than £120 per week, compared with well over half the forty-three Woodford families. The median net income for the Bethnal Green families was approximately £90.50 and for Woodford £160 per week.[33]

All the single mothers were in the £60 or less income bracket. All were on supplementary benefit. Those living with relatives were in receipt of their personal and child allowance, less their child benefit and the one-parent benefit which had just been introduced as interviewing began. The amount varied according to their age and also whether they were living on their own or with relatives. May Riley, in her own Bethnal Green council flat, just scraped through on the right side of £55. Her counterpart in Woodford, June Pratt, had £53-odd per week. The remainder were on the appropriate basic rate current at the time, which ranged from £2.40 per week to £24.35 per week, with or without any small statutory or other extras.

Only six two-parent council tenants had a net income of more than £120 per week compared with twenty-five home-owners. Moreover, all of these last except four had more than £140 per week coming into the home. Only two home-owners – the Selbys in Bethnal Green, and the Shadwells in Woodford – were in the £61 to £80 per week bracket, compared with fourteen of the council tenants. The median net income for the home-owning families worked out, very approximately, at £157 per week, and that of the two-parent council families at £81 per week.[34]

The majority of two-parent families in tenures other than owner occupation and council tenancies, particularly the sharers, brought home less than £80 per week. Three notable exceptions among this group were the Patels and the Russells, both living with parents, whose net incomes topped £120, and the Farrows in Bethnal Green (in tied accommodation), who netted over £150 a week.

These then were the cash incomes as reported to the interviewers. But they do not necessarily reflect the financial security or otherwise of the families. The most important underlying difference lay in the possession or not of the home. The home-owners had a marketable capital asset. There were also savings. Though there was relatively little difference between the areas in the proportions of two-parent families who had once had savings, twice as many in Woodford as in Bethnal Green had them at the time of the interviews. There was a further difference where amounts were concerned – as far as these were ascertainable. Roughly similar proportions named sums between £25 and £1,000. But possessing

£1,000 or more (going up to beyond £4,000), there were only two Bethnal Green families compared with twenty-one in Woodford.

Social class

'Any observer', my predecessors noted, 'would confirm that Woodford had a "middle-class" character as surely as Bethnal Green had a "working-class".'[35] A quarter of a century later, the same statement can be made. The working-class character of present-day Bethnal Green has been made more striking, if anything, by the dominance there of council flats. The 'gentrification' of some of the little houses has made little impression on the general character. There are too few of them, just as in Woodford the council estates are too few to affect the general middle-class impression produced largely by the houses so obviously in owner occupation. But if housing tenure gives substance to visual impression and is a recognised means of allocating people to social classes, it is not the one most commonly used. That is occupation, which has generally meant men's occupations except in the case of single women. On this basis, the difference in character between the two places in the 1950s was borne out by the proportions of manual and non-manual workers in the two study general samples – 38 and 62 per cent respectively in Woodford,[36] 82 and 18 per cent in Bethnal Green.[37] The contrast today is only slightly less strong. Census data show 36 per cent manual and 64 per cent non-manual in Woodford, 81 per cent and 19 per cent respectively in Bethnal Green.[38] These proportions are reflected in those of my sample fathers (see appendix 2, table 2.5).

This standard classification, however, seems unsatisfactory for my purposes. First, my study gives more weight to the mothers. There are more of them and more were interviewed. Their attitudes may be influenced as much by the ambience of their own working life as by their husband's or father's. Most mothers had or had had an occupation in their own right. Using the manual/non-manual classification to denote 'middle-class' and 'working-class' for the mothers, a quite different picture of the families' social class emerges from that where the father's occupation was used as the measure (see appendix 2, table 2.6). Whereas by the father's occupation, 26 per cent of the Bethnal Green and 60 per cent of the Woodford families are middle-class, when judged by the mother's, these proportions are increased to 55 and 92 per cent respectively.

But my second point is that the use of hands to define class membership no longer seems appropriate. By abandoning the manual/non-manual division and using a three-fold classification more like the old 'upper', 'middle' and 'lower', present realities are more nearly approached. Goldthorpe and others[39] create a 'Service Class', and 'Intermediate' Class' and a 'Working Class' from their seven occupational categories. The Service Class includes the Registrar-General's classes I and II, the professionals and managers; the Intermediate Class the non-manual and manual sides of class III; and the Working Class the semi-skilled and unskilled manual workers, classes IV and V. I have combined the mothers and fathers into these three divisions with two noticeable results. First, as would be expected, in the sample as a whole the largest single group of mothers and fathers (50 per cent) is the Intermediate Class, from which one may suppose, correctly, that there is considerable intermarriage between the non-manual and manual sides of social class III. Secondly, the distinctions between the areas are concentrated in the two 'outer' classes, the middle one holding roughly similar proportions. This approximately reflects the 1981 Census data where, if men and women are put together in Bethnal Green, 49 per cent would be in the 'Intermediate Class' and in Woodford 48 per cent. But the proportions in the two areas belonging to the 'Service Class' and the 'Working Class' are in almost exact inverse ratio, 39 to 9 in Woodford and 9 to 38 in Bethnal Green.

Housing tenure thus mirrors the occupational class differences, but only up to a certain point. There is a clear social class 'polarisation' between owner occupation and council tenancy at the two extremes. The middle ground, however, is taken up more or less evenly by both tenure groups (see appendix 2, table 2.7). It is buildings and their uses, therefore – high-density council estates and all the trappings of industrial and commercial enterprise on the one hand and spread-out privately-owned houses on the other – that still so clearly define working-class and middle-class character in the two neighbourhoods. But the changing relationship between this and the occupational structure of the women and men who live and work in the buildings should not in my view be overlooked.[40]

Self-ascribed social class

What class you are assigned to by objective classification is one thing. Where you place yourself is another. Lopreato and Hazelrigg suggest that the history of any class structure is to a large extent the history of the interplay of class consciousness and social mobility.[41] Members of the general sample in the earlier Woodford study were asked to assign themselves to a social class. They were then prompted with the finer sub-divisions of 'upper, upper middle, middle, lower middle and working'. Forty-eight per cent of the manual workers called themselves middle class, 3 per cent upper middle, 35 per cent middle and 10 per cent lower middle.[42] Woodford at that time was not unique in having manual workers who put themselves into the 'middle class', but it was in the high proportion doing so. I therefore thought it would be interesting to know whether things had changed twenty-five years later. They had; but to me at first sight in unexpected ways. Far from the earlier substantial proportions of manual workers who assigned themselves to the middle class, only nine out of the sixty-five mothers and fathers did so – 14 per cent.[43] This is not only very much less than in the earlier Woodford study, but is also less than in other studies.[44]

But more noticeable in my findings was the proportion of the ninety-five non-manual workers (mothers and fathers) replying to the question who called themselves working class – 46 per cent. The mothers ascribed themselves more often than the fathers to a different class – either 'up' or 'down'. In the earlier Woodford study the 'upward' rating (and its exceptionally high proportion) was explained chiefly by the influence of the dominating class of the district. The families tended to 'have some of the possessions that go with a middle-class style of life',[45] and to display other traits – in housing tenure, church and club membership, for instance, and in family relationships – associated with the middle rather than the working class. Townsend similarly identifies a number of factors which 'play a substantial part, or some part, in shaping images of class membership'.[46] These are: level of education, housing tenure, membership of either a trade union or a professional association, church attendance, deprivation index and net income level. He places the greatest emphasis on the last, and plays down altogether the relevance of occupational class.[47]

In my sample, income was clearly relevant. This was particularly so for those at the lowest net income level (under £60 per week), who called themselves working class, and the highest (over £140 per week), who called themselves middle class. The great majority of self-ascribed working class were also council tenants, which has relevance to the point about Bethnal Green's working-class character. But there was a lower correlation between owner occupation and middle-class self rating. Of these mothers with a definite view, just over half described themselves as working class. Twice as many home-owning fathers, on the other hand, assigned themselves to the middle class as to the working class.

Not too much should be made of all this because of the size of the sample and its bias towards one period in the family cycle. This bias may well account for the unusual proportions of working-class self raters with unlikely associations. Class loyalties are strong and the fact that this seems to work more for my sample than for others may have something to do with the relative newness of most of the households. Woodford mothers tended to be particularly articulate about the persistence for them of old values. Mrs Macintosh was one. She told us that she had been 'born into the working class but am by education and profession out of it, though my husband is a craftsman and a weekly wage earner. But neither of us is integrated into the middle class. We're a bit out on a limb, but it's quite a happy limb. We don't find it presents problems.' Or there was the sophisticated left-wing economist, Mrs Turner, born and brought up in Limehouse who, in telling us that she had 'working-class values' and assigning herself to the working class, sympathised with our dilemma – 'I know how difficult it is to classify class. I've done it myself.' There was, however, no indication among this group of mothers that they had carried their working-class allegiance through to their way of life and it could be that in a few years' time they would give a different answer to the question.

Minority groups

From time to time in this chapter I have referred to families who could be assumed to have a different skin colour or who had come from overseas since adulthood from countries with different cultures from that of the west. The circumlocution of the last sentence is deliberate as I wish to avoid the trap of considering them as a single group. Four examples will suffice to show how little they had in common. Tina Sydney, black-skinned, had been born in Bethnal Green. She had a strong cockney accent and behaved as a natural and confident Bethnal Greener. Mrs Bakali had been orphaned as a child in Bangladesh. She had been brought up by peasant neighbours, had been married to her husband at an early age but had only very recently joined him after a ten-year gap. She was extremely shy, hiding behind her sari, had had no schooling and could speak no English.

Mrs Benkarin, on the other hand, spoke quite good English. She had been in London for three or four years and had worked before her marriage. She dressed in European style. She and her husband had furnished the living-room of their council flat with upholstered *banquettes* against the four walls, and I immediately felt transported to their native North Africa. Mrs Patel had come with her husband from India. Her father was a doctor, and rich. She had been to university and by her own account suffered, though only mildly, from the clash of a sophisticated education and the traditional submission of a wife to a husband.

Obviously those of the families who had come recently from overseas[48] had their own kind of family and kinship network, for the most part severely disrupted by their migration. But they were usually not the only members of their family to have come. Some relatives or friends – it was sometimes difficult to tell which – were nearly always present during the interview with the Bangladeshi wives. They had also been largely dependent on these networks for their present shelter; a common pattern among this group of newcomers.

One Asian mother told of a housing official who had said, 'A lot of people like you have about ten children.' Otherwise none volunteered a complaint either of discrimination by the authorities or harassment by fellow residents, though the questioning gave them opportunity to do so. When pressed, however, one father from Bangladesh revealed that the windows of his flat had been smashed. He had made no formal complaint. I shall return to this subject in later chapters.

To sum up. Some change for the better in both places has occurred since the 1950s; in standards of physical health, for instance. In their personal characteristics, however, many families still belong firmly to each neighbourhood. If you are poor and have not got far in your education and are a single mother, you are more likely to live in Bethnal Green than in Woodford. Bethnal Green's 'working-class' character and Woodford's 'middle-class' still find their basis in the occupations of their residents and types of tenure at the two extremes of the social-class scale. It is, however, important that in both places when social classes are grouped into three occupational divisions the most substantial group of families belong in the middle. They are to be found in council tenancies and owned homes in almost equal proportions.

3

HOUSING HISTORY

Why were the families in Bethnal Green and in Woodford? Had they started their new family life elsewhere and, if so, how many homes had they had? How long had they been in their present home? In view of the nature of the sample this time should be relatively short. Eight of the single mothers were in their parents' home where they had always lived. If these are discounted, 67 per cent of the families had, in fact, been in their home for less than three years.

Only Mrs Poulter had been in her present council flat, which had belonged to her parents, for more than twenty years. By the time her husband had moved in, her father had died, and when I first met her her mother too had recently died. She and her husband were still living in the flat, but she said they had been refused the tenancy. By the time of the second meeting, however, they had been to the local Law Centre and 'the next thing I knew, they had called me to come and sign the agreement.' Two other couples had also been in their home for a long time: the Selbys, as owners, for ten years, and the Powells for sixteen. Recently married, though both over thirty-five, they had a similar housing history to the Poulters in that their council flat had belonged to Mrs Powell's mother before she died. There appears, correctly, to have been no problem for them over the transfer of the tenancy.

These three families happened to be living in Bethnal Green but generally for the sample there was relatively little difference between the two neighbourhoods for length of time in their present home. The mean time for Bethnal Green was 3.0 years and for Woodford 2.6 years. It should, however, be noted that there is a difference among the newest households according to tenure. All the Woodford council tenants had been under a year in their present home and so had well over one-third of those in Bethnal Green.

This was so for only four – all in Woodford – of the thirty eight home-owners. I shall return to the importance of this difference in the next chapter. A majority of the couples had had more than one home since marriage – over half in Bethnal Green and two-thirds in Woodford. For most of these, there had been only one other. A few, nearly all in Woodford, had had three or more homes since setting up house together.

Irrespective of the number of homes, there is the question of tenure. The aim of a newly-formed family is obviously to set up an independent household, and their final goal – their 'destination tenure'[1] – will most probably be a council tenancy or an owned home. They may succeed at once, but they will more likely have to wait and make do with privately rented or shared accommodation – a 'transit tenure'.[2] Their progress has been described as a 'tenure pathway'.[3] Only twelve of the thirty-eight home-owning couples of my sample and thirteen of the thirty-six council tenants managed with no transit tenure. Taking the sample as a whole, over half had spent some time in shared or privately rented accommodation or were still there. This matches well with roughly equivalent groups. Madge and Brown, for example, studied a sample of 914 young couples in three different areas, a substantial proportion of whom were re-interviewed twice during the first two and a half years of their marriage. They also found that more than half the couples had spent a period of time since marriage in a transit tenure.[4] Private rental, however, figured more often in their sample than in mine though there were differences between their three areas. I, too, found area differences. Reflecting the general tenure patterns of the districts, only one Bethnal Green couple had been in private furnished accommodation, compared with ten in Woodford.

In other ways there are parallels between the two samples: in the minimal movement, for instance, between the two main destination tenures. Only the Turners in Woodford and the Georges in Bethnal Green had moved from a council tenancy to home-ownership. Among the Madge and Brown sample only six couples had done so at the end of the first two and a half years.[5] None of the families in my sample had exchanged an owned for a council home, compared with 1 per cent of the Madge and Brown couples.[6]

There is nothing new in having to postpone the creation of an independent household. In the 1957 Bethnal Green marriage sample twenty-one out of the forty-five couples began their married life in a shared home.[7] Among the Bethnal Green couples of the present sample, twenty out of thirty-nine had to share. So there is no change to speak of on that count. There has nevertheless been some. In the 1950s it was the parents' home that was shared and, moreover, fifteen couples lived with the wife's parents and only six with the husband's.[8] Amongst the present Bethnal Green couples, only three-fifths of those in past or present shared households were or had been living with parents; of these five were with the wife's parents and seven with the husband's. The rest were or had been with friends or relatives. The numbers are too small for firm conclusions, but the pointers are interesting. I shall return to them in chapter 6.

Home seeking in Bethnal Green

I was also to find little change in Bethnal Green between the two periods in another aspect of housing history. Long residence was common there in the 1950s.[9] In the 1980s there is still strong evidence of this kind of continuity. As indicated in chapter 1, the great majority of the sample families were living in Bethnal Green because one or other of them had been born or brought up in the locality. Only eight couples had had no previous connection with the neighbourhood. The accident of birth, therefore, had placed them there in the first place, but a decision – if only by default in not deciding to move out of the area – kept them there. Like Jane Mason, who told us that she had always lived in Bethnal Green except for one year when she had moved with her parents to Ilford. But back they had come – 'It was too quiet; I didn't like it at all.' When she married another Bethnal Greener there was no question but that this was where they would live.

For the remaining families the inevitable mixture of chance and decision had brought them to Bethnal Green. Like the three home-owners, or like Mr and Mrs Lopez, whose journey had carried them to and from Bethnal Green and back again, via the West End, North London and Scotland through a series of homes – six in all – in the space of fifteen months. They had gone to Scotland when Jean Lopez became pregnant, as that was where she wanted to have her baby. But they returned because the house they had been sharing with her aunt was badly overcrowded. It was then that they came to Bethnal Green because there were friends to come to. But that, too, according to Mrs Lopez, had been 'getting over-crowded, you know, so we went to the Homeless Families and they wouldn't give us a place – we must go back to Scotland, so all we could do was get a squat.' Evicted from there they transferred themselves, again as squatters, to their present council flat. On the day I first met them they had just successfully countered an eviction order and had become the legal tenants.

Others of the non-local families had come from overseas or other parts of London or the UK following the usual pattern in inner London, seeking work, joining friends or relations. The Bakalis and the other three families from Bangladesh were among these. Also Mr Benkarin who, having come originally from North Africa, had, before marriage to his present wife, progressed slowly eastward within the metropolis. Or as with the three couples who had deliberately chosen the neighbourhood to buy a house in.

Local authority responsibility for housing in Bethnal Green at the time of this study was still divided between the Greater London Council (GLC) and the London Borough of Tower Hamlets, which I shall refer to as the Borough. Twenty-seven of the families either held the tenancy themselves or were sharing flats in sixteen GLC estates, and the remaining fourteen were spread between seven Borough estates. There is some difference between them in their policies and in their administrative practice; in the criteria, for instance, that qualify for registration. These distinctions will vanish in 1985 when the dual system becomes one – with the Borough taking over all. Meanwhile, the families had two bureaucracies they could exploit, and they did so with a greater or lesser degree of confidence and prior knowledge and sometimes, like Mr Lopez, with a formidable belligerence. He graphically amplified his wife's account of the acquisition of their GLC flat.

'We applied to Tower Hamlets. And they said we were not entitled because we weren't in the area long enough, weren't squatting long enough. Then we went to the GLC. No, the guy wouldn't take it – well he was a bit of a dope. He was one of these "just left University with my degree" sort of people, "move on and go and see them upstairs". Just a freak – I felt like dragging him over the counter and beating the hell out of him. He was one of these people, you don't know what he's thinking – a mindless person – he said that we were going to be evicted and there's no point going on the list because we'd be waiting years.

So the best thing to do was go upstairs – to homeless people. Because we were squatting here and we had a bairn. If it hadn't been for the child we wouldn't have got it. But we were determined. I told the GLC guy that came here we were the squatters that had been in the other place and now we'd moved here and that we were determined to get a place, so you can throw us out 50 times and we're still going to squat. And finally he went back to his superiors and explained the case and we got the flat.'

If you are in the early stages of forming your own family and live in or near Bethnal Green, many forces press you into a council tenancy even if you may have to wait for it. Twelve of the twenty-seven mothers in council tenancies gave as one of their reasons that there was 'nothing else possible' – a fair comment on Bethnal Green's tenure pattern, though the statement sometimes meant that it was not possible for *them*. Thirteen mothers said that they 'couldn't afford to buy or rent privately'. Most were referring to house purchase, but one father told the interviewer that with his wife pregnant there was 'no way they could have afforded private rent'. According to him – 'The thing is basically that if you rent private the landlord can put up the rent whenever he feels like it and I'm used to paying rents of £40–£50 a week and you get nothing for it.' It was unclear whether he was referring to unfurnished or furnished renting. As a 'regulated' tenant[10] in an unfurnished flat, he would have had protection from arbitrary rent increases though he could well have been asked for key money. However, with a baby on the way, the chances of his finding an unfurnished flat at an affordable rent would have been negligible. Furnished flats are less subject to controls despite possible recourse to a rent tribunal,[11] and again children are rarely welcome.

There is another force guiding Bethnal Green families towards council homes, much more difficult to pin down, which has to do with the association in peoples' minds of council housing with 'the working classes'. It was to the council you went when you were ready to set up house. This was behind Vivienne Stokes's comment – 'No, it didn't occur to me to look for private renting. The main thing when you get married is to get on the council or, if I'd taken my mum's advice, the Borough.' Sometimes it was thought out. Mrs Price told the interviewer that at the time they were applying for a council flat she had been working in a bank and she 'could have got a mortgage. So if we was desperate we could have bought, but we didn't want to.' But whether they were knowingly or unknowingly steered towards the local authority, the dominant reason given was for a 'home of our own'.

To get a local authority home you have to put your name down on the waiting list. Since the 1963 Local Government Act there has been an obligation on housing departments to provide one. The lamentable game of match-as-match-can goes slowly in one decade, fast in another. Whatever the state of play, for every winner there always appear to be more losers; the waiting lists grow longer and longer,[12] though this varies from borough to borough and is not necessarily a true measure of the supply. But since the Homeless Persons Act of 1977 the local authority is obliged to house people who are technically homeless whether or not they are on a waiting list though, as with the Lopezes, there are loopholes. Since the Conservatives first took office in 1979 the sale of council homes has been accelerated, thereby reducing if not the absolute number of properties available then assuredly the absolute number of desirable properties.

Both the Borough and the GLC housing departments had a points scheme for applicants.[13] There were, however, various possibilities for jumping the waiting-list queue. The GLC 'sons-and-daughters' scheme was one. In this the children of GLC tenants if about to set up independent households were given priority – a practice that echoes the 'speaking for relatives' by tenants of private landlords and housing trusts in the old Bethnal Green,[14] and which still occurs. The Borough's engaged-couples list, now defunct, was another. This was a ballot in which you could take part on becoming engaged to be married. Both authorities ran difficult-to-let schemes. These were for properties in poor condition or high up in tower blocks or otherwise likely to be unpopular and were not intended for families with children. Mr and Mrs Moore tried first one scheme, then another.

'What happened was we had our name down with the Borough and our name came up in the ballot draw in the first month, but then they went on strike. So they suggested we put our name down on the GLC and then we got our names down on the sons-and-daughters list and got this place, because his mum and dad live on this estate.'

And so did the Clarks.

'Well, that's how we did it. We applied for difficult-to-let on the Borough one and we forwent that for the sons and daughters. You can't be on both. We applied in February because we were getting married a year later. We both applied on our estate; we both lived on different estates.'

But ignorance of procedures nearly landed the Poulters in trouble.

'I didn't understand half of what you had to do. I rang the GLC up a couple of times and asked how to apply. They said I should have given them six months notice before I got married. But because I rang up *after* I got married I didn't qualify for "daughters-and-sons" scheme. Then I had the borough council come down and they said they'd try to get something before she was born, and she'd been born since April. As far as they were concerned I was living here illegally and I thought they'd push it then but they didn't. So of course when the GLC offered me this we took it up.'

The majority of mothers and fathers said that they had started off knowing little or nothing about how and when to apply. They relied on friends and family for information. It was thus that Clare Price had got the impression that 'Harlow give you a second-generation place' so that if they had not got their Bethnal Green home they would have been 'given one there once we were married'. About one-third of the families had found one or other of the housing departments 'helpful', but there was much criticism – of individuals and the system, if not in such aggressive terms as those of Mr Lopez. Mr Clark was fairly typical of the dissatisfied ones, not only in his view of the housing department but in his determination.

'I think both parents would have had us but I don't think it quite works because I think that brings a lot of pressures and problems. We did apply to other places – tried whatever we could and see what came up first. It's very hard to get housing so you have to get what you can. I did want to get on the council mainly because you've got a bit of scope. I mean if you was to get a couple of rooms like a lot of people get, well, at our age [Mr Clark was in his forties and Mrs Clark in her thirties] we was obviously going to start a family, well, then you're restricted. If you're in a couple of rooms how are you going to get out of there whereas when you're on the council once you start a family you're in a position to get a transfer.'

When asked if the department had been helpful, he replied:

'No, not at all. In fact we went round to various places. Someone told us of a place in Commercial Road, an information place. We both went up there and even in there I was asking the man questions and he gave us no chance apart from what we'd done – gone onto the Borough. I was trying to see if there was any way I could get to the GLC because I wanted more openings and I should have imagined we must have been in there three-quarters of an hour and I was going on and on and on. It came up about the sons-and-daughters scheme. But it wasn't advice that was offered. I felt I had to put pressure. I felt that whatever I did I had to put on pressure to get it.'

Mr Hill expressed bitter resentment.

'I got a letter from the council saying they didn't believe I was living there all that time. We went up to Cheviot House. They've got a big long desk with three people sitting there. Every time we went up we see someone different. We never got nowhere. We filled in a form when we first went up there and that. They came round to my house and wanted proof that I lived there. A letter with a stamp and my address. We got a letter back saying it wasn't sufficient evidence. Then we waited months. Then we had to go up again – I was on at them all the time. This went on for months and months. Eventually we were offered this place.'

Officials have to implement a policy which they do not draw up. Undoubtedly some do it with insensitivity, as David Donnison found when he was Chairman of the Supplementary Benefits Commission, though he also found the opposite.[15] How far the policy itself should and can be modified is something I shall discuss in chapter 8. Meanwhile, it is only fair to record that in conversations with senior local housing officials I was impressed by their compassionate approach to many of the problems they have to deal with. It must be faced that in an understandable effort to beat the system deceptions are practised. When they got married, the Brogans had lived with her parents because earlier registration on the difficult-to-let and the 'ordinary' housing lists had produced nothing.

> 'And we had to keep lying to them and saying that we were living separately. When we said we were getting married they asked if we could live with either of our parents, and we had to say no we didn't get on with them and that. Because it's obvious isn't it, with three bedrooms in my mum's place they wouldn't think they had to give us a place of our own. It was terrible lying but what else could we do. Yes, they knew we were married and that I was pregnant.'

These, however, were the successful applicants. What of others? The Farrows and Mr and Mrs Michialos were in their tied flats because of the job. There were also two couples in Crown properties, and the Carlyles in a private tenancy – all three with a history of long residence in Bethnal Green. All had tried for council homes. The Mitchells had been 'on the list for 10 years' but had 'heard nothing'. Neither had they made any further contact, though should a ground floor flat or maisonette with a garden in their present neighbourhood become available they would 'leap at it'. Family connections had got them their present flat – 'My mum has always been a Crown tenant and when we decided to get married we put our name down and got it about six weeks before we married. This was all we were offered.' This was the Watsons' second tenancy (also obtained originally through family connections) which they had got just by 'keeping on at' the Crown for a transfer because they wanted something better, including the share of a garden for the sake of the baby. Both families had contemplated buying a home. The Watsons had cancelled an application to the building society four years previously. 'Everything went up at the same time – it was just too much.' And the Mitchells, too,

> 'discussed buying a house and everything at the time, but my husband was more intent on buying furniture. I know people who have got houses and more or less nothing to go in them

so I thought, well, leave it for a couple of years. But they've gone well out of our price range now. I'll have to be a Crown tenant now. Maybe when I become a millionaire – or my dad does!'

The Carlyles also had rejected the purchase of a home. 'We probably could afford it, but it's if anything goes wrong.' They had rejected the idea of going on with a local authority home after they had actually lived in one in Spitalfields for a couple of years.

'I think both of us were a bit disheartened with the area. It's not all that nice, it's a bit dull and drab round there. All the people in the flats were coloured or problem families, there wasn't anyone to talk to much. It wasn't too bad at the beginning, there was the novelty of being married and having your own flat and then we started noticing the area, and it turned us off a bit. I didn't mind the being alone at night. It was just what was going on around. There was always trouble and all that in the area, that was what worried me more than anything. There was always noise downstairs or fighting in the grounds. It was really terrible down there.'

Mrs Carlyle went on to explain how they got their present private tenancy:

'Well, my husband, his father had an upholstery place and he used to do work for the landlord. My husband was good friends with him and that was how we come to ask him for the place when it became vacant. My husband used to work for his dad as well. We knew the people upstairs before we moved back. Both living down the street before, they saw us grow up. The people round the back saw my mum grow up as well. Everyone knows each other.'

Their roots kept these three families in the neighbourhood; they were all in the tradition. But attempts to get a council place by those with no home of their own, whether they had roots in the district or not, had also failed. All the two-parent families had applied, clearly with the dominant wish to have a home of their own. None could 'afford to buy'. All – single and married alike – deplored their 'lack of privacy'.

Why did the three home-owners in Bethnal Green decide to buy in the first place? The Georges had made the decision after three years in a 'difficult-to-let' council flat in Bow, wanting to stay in the East End but despairing of a transfer. It was not only because the accommodation was poor but because they wanted a house. They also thought of it as a financial investment. The Selbys had been living in Kent in furnished accommodation. Mr Selby did not like 'giving money to other people – you just pour it away. There was no way we was going to get a council place then because we didn't have no family.' They had seen two houses before their present one. The 'finance company who were selling the house did it all – we didn't need no advice or nothing. We just pay our £17 a week – just like paying rent.'

The Benthams had been in a private furnished flat, wanted more space, disliked private renting and had not pursued Mr Bentham's registration on the council's difficult-to-let list because of the 'lack of choice and mobility' involved in council renting. They had looked at about 100 homes.

> 'It took a year. We went through several other places, mostly in this area but not all. The first one we tried to get went to a cash buyer. The houses were on an estate being sold for conversion. They sold very quickly. They came on the market initially at £15,000 and within a month they were up to £22,500 which was beyond us because we wouldn't have had the money to convert. So that killed that estate. We got as far as getting a mortgage for another house from the GLC. That didn't take. My cousin is a surveyor and came and looked at anything for us. That was murder, that house. You could tell we were dealing with a property company. They initially didn't tell us we were in a contract race and then did tell us. Then they wanted some extra money and did the roof when we didn't want them to. Then they wanted more money. When the extra was wanted it looked like we were going to break the conditions of the GLC mortgage, then two days later they told us they'd sold it to someone else anyway.'

Home seeking in Woodford

Long residence was much less in evidence among the Woodford families than among the Bethnal Greeners. If the locality is defined strictly by the Wanstead and Woodford boundaries, there were only eight couples of whom one or both could qualify as local. This was increased to seventeen by the inclusion of neighbouring districts such as Chigwell and Ilford. So for these seventeen couples it was on the face of it simply a question of staying where they had always been.

An important group of Woodford families had been part of the movement from inner to outer East London – thirteen families in all. Five couples had themselves made the move. They were also part of Young and Willmott's 'slow march',[16] moving upward socially as well as outward geographically. All had spent the greater part of their childhood in the East End. All had gravitated outwards in search of a home to buy. Clarice Berman, for instance, 'didn't want to have children in the East End.' Mr Shadwell's parents still lived in the East End in a council home, as did six of the other ten sets of parents.

Then there were the families where the parents had migrated while their children were young, not then only to buy; three sets of parents had moved to council estates. At least three of the families had moved from privately rented homes, and the evidence suggests that this had been so for five more.

The remaining families came from further afield, landing up in Woodford for a variety of reasons. Mr and Mrs Patel, for instance, had come to England recently from India with the intention of setting up in their own business. They had chosen Woodford because they could take temporary refuge with his parents who were living there in a house they had owned for some years. Or if the families were seeking a home to buy with prospects of an addition to the family the suburb had considerable appeal. Over the period during which the families were buying, house prices were more likely to be within their range than in many other parts of London.

Three home-owners in Bethnal Green were exceptions. Thirty-five in Woodford conformed to the prevailing tenure pattern of that district. But their decision to become home-owners and the predominant reasons offered for doing so were pretty much alike whether they were the minority or the majority group. Thus in Woodford two-thirds of the mothers, and a similar proportion of the fathers, gave financial reasons. It was 'an investment'; there was no point in paying out on a rent when what you pay out on a mortgage gives you your house in the end'; 'we wanted to get on the house-purchase ladder'. Mr Rush, who had bought his house six years before, paying £12,000 for it, spelt it out. 'The mortgage is not dead money. Even if a mortgage were double your rent you're still getting something back in the end. I mean I'll only be 46.' The Perrys had bought two years previously, paying in the region of £35,000. For Mrs Perry it was 'just daft not to buy these days, but of course we were lucky to be able to afford it.' But she thought they 'deserved it' as they had 'both worked very hard for all those years'. And Clarice Berman, referring to the decision taken eight years earlier to buy their previous home, said it was 'obvious. You buy property to escalate, don't you? Our main aim is to get better financially as we get older.' For Mr Henry, too, it was 'a natural progression as one gets older. As one takes on responsibilities one has to see some sort of value in your everyday life.'

A few suggested that home-ownership gave greater mobility. Mrs Macintosh said they had had to move because of their jobs and this was feasible only through buying. She 'didn't really want to own', though she conceded that 'it seemed better to be paying "rent" to the building society than to anybody else.' Mrs Berman, for all the 'obviousness' of their buying decision, had never 'consciously decided, "Oh my God, I don't want to live in a council place".' But there were others – nearly one-quarter – who had abandoned all thought of a council home not only because they did not like the idea of council renting, but also because they despaired of ever achieving one.

The London Borough of Redbridge also has its housing waiting list. Mrs Bell had discovered that, as in other places, a childless couple stand little chance. They had been on the list 'for years. We were told to go away and have some children. The fact that we had to live in one room at my mum's and had to dive from the door to the bed didn't count for anything.' The Winthrops had decided a council place was 'not worth it'. Margaret Winthrop's parents in Bethnal Green 'had been on the waiting list for 15 years before getting a place.' And the Oakses also 'didn't want to be council tenants. The chances of getting in round here are extremely remote anyway.'

The ability to choose initially and the freedom 'to do what you want with the place' once you've got it were reasons given by one-third of the Woodford home-owning mothers. For six, the idea of a council home, 'had never occurred to them'. Mrs Green told the interviewer:

'It was just taken for granted that we would always buy our own home. That was true for both of us. Whether or not you buy your own home depends on your upbringing, what you've been used to, always living privately rather than in rented accommodation. I don't really like the idea of paying out rent and not owning anything at the end of it. My parents were tenants in a pub, and my husband's parents have always lived in a private house that they've owned. When we first got married there wasn't a lot of money about and it was a question of saving up to get the deposit. We'd only been going out for about 10 months before we got married and we didn't have really enough time in that space of time to get together a deposit. So once we were married we settled down [in a privately rented furnished flat] to saving up for a deposit towards actually buying our own house. That took around 10 to 11 months.'

She thought she would not 'really like to live in a council house, even though it might be a bit snobbish.' Mr and Mrs Enright had both come from families where they 'all own their homes and it was just accepted that one gets a house and pays a mortgage.' To Mrs Enright, 'a council list is for someone who just hasn't got the wherewithal to own their own property or pay a high rent.' What came through, though not perhaps so clearly, was the obverse of the Bethnal Green association between council housing and the working class.

In Bethnal Green the majority of council tenants had felt themselves ignorant of how to go about getting a home. By contrast, the majority of Woodford home-owners felt they had known enough when they started to buy, and those who did not had been untroubled by their lack of knowledge. Mr Grainger had thought of it as 'an apprenticeship'. Well over two-thirds had taken some time over their search and had seen a lot of properties. It was a not untypical story of house-hunting in London in the 1970s and 1980s. Getting on for half had lost one or two properties they would have preferred because of mortgage problems, for instance, or through their position in the chain of purchasers or because they had been gazumped.

A variety of opinion was expressed about the professional help they had had. Some was good and helpful, but Mrs Turner, for instance, would 'cheerfully have stuck a stick of dynamite up the solicitor's backside.' He had been recommended by the building society and it appears he delayed paying over the deposit because, in Mrs Turner's view, he could earn interest on it. There was, however, no clear weight of opinion either way. It was the same regarding the expense of the whole transaction.[17] Some had found it very high, others 'not too bad'. Building societies usually came in for considerable praise, though again, not all of them. But for all the home-owners the outcome had been worth it.

It is a long way from home-ownership to accommodation for the homeless provided by the local authority – a very temporary form of transit tenure and among the least desirable. The Reads, after a row with their private landlord, found themselves in a 'half-way house', so called because it is half-way between a hostel and a self-contained flat. The second sharing couple – the Russells – had managed to avoid such a fate. They had returned from Kent eight months previously for want of employment, and had moved in with Fred's parents as there was 'nowhere else to go'. They had immediately put their name on the housing list, but after the arrival of the baby they had been transferred to the 'Homeless Family' list.

'They said you won't be on that very long. What they're saying now is we'd have to go into a hostel first. But I'm not doing that – no way – not with our baby. They said, "Well there are some who go there straight after they come out of hospital." "Well," I said, "that's up to them, but I'm not doing that."'

The Russells and the Reads were not alone in Woodford in being classified as homeless. Four of the nine council tenants had acquired their flats by this means. Nor were the Russells the only couple who were prepared to resist or fight the various pressures put on them. The MacEwans had been in a hostel. This was where they began their fight.

'The place they offered us wasn't a formal offer. I wouldn't let them make it one because in the hostel you have to take your first choice. And if you don't take that you've had it. They tried to make it a formal offer but I played up and argued so much I said it's not fair to us. And I really did play hell over it. I wouldn't have gone there to be honest. Yes, we know people living there and we've heard even worse stories than what I did before. A terrible place to live. And yet the flats are so nice. It's the people that are rubbish. They're just scum. I mean I'm a friendly person, I want to enjoy where I live. And you can't do that where you're not safe. A lot of marriages have ended there and suicides and what have you. I think it's unfair that they should stick young married couples in there for their first home. It's mostly trouble-makers that get put there, but there's a lot of newly-marrieds too and it's not fair. But the council were quite sympathetic in the end.'

The flat they obtained was in a small estate with much to recommend it. Another couple had accepted a flat in the estate rejected by the MacEwans and found the council reasonable to deal with. Their troubles had occurred earlier at Christmas time in a private tenancy when they had been refused entry by the landlord on returning one evening and had had to sleep the night in the car, 'not the best time of the year! It was a terrible aggravation.' But they had succeeded in establishing their eviction as illegal and the landlord had been fined £100. The experience of two other Woodford couples in council tenancies echoed the insensitivity – and worse – of Tower Hamlets officialdom as described from the point of view of the injured party. Here is Jenny Steel.

'We went up there when I was pregnant and they wouldn't give us anywhere until we got married. They told us it wasn't their problem and they wasn't a charity. So we had to get married and take up our marriage certificate. They wouldn't believe I was pregnant, even when 7 months. I had to take a letter from the doctor.'

And Pat O'Kelly.

'It's really embarrassing to get a place. They don't believe a word you say. You go up and you explain to them and they just make it as hard as possible for you. They were going to put Lorna in a hostel when she was four months pregnant.

Her grandmother didn't want to keep her. I disagreed and phoned the Chairman of Housing. Argued on the phone for two hours and they finally gave us this.'

Perseverance, 'pestering', a tough refusal to accept the inevitable were thus put to good use. None had been on the waiting list for longer than eighteen months. Here is an unabashed piece of manipulation.

'You ask people you know. To get anything from the council you've got to tell a lot of porky-pies. You've got to walk in, like, sobbing. It's no good saying you're happy and that – that's how we got this place really. Nothing's above board with the council. Whatever they ask you, you've got to answer as they want to hear it. It's the same with the social [social security]. I went twice when I was about 16. I've never been again. I hate pleading.'

It did not always work, of course. Mr Reagan was not pleased with the result of his struggle.

'I went down to the council dozens of times. They suggested we should go into a hostel and we'd be on the homeless persons list. I wasn't going to agree to that. We came to a decision then, me and the feller up there, that we'd be housed as soon as the baby was born – as soon as they knew the baby was OK. He said to me – I'll put it to you straight, if the baby lives you can have a place – if it don't, you can't. So I said that's fair enough. Some people might get a bit upset about it, but I thought it was fair. But when I went back down there after they didn't want to house me. They wanted me to wait another three or four months. So I said – Well, where's my wife going to go with the baby? I said, She'll have to stay in hospital. So he said – Well, the man dealing with your case is on holiday for a fortnight. So I said, That's not good enough, you'll have to get the next bloke in charge down.

So he said I can't do that, so I said I'm not leaving here till you get someone down here. Some geezer came down and I said you promised me to have one as soon as the baby was born. I've brought the birth certificate up like you've asked. So he said all we can offer you is the 11th floor. So I said, I'm going to have to take it, aren't I? I knew they had the vacancies;

they were just being awkward. Really they don't allow babies up this high. But because I didn't wait for the three months they slung me in here. And it was a right hole when I got it.'

Only four mothers and three fathers in Redbridge Council tenancies actually referred to the alternative of buying a home and then only to reject it as a possibility.

As for private renting, that was also rejected by a similar proportion. Mr MacEwan had had 'a taste of it. They just charge too much. I was living in a landlord flat when I met Vi – and it was in a right state – mice-infested and the lot, and a lot of landlords are too selfish these days. And if we could get a council house, then we might be able to buy it.'

Finally, there were the three Woodford families whose decisions brought them to that relatively new form of tenure – the housing association described in the Introduction. The Bakers were in one sense council tenants in so far as the property – a large, attractive, dilapidated Victorian house – was owned by Redbridge Council, though the immediate landlord was a housing association. Hannah had taken the flat as a single girl and had since married her 'landlord'. He had come to England from Australia some years before and had become involved in housing the homeless through close association with an ecumenical Christian group. The main association, set up and funded under the 1974 Housing Act, now owns 1,400 properties. It grew out of the much smaller organisation, managed by Jim Baker, which exists on the income from eight or nine properties and which would cease if these were taken back by the council.

Wendy and Len Black gave slightly different accounts of how they came to be in a housing association. With her it was 'sheer luck' and some friendly advice from someone in the housing department; with him it was 'a lot of hard work and searching'. One thing, however, is clear, and this is that they took the initiative, first in 'tearing up the council application form', and secondly in trying 'everything, the local paper, every bureau we could think of. But they take so long. They just try to get your name down on their books and then they want a fee, a percentage on the rent of the property which they get you. They've never done nothing for us and we're still on their books as far as we know.' When they finally reached the housing association's office through a casual recommendation, they were told they could be given a flat before the day was out – 'We were really lucky, really lucky. Everybody expected us to come out smelling of roses.'

The Sadlers had been desperate for 'somewhere to live together'.

'My husband, he lived with his parents. I had to live with my parents and none of the rooms were big enough to take the two of us, no place to live separately. It was a bit of a strain for nine months: the build-up to the wedding and then after the wedding it was like we hadn't got married, you know. He went home at night and I went home to me mum. We'd been on the council list in Camden for ages, nearly two years, and we only got offered sort of old slum flats. Like we both had pretty nice houses so we wasn't going to go for something worse than what we already had, so we looked around to buy and that but for what we could afford, it was just bedsits. It wasn't really worth paying out for a bedsit. We wrote off to quite a lot of co-ownerships. There's loads of houses . . . all over London. We was on quite a few of those and this one came along first. We both wanted to stay in London but this came along so we took it.'

More will be learnt of this particular scheme in chapter 5.

The grandparents

There were no co-ownership schemes in Woodford or Bethnal Green in the days when the parents of the sample mothers and fathers had been forming their families. There had been other differences, of course, as is shown by the housing histories of the eight grandmothers and one grandfather. They were asked to describe their experiences at the birth of their first child. The earliest was born in 1936; the most recent in 1963. But their housing experiences at these varied times had been singularly alike in one respect, and for most had been of a kind that the present-day families would have found unacceptable. The common feature was that, with the exception of Mrs Hammer of Woodford and Mrs Sutton of Bethnal Green, they had all returned from hospital to a home that was not their own. Mrs Hammer had been the only owner occupier and Mrs Sutton the only council tenant. Six out of eight had been living either with parents, in-laws or in one furnished privately rented room. This contrasts with the present sample of eighty-eight couples, only seven of whom were not in a home of their own by the time their first child was born. I have, of course, no means of knowing how representative of the remainder of the families these eight grandmothers are, but the proportions in the earlier Bethnal Green study who had started their married life in the parental home suggest that they are probably not untypical.[18]

Thus, for example, Mrs Cohen told the interviewer that in the mid-1930s nothing but one room with no facilities in her sister's home had been possible. Mrs Macintosh, alone in Perth with no friend or relative near, with her husband in the Air Force and living in one unfurnished room, 'just had a bed and the bare cooking facilities. There was an outside toilet and a pail for emptying your slops in, but it was clean and I was quite happy there.' Tina Sydney's elder brother was born in 1963 in Mile End Hospital, whence her mother had returned to 'one room in a house belonging to some Indian people'. 'It was all right,' Mrs Sydney said, though 'all right' seems overpraise for a home consisting of one room for two people and a baby, without a kitchen ('there was a cooker on the landing') and bathroom. Their subsequent housing careers traced in the ensuing pages take us further, of course, than we are able to go with their children's.

In chapter 1 I described how the Shaws – Mary Clifford's parents – had migrated to Wanstead from the East End and changed tenure eventually from private renting to owner occupation. Mr and Mrs Cohen, also with a home-owning daughter living in Woodford, took a similar outward-bound pathway. But their journey had taken much longer and followed what might be called the alternative standard route, bringing them to a different destination. It had begun in Shoreditch at a much earlier date – 1936 – in one room. Six months later they had been able to move into a couple of rooms with their 'own toilet, wash place and cooker. There was more room for the baby and ourselves.' Eventually, after the war and several moves, they had obtained a council flat in Whitechapel and there they stayed for twenty-seven years. Now they are in Debden, still tenants of the local authority. You could say that their goal had been more modest than that of Mrs Shaw. It certainly took longer to reach, but they too were satisfied with what they had achieved. With them there was nothing to be deplored, as there was with Mrs Shaw, in the fact that the East End had caught them up. They had brought it with them and were glad of it: 'It's mostly East End people who've moved here. We're all more or less the same kind of working-class people.' Mrs Cohen liked it because of the neighbourly atmosphere, the gardens and 'because you get to know one another more in a closed community like this.'

Apart from the similar experience of returning from hospital after the birth of the baby to a 'home' that was not their own, there is much that is different in the histories of Mrs Macintosh and Mrs Stubbs, Jill Reagan's mother. Mrs Macintosh, a widow, represents a third kind of population movement. Or rather, her son and daughter-in-law do. For they came south from Scotland seeking work and a different life style, and this is how they and Mrs Macintosh senior came to be part of this study. The young couple owned their Woodford home. His mother was a gentle lady from the far north-west on a short visit to London. After describing the forlorn circumstances attendant on the birth of her first baby, she gave an account of her subsequent progress through a series of homes. These were peculiar in some ways to the Scottish urban scene – witness her 'single end' in an Edinburgh tenement, 'just a single kitchen-cum-living room. There were two toilets on each landing, a wash house, a huge balcony and a great big communal green.' Finally, in 1946, after weekly requests at the letting office where she paid her rent for the single end, she got a house. 'And that was a lovely house. I thought I'd collapse.' When her husband came out of the RAF, they managed a small family hotel in Perth and this was the childhood home of Alex, the sample father. Now she had a five-room council house in the same city.

Mrs Stubbs was the only Woodford grandmother whose childhood and youth had been spent in the same street. The council estate in which she lived is pleasant, brick-built, self contained with gardens and trees. Mrs Stubbs appreciated its qualities – 'I know it doesn't look like a council estate.' Nevertheless, she 'would rather it wasn't one. I suppose it's snobbery. That's the only reason.'

Mrs Stubbs had not only been brought up in the locality; she had been born there, as had her mother before her – three generations belonging to the same outer-London suburb, not a usual pattern. Are she, her mother and her daughter auguries of the future pattern of generations in Woodford and its sister suburbs? Or will the 'centrifugal movement' continue, as Mrs Shaw thought it must, thus maintaining the heterogeneity typified by the Woodford sample families – jobs, marriage and the search for better housing taking the next generation still further out, and bringing in others from elsewhere? Mrs Stubbs would not want to live anywhere else; her daughter said that she did not mind.

There is, however, a direction evident in Mr and Mrs Stubbs's housing history, relatively stable though this had been, which does correspond to a national trend. In its early stages they had taken the common route from their transit tenure – shared accommodation – to their 'destination tenure' – council tenancy. But the last stage exemplified a recent aspect of shifting patterns and that was the move from council tenancy to ownership, along with a growing number of others on the estate, through purchase of their council house. Moreover they typify this particular pattern in another sense. It is the long-standing, older tenants who buy.[19] Mrs Stubbs's daughter and son-in-law are council tenants, but there is no prospect at all at the moment that they could convert their tenancy into ownership.

The last Woodford grandmother, Mrs Hammer (Judith Sharman's mother), was the only one of the eight who had, with her husband, owned the home she was living in when her first baby was born in 1952. They now live in Woodford, in her daughter's opinion in a 'much posher part' than hers. They are a relatively affluent family from East Africa. Their housing history and outlook, therefore, were very different from those of the other grandmothers and their families. From her 1950s home in a 'newish suburban housing estate', where all her friends had small children, they had gone out 'day after day and visited and sat under the trees and drank tea, and the kids had biscuits and cold drinks. And then at five you went home again. This was a daily pattern. There were always children for the children to play with.' When they had decided to emigrate to the UK there had been no automatic assumption of buying a home, as I suspect there would have been had they come twenty or thirty years later.

'We imagined ourselves being content with a couple of rooms to rent. We knew housing was difficult, but we hadn't envisaged buying. But after being in one room in hotels with the children, we realised we had no option but to buy a house. For one thing one would never have been able to rent suitable accommodation; landlords in those days were very tricky and choosy and with children of six and eight we wouldn't have got a flat. Secondly, by this time, because they were so dependent on us for affection – whereas in East Africa they'd been used to family around – the children were thrown immediately on our resources only and became rivals and fought. Until then they had been perfectly good friends. With a house they would each have their own room and get out of each other's hair. Also to us, a flat was a purpose-built edifice, whereas flats at that time were 99 per cent conversions. We didn't like the prospect of this. We would never have bought a terraced house but were reasonably content with a semi-detached – not that close to your neighbours on both sides.'

Her comment on flats is relevant to the strictures on council-owned 'purpose-build edifices' which were, it is true, only rumbling at the time but which were soon to become part of the conventional wisdom. So, for the Hammer–Sharman family, there had been continuity in tenure. Their daughter and son-in-law also owned their present home – their first. Whether they will become established as a two-generation Woodford family remains to be seen. At the moment, all the younger pair would commit themselves to was a move to 'a better area', which could be quite near by, at some future date.

The Bethnal Green grandmother-families present a very different picture – an inner-city picture as you would expect, but, in their immediate circle anyway, without the twist of migration to the suburbs. This little group, then, were the 'left-behinds', but they demonstrated also the pull of the known and loved neighbourhood. They may have lived there always or they may have come more recently, but they had stayed and were staying because this was what they wanted.

Mrs Sydney was typical of one very important component of inner-city life – the successive waves of immigrants who have sought refuge or work. It is true that these tend to move out as new groups come in. But some also settle, become assimilated and may themselves look askance at the newer arrivals. Mrs Sydney and her husband had come in with the great influx from the Caribbean in the 1950s and 1960s. Her parents had died before she came; her husband's were alive but had never left the West Indies. After the birth of their first child in 1963 they had stayed in their one room for three years and then moved to yet another single room in Hackney, the family increasing in size the while. Finally, in 1969, they had got their present council flat. Though she 'could do with another bedroom' and would have preferred a maisonette, she was content and would never leave the area. Nor would her husband. And what of their daughter? It is too soon to say, for Tina had her baby when she was only sixteen and was still living with her parents.

Mrs Gedge, Mrs Mitchell's mother, and Mrs Sutton are true East Enders and proud of it. Both were in tenancies usually included in the general category of private, though they differ from each other. Mrs Sutton's landlord was a long-standing housing trust; that of Mrs Gedge was the Crown.[20] Here was a tale of continuity, for her Bethnal Green childhood home had been among the first to be taken over by the Crown from a genuinely private landlord. Apart from a brief 'terrible' stay in a council flat, where they had been placed temporarily while work was done on their house, she had lived in Crown property ever since. Her daughter and son-in-law also rented from the Crown and neither they nor Mrs Gedge would have wanted to move far from the area.

Mrs Gedge – 'call me Daisy' – was a lively, voluble widow who obviously revelled in her reminiscences. Her mother had died in childbirth, leaving seven children under sixteen. Daisy was the last of the sisters but had two younger brothers. She had lived with her father, bringing two husbands into the home, until her father died. And there she was living when, by her second husband (the first had been killed in the war), she had her first child in 1949.

'My father, he was mum and dad to us. I never went to work. When I was 14 I kept house for him and my brothers. There was never no trouble living with him, he was a good help to me. I never washed a nappy in my life!'

Mrs Sutton and her husband were the second and only other set of grandparents who had been in a home of their own – a council flat in Dalston – consisting of two bedrooms, a front room, kitchen and WC, when her first baby was born in 1959. They had been re-housed from war-damaged property fifteen months before the baby's arrival, and they had stayed on there through the children's early years. Then the need for somewhere for the children to play and a desire to be near relatives because of the onset of arthritis had brought Mrs Sutton and her family to the corner of Bethnal Green and the little three-storey house where I met her. Unusually, the move took them from a council to a private tenancy. Here her son and daughter-in-law – Dan and Julie – were living when they had their first baby. Mrs Sutton would never contemplate a move from the East End but, now that her children were grown up, she would welcome a change of house. 'I think I'd go for the antique; just enough for my husband and myself and a spare room.' Only a 'win on the pools', she said, would bring that ideal within her grasp. Dan, not yet twenty-one and out of work, and Julie had higher aspirations and greater confidence.

So here, encapsulated in the housing careers of the sample families, are hints of some of the trends in population movement and housing circumstances over the past thirty years or so – centrifugal metropolitan expansion incorporating moves from working-class privately rented accommodation or local authority estates of flats to middle-class owner occupation or working-class estates of houses and gardens;[21] immigrant movement into the inner city; cross-currents of movement in and out of the suburb and within it, carrying with them predictable, or less predictable, tenure shifts and fluctuations; a steady inner-city residue – some there from choice, particularly among the older generation, some reluctantly.

Perhaps what stands out most clearly so far from the housing careers of the second-generation families is the problem of access to housing for those with limited status and low incomes, a problem which is inevitably more apparent in Bethnal Green than in Woodford. This takes on more meaning in the next chapter.

4

FAMILY BUILDING AND HOUSING

It is only in the past few years that researchers have concerned themselves with the interaction between housing tenure and 'fertility', a blanket term involving the study of such variables as family size and the rate of family building and the part played by individual intention and control over the size of family and the timing of children. The influence may be of housing tenure on fertility or the reverse. Payne and Payne[1] and Ineichen[2, 3] were concerned with the effect of fertility on selective entry into different forms of tenure. In other words, how far is 'choice' of tenure or ability to enter a particular sector a response to decisions to have a first or subsequent child? On the other side Cartwright in *How Many Children?*[4] considered housing tenure as one influence among many, but an important one, in family formation and on the size of families. In my sample the bias towards one particular stage in their lives and its small size severely limit any approach of this last kind. All I can do is speculate about what the mothers say of their intentions and desires.[5]

Family size

Families have been getting smaller over the past decades.[6] Certainly in *intentions* this was reflected among the Bethnal Green and Woodford families, the great majority following the general pattern of two children altogether.[7] Mr Mitchell, a Crown tenant, sharing his wife's views, gave a commonly-held opinion on the desirability – or expediency – of the two-child family.

'I think two's ideal. Especially the way things are going. Well, the way schools are going for a start. They seem to be laying off teachers with all these recessions. I don't know what things are going to be like by the time she gets to school but the future doesn't look all that happy for this country, just the way things are going – rates are going up, jobs are threatened.'

A few wanted only one child. Here are two typical reasons given by council tenants with their options nevertheless kept open. By a father:

'You can give one everything. With two you have to divide it. It's the money, it don't buy a lot. I won't ever have another. I used to want a little boy but now I don't. The idea's gone out of my head. I don't think I'll ever change my job either. It's the same amount of money. You don't come out any better if you get a wage increase; rent goes up, food goes up, clothes go up. If I did change my mind it would be in the next year to year and a half. I'd want the baby to grow up with the other one.'

and by a mother, 'I dunno. I think it's cruel really to have more. We're both out of work now. I don't think I'll have any more – not yet anyway.'

With my small sample there was no difference in family size intentions between tenures. There is, however, evidence from other studies that family size differences go with tenure. Cartwright suggests that 'there are probably three ways in which housing might influence family size decisions – amenities, security and economics.[8] On the second of these, security, there is not very much to choose between private ownership and local authority renting.[9] It is in private renting that people feel most insecure, but on its own the question of security seemed not to play a large part in family size decisions. When we come to 'amenities' and 'economics' it was not those with better amenities and higher incomes – the home-owners – who wanted larger families. Cartwright found that council tenants had and wanted more children than families buying their homes on a mortgage.[10] But within the groups things were no longer so straightforward. Under 'amenities', for instance, mothers who already had two children were most likely to be deterred from increasing their families by an intermediate quality of housing, neither very good nor very bad (in their opinion), for rearing children. Under 'income', too, deterrence seemed to be strongest for those in the middle range. Mothers at the extremes, married to

84

unskilled workers at one end or to professional workers at the other, wanted or had more children than those in between. Cartwright's interpretation of this seeming anomaly was that different groups had different standards about what they *felt* they could afford in the way of children, the higher incomes for different reasons coming together with the lower on this point.[11]

In this connection it is, I think, important to note that in some estimates derived by Murphy and Sullivan on final family size distribution the predictions show similar proportions of council tenants and home-owners with one child and a higher proportion of home-owners with two or three children. But the proportions are in reverse for families with four or more children.[12] It is the same with social class differences. Using the three-fold division (see chapter 2), fewer of the working class – the semi-skilled and unskilled manual groups – are estimated for a family size of up to three children. But only for numbers higher than that do their proportions markedly exceed those of the other two classes.[13] Clearly there are innumerable influences and counter-influences at work, not least what is held to be the norm by a particular collection of people.

Murphy and Sullivan also suggest that the spacing of children after the first birth is not influenced by tenure.[14, 15] When it comes to a consideration of the reverse influence, however, the effect of fertility on entry into different tenure groups, birth timing of the first child is very much something to be taken into account. For this I am able to draw on the data from my study.

Birth timing

As seen in chapter 2, Bethnal Green mothers are considerably younger as a group than those in Woodford. It is therefore no surprise to learn that the average age of the owner occupiers is higher than that of the council tenants or those not yet in their own home. Not far short of three times as many home-owners as council tenants were aged twenty-five or more. Only one out of the eighteen mothers with no home of their own was in this age group, and three of the eight other tenants. This was their age at the time of the interview. Adjusted for the time of the child's birth, the proportions remain the same.

With birth timing it is important to know for the two-parent families how old they were when they married, or for the nine cohabiting mothers when they set up house together. Similar kinds of differences between the tenures are evident. Over half the council tenants married under the age of twenty-one compared with only just over one-sixth of the home-owners. The majority of mothers now in owner occupation married between the ages of twenty-one and twenty-five and quite a substantial minority – eleven out of thirty-eight – married at the age of twenty-five or later. Only five of the mothers now in council tenancies were in this later age group.[16] Put another way, only one-sixth of all those who married under the age of twenty-one are now home-owners (see appendix 2, table 2.8). By contrast, of those marrying over the age of twenty-five, nearly twice as many are now in owner occupation as in other tenures. Though the differences between the two tenure groups were not so great, Holmans, in his analysis of material from the Family Formation Survey, found that there was a greater chance of becoming an owner occupier if age at marriage was twenty or over, and a greater chance of becoming a local authority tenant if age at marriage was under twenty.[17] So there is already considerable potential for a difference in fertility patterns according to tenure. But, to translate potentiality into actuality, age at marriage must be related to age at birth of the first child.

Six times as many council tenants as home-owners had their first child within the first two years of their marriage (see appendix 2, table 2.9). Council tenants tend to marry younger. There is also evidence from other studies that a greater proportion than among home-owners conceive their first child before marriage.[18] In my small sample over one in six of the council tenants had done so, compared with only one of the thirty-eight home-owners. None of the six home-owners who had married under the age of twenty-one had had a child within the first two years of marriage, compared with fourteen of the nineteen council tenants.

So the evidence from this study agrees with that from others that families in council tenancies tend to start their families sooner than those who own their homes, and that consequently movement into the two major tenure groups is 'highly fertility specific'.[19] This in itself is not surprising. Earlier birth timing has strong associations with low income level, low occupational status, low employment status, and so on.[20] Its association with council tenancies could simply be an extension of this general association already apparent in chapter 2. Only one mother of the twenty-one belonging to the 'Service Class' had conceived before entry into her destination tenure; in the 'Intermediate Class' the ratio was nine after to four before, and for the 'Working Class' seven after to ten before.

Further research, however, notably that of Payne and Payne and Ineichen,[21] suggests that there is a more direct connection between fertility and housing tenure, that 'despite some overlap of age, income and occupational status, owner occupiers and council tenants develop as groups with contrasting social characteristics, partly as a response to structural factors within the housing market.'[22] One message coming clearly through these two important pieces of research is that, in order to achieve entry into their particular tenure, aspiring home-owners will defer the birth of their first child so as to save enough money, while those headed for council tenancies will find a child, or children, an advantage – or even a necessity – in the achievement of their goal. How far these two goals are chosen freely in the first place is another part of the story, which has already been touched on in chapter 3 and will be discussed further in chapter 8. The view can be summed up in the Paynes' 'third principle of the housing market', which is that 'access to ownership is by economic capital; access to council tenancy is by human capital'.[23]

It is particularly important for the above thesis to know at what point the couple *enter* what is likely to be their final tenure. It is not only a question of when the baby was born but when it was conceived. Only two out of the thirty-eight mothers in owner occupation, both in Woodford, conceived their first child when in a different tenure. Dr and Mrs Grigson had been in tied hospital accommodation intent on buying a home as soon as it was possible. The Turners had been in an East End council flat. The decision to have a child precipitated their move into home-ownership in search of more space and a more congenial environment. Twenty out of the thirty-four mothers in council tenancies, however, had conceived before entry. So, in so far as proportionately very many more council tenants than home-owners started their family before achieving their first council home, my findings correspond with those of the other studies.

Council tenants

On the question of 'before' and 'after' proportions *within* the local
authority sector it is more difficult to draw comparisons with other
data. Holmans, Madge and Brown and the Paynes were each
concerned with entry under somewhat different circumstances from
those of my sample.[24] Ineichen, on the other hand, was looking at
pregnancy and birth timing, but our proportions differ. In his
sample as many as twenty-two out of twenty-seven couples had
had their baby before getting their council home,[25] compared with
two out of thirty-four in my sample. One thing that may go some
way towards explaining the difference in the proportions is that
Ineichen was following through recently married couples, whereas
I began with the birth of the baby. Thus the parents could have
been married for some time and would be more likely already to
have acquired a home of their own. Moreover, as will appear later,
my sample proportions are modified when the families still in their
transit tenures are taken into account.

A further factor may also help to explain the relatively high
proportions of the sample families who achieved a council home
either before or soon after the birth of their child. This has to do
with whether or not the birth was planned; a point which seems
not to have been given much prominence by other researchers
looking at the influence of fertility on entry into different tenures.
Madge and Brown state that they could 'not tell whether the babies
were planned or not';[26] the Paynes refer to the 'social class differen-
tial' in the use of contraceptive services, women whose husbands
were in semi-skilled and unskilled occupations being less likely to
seek contraceptive advice.[27] They also found that, in the timing of
their first pregnancies, couples in the same group tended to have
children earlier in their marriage than the other social classes. They
go on to say that 'this group would also be the most likely to
require a council house and, given the present allocation system,
their reproductive behaviour can be seen as a rational way of
becoming eligible for a council house.'[28] But it is not clear what
proportion of their sample actually planned their babies. Ineichen
has data on 'fertility intentions' which show that an extremely
large proportion of council tenants relative to home-owners either
already had a child or expected to have one within the first two
years of marriage.[29] But he does not indicate how many of the

children already born within the first two years of marriage or at the stage of a later interview had actually been planned. My sample mothers were asked directly if the baby had been planned. The overwhelming majority of home-owners had planned their first child, nearly all deferring them for at least two years from the date of their marriage, nearly two-thirds in fact for four years or more. Of the mothers belonging to the thirty-four two-parent council tenants, many fewer said they had planned their babies. Nevertheless, more, in an approximate ratio of four to three, had done so than had not (see appendix 2, table 2.10).

I looked to see if there was any apparent correlation with religious beliefs, but found nothing of any import. Half the sample said they had no religion or had lapsed in their Church of England or Roman Catholic beliefs. Roughly similar proportions of believing and non-believing mothers said they had planned their babies and it did not seem to make very much difference which religion they belonged to. The only two single mothers who said they had planned their first birth were believers – June Pratt was Jewish and May Riley a member of the 'Church of God'.

In order to establish the connection of family planning decisions with local authority tenancies it is necessary to know, for those conceiving before getting a tenancy, if and when an attempt had already been made to obtain a council flat and, for those conceiving after, when and how they had got their flats. There were fourteen of this last group and there is obviously less reason to be concerned with their family planning decisions. All lived in Bethnal Green and all except three were tenants of the GLC. Five mothers had been long established as council tenants – three as second wives; Mrs Poulter and Mrs Powell through having taken over a parent's tenancy. Seven families had obtained their flats, for which they had applied when they were courting or engaged, though one or other of the special housing lists referred to in chapter 3, sons-and-daughters schemes, engaged-couples ballots, difficult-to-let lists. Alice Tooley had acquired her flat by this last means with three friends five or six years previously and now lived there with Rob and the baby, which had not been planned. 'We'd only been living together for about eight months,' she told the interviewer, 'and I think I'd have liked to have a little longer.'

This leaves only two families of the 'post-entry' group who applied for and obtained their home through the 'normal' channels of the housing waiting list. Both had applied when they were courting; the Stokeses four years previously having waited about two years, the Farleys more fortunate with a delay of only a few months.

Thus, with these fourteen mothers, marital status, age, deliberate decisions, special allocation policies and good fortune had all played their part in the timing of the conception of the first child so that it occurred after they had reached their destination tenure. Three of the four non-planners among them would have 'preferred to wait a bit longer' before starting, but that had nothing to do with their housing circumstances. Mrs Powell, long married, had not been taking precautions and was well pleased.

Now what of the twenty families who had conceived their first child *before* becoming council tenants? At what point and how did they get their flats? An initial distinction here between planned and unplanned babies is necessary, and I shall take the planned babies first, of which there were nine altogether, five in Bethnal Green and four in Woodford. All said that they had decided to have a baby, mostly within a few months of their marriage or the start of their cohabitation, because they 'just wanted' one. This in fact was by far the most often cited reason for their decision by all the council tenants who had planned their baby irrespective of the timing of their entry into the sector. None of the planners referred specifically to their housing circumstances. None suggested that they had planned the baby in order to achieve their end.

Of the five Bethnal Green families who had planned their baby, three, all now GLC tenants, started it some time after marriage. They had put their names down on the 'Borough waiting list' when they were engaged. The Sellars and the Tomlinsons – by dint, they said, of the usual 'pestering' – were given a flat a month or two before the baby's birth; the Botts got theirs at about the same time through the GLC engaged-couples ballot. The remaining two families were housed through the Homeless Persons Register.

In Woodford all four families had been on the Redbridge Council waiting list, three for at least a year before starting their child. For Mrs O'Kelly and Mrs McEwan this had been their second pregnancy, while Eileen Scott and Tom Peters had been living together with her parents and had applied when she became pregnant. Only the O'Kellys had failed to get their flat before the baby's birth.

Mick's running battle with the housing department finally produced it two months after the baby's arrival.

And finally there were the eleven mothers who conceived unintentionally, all, except two, a short time after they were married or began living together. One or two were 'quite pleased when it happened'. Others would have preferred 'a little longer' – time, for instance, 'to finish the flat properly' or just 'to be a bit older so I could understand a bit more about a few things.' Mrs Shelley would have liked a wait of five or six years.

> 'I'm quite selfish. I wanted to do a lot of things, like trying to save up to get our own place, to go on holiday, do all them things first. I still wasn't over-keen when I knew I was going to have a baby. I couldn't have been more surprised. As I was going through the pregnancy, I thought Oh, what have I landed myself in for.'

Seven of these families were Bethnal Greeners. Four had put their names down for a flat when they had been engaged or on marriage. Mrs Brogan and Mrs Langley had been pregnant and single when they applied; the Lopezes' history had involved an application after marriage and after pregnancy. They did not obtain their flat until after the baby's birth; the rest from one to four months before, except for the Hills and the Shelleys who had been lucky through one of the special schemes in getting theirs almost immediately after the start of the pregnancy. In Woodford, Mr and Mrs French had got their flat as 'homeless persons'; the remaining three had applied after pregnancy began and obtained their flat just before or just after the baby's arrival.

So the picture for the twenty families who started their family before reaching their destination tenure is more confused than for the 'post-entry' group, but it is possible to distinguish certain features. First, though conception occurred before getting a tenancy, nearly all the babies were born after getting it. Secondly, they had all achieved their homes through the ultimate recognition by one or other of the local authority housing departments that the accommodation they were in was unsuitable. Thirdly, more than half the babies were unplanned and there was a higher proportion of 'emergency' applications among this group than among those where the baby had been planned. However, the various possible means of entry – application when engaged, special schemes, Homeless Persons Register – were common to both groups. Fourthly, and the evidence for this comes as much from chapter 3 as from this last analysis, persistence on the part of the mothers and fathers seemed to pay dividends. Finally, it is clear that the imminent arrival of a baby was the key factor in obtaining a council home for all but three of the families, and they had succeeded in the sons-and-daughters and engaged-couples schemes. 'We wouldn't have got it if I hadn't been pregnant' was a typical comment. Mrs Bell, after all, now a home-owner, had been told in applying for a council home to go away and have some children.

Transit tenures

The above picture is incomplete without reference to those families still in transit tenure, since their experience reflects the earlier position of so many of those families who had achieved their destination tenure by the time of the interviews. Something is already known of their housing history from chapter 3. It is also apparent from chapter 2 that their incomes varied considerably.

Among the two-parent families all except the Patels and possibly Mr and Mrs Hafiz were hoping for council tenancies. The three Bangladeshi mothers had clearly intended to start a family.[30] Application for a council tenancy had been made in each case not only before the baby's conception – between six months and three years previously – but before there could have been a possibility of this, since the husband and wife had been separated by thousands of miles. It is true that Mr Aslam and Mr Quereshi had each rejected one offer, but for what seemed to be good reasons. Neither baby belonging to the two young indigenous Bethnal Green couples – the Suttons and Mandy Wallace and her boyfriend – had been planned. The former couple had applied to the council after conception and before marriage, the latter only after the baby's birth, so for them it would have been little short of miraculous if they had already achieved their goal by the time they were interviewed. Neither of the two single mothers desirous of her own council home had planned her baby. Both, however, had had applications in with the council before conception. In Woodford, the Reads – in temporary accommodation – had planned their baby while still living with Stan's father because they 'just wanted one'. The Russells had applied to Redbridge Council five months before their baby's birth (which had not been planned), but in their case the usual persistence had not so far succeeded.

One year later both these couples had been rehoused by the council, the Russells already with a second child. In Bethnal Green the Quereshis had been given a council flat in Spitalfields very soon after the main interview. The Aslams had just left their friends when I called about a year after first meeting them, she to return to Bangladesh, he to some other destination outside London. I was unable to learn more. Mandy and her boyfriend and the Suttons had obtained council flats.

I have dealt at some length with the fertility/tenure relationship of those families already in the local authority sector or heading for it because the idea behind the thesis – that the starting of a family by couples who 'cannot afford' owner occupation while still in their 'transit tenure' is necessary to obtain a council home – is often represented as an artful ploy to jump the queue. And this is not only by people unsympathetic to the plight of such families. Ineichen himself suggests that 'pregnancy [is] sought as the only technique for obtaining a suitable home' and refers to a 'not altogether serious charter for "working the system"' composed by Niner.[31] I come back to this at the end of this chapter. Meanwhile I look briefly at the sample families already in the second of the two main destination tenures – owner occupation.

Home owners

The connection between family planning decisions and movement into owner occupation is by now more or less taken for granted. Ineichen, as mentioned above, discusses the deferment of the first child and from his data is able to give a percentage (40 per cent of the sample) who said they were deferring their first child for housing reasons.[32, 33] This certainly figured prominently with my sample mothers in the reasons for their choice of time to have a baby. Well over one-third mentioned something in connection with housing, either the need to save for a house or, if they had already bought a home, to improve it or move to a bigger one or from a flat to a house. Thus Mrs Grey, who had married under the age of twenty-one, told the interviewer that they had been married about five years and had 'built up the home' as much as they wanted and then had 'decided to have a baby'. The Shadwells had not married until she was twenty-five and he twenty-six, four years earlier. They had moved a year or two previously from their first home – a flat, also owned – since they wanted a house and did not like the area. Mrs Shadwell 'had always wanted a baby,

> but my husband said we've got to get to a certain stage before we could have one. I wanted to have a baby as soon as we moved into the house, with no electricity or water or anything, but we wanted to get as much work done so that it would be in a liveable state anyway. I helped quite a bit with the house, concrete slabs in the front, windows, made a wall at the back. We got to a certain stage and he said, "We should go ahead because we've got what we want." We'd achieved the goals we'd wanted to achieve.'

Other reasons, however, were given very nearly as frequently as those to do with housing. There was often more than one. Just under one-third of the mothers, for example, referred in one way or another to the advantages of no family responsibilities or the wish to establish themselves in a career.

Mary Clifford, who had waited five years and was about to return to paid work, combined several motives in her reply.

> 'I don't know really – when we got married children were somewhere in the future. We'd moved here and we were very happy and we wanted to get this just as we wanted it. At one time we said next year, 1982, perhaps, because that's when we'd aimed to get the place finished. But it's very easy to say next year, next year. We were used to just going out and doing what we wanted. I don't really miss that, particularly when I get back to work as I put so much into the job in the evening.'

Mrs Reeves, however, said that with them there was no question – 'consciously anyway' – of saving up for a house.

> 'When we first married we didn't even really talk about it. I suppose we always thought we would. I suppose we've spoken about it from about six years onwards. We enjoyed our social life, we realised that having a child would be a tremendous loss of freedom. We kept postponing it and we were happy as we were. But then I suppose we felt we were just going on and on and couldn't really see what we were aiming for and I

suppose we thought that a child would sort of bring us something more.'

Mrs Green, an ex-teacher who had moved straight into an owned home on marriage four years previously, told us that she 'felt settled and ready to have a child'. 'Prior to that,' she said,

'I had other things on my mind – my career, wanting to get on, to make the most of that for a number of years. I got to the stage where I thought now is the time that I'd like to have children. I suppose to some extent age came into it. I was 27, that's not old, but at 27 I was just perfectly ready to have children and hopefully cope with them. We always both wanted children, it was really just the "when". The decision was very much up to me. My husband was ready to have children whenever I wanted to and decided to go off the pill.'

And for Jean Macintosh also, the motives were mixed.

'In 1978 I was 30. Thirty is a very traumatic year, really. Many reasons, but I think that was the main one. I'd got so far in my work. We were quite settled, I'd always wanted to have Alex's child. We both wanted to enjoy our relationship first. I would put my twenties into developing a career, take a little time off, making sure that I had something that was well established before I broke it. I felt strongly I didn't want to sacrifice the one for the other, a job and independence and everything that goes with it to an impoverished few years with a young baby. Equally, I didn't want to sacrifice not being a family for the sake of a job. It was just a matter of the right time.'

Mrs Bates and Mrs Rush expressed a view, from slightly different angles, shared by a few others who were unable to think of any specific reason other than the important one of enough money. Both had started their married life in their present home. Here is Mrs Bates:

'John didn't want children at first, and it took five years to get round to it. I always wanted children but I just had to be patient. The time was right, we just felt we were settled and had some money behind us. I don't really know how you decide these things.'

95

And Mrs Rush:

> 'We wanted to have enough money in the bank and to be used to being married and being with one another. We had a good four to five years together. Now that the baby takes up a lot of my time Harry could feel left out but he doesn't because he knows it's not going to last, and as he had me on my own for five years he doesn't mind taking a back seat for a while.'

Discussion

It is argued that families belong to a given tenure group less by their own free choice than because of certain initial constraints. These have to do with such factors as income level, occupational status, educational and parental background.[34] They also result from certain structural factors in the housing market which influence the fertility patterns of families seeking a home of their own, thereby compounding a process of stratification already set in train by those other factors. From the point of view of the aspiring householder, entry into the ownership sector is governed largely by the ability to afford the initial deposit cost and the continuing mortgage interest and repayment costs. Entry into the local authority sector is governed largely by the availability of housing stock. Since there is rarely enough to go round, availability is in turn governed by local authority allocation policies which restrict or facilitate access according to a set of rules – nearly always taking the form of a 'points system' – in which children and family size invariably figure.

The evidence from this small sample certainly supports the view that there are distinctive fertility patterns belonging to each of the two main destination tenure groups, owner occupation and council tenancy,[35] even though some of these are entangled with differences between socio-economic groups. There is a relationship between age, birth timing and tenure group. Home-owners tend to marry later than council tenants and to defer the birth of their first child for a longer time. The former for the most part took precautions to postpone conception until after becoming home-owners. Council tenants, present and potential, were more likely to have conceived before than after getting their tenancy.

There were, however, some differences in my findings which

while they do not, I think, fundamentally affect the argument may perhaps modify it.[36] In my sample a larger proportion of the council tenants than in other studies conceived after becoming tenants; furthermore, just over half the conceptions occurring beforehand were unplanned. Among the reasons given by the 'planning' mothers for their choice of time only a minority of the home-owners mentioned housing, and no council tenants actually said that they had started a family as a quick way of getting a flat. None the less, unlike those in other studies, a considerable majority (35 out of 44) of my sample families who had sought or were seeking a council flat had obtained one either before or very soon after the birth of their child.

The upshot is that fertility is certainly connected with the housing people get. But it is not a simple matter of some people having children early so as to bolster their claim for a council tenancy, and of others postponing children until they have saved enough to pay deposits and buy the accoutrements of a satisfactory home. There are two stereotypes, and some people actually conform to them. But the relationship is much more complicated than that. First, where the first child is planned, a variety of reasons may affect the choice of time for potential home-owners and council tenants. The financial advantage for the former of postponing conception could be the main reason, one of many or not consciously one at all. For potential council tenants the 'qualifi-cation' advantage of expediting conception seems more likely to be a *post hoc* rationalisation than a conscious decision. This last point of course has particular force where the baby is not planned.

Secondly, allocation practices vary. In the particular areas of my study newly-formed families seemed to stand a better chance of getting a council flat than in some other areas. Nevertheless, as elsewhere, the relevant housing departments used the absence of a family as an automatic rationing device. It is the providers rather than the home seekers who take advantage of family building prospects.

Thirdly, even though among my sample the great majority of council tenants had a place of their own by the time their first child was born, for most it had been a scramble; they had had little or no time to enjoy the making of a home before the advent of the baby. But most of all they had been virtually unable to choose what kind of home they would like from the point of view of dwelling type, area, location, accommodation or anything else. Those of the sample still awaiting a council home faced the same prospect. The next chapter will show what this meant for the families in question.

Finally there are, it appears from my study and the results of the others cited, still distinct styles of life. Early conception linked with poverty and poor education and poor jobs is associated with council housing while the opposite is associated with owner occupation. The division into the two main types of housing reinforces the division between styles of life which run deep in our society. Bethnal Greeners are once again at a disadvantage, a disadvantage shared by an important Woodford minority.

5

THE HOMES

The various aspects of housing tenure – location, dwelling type, accommodation and facilities, costs – are of course interdependent. For the sample families, to be a council tenant was to be a flat-dweller (except for one family in a maisonette). In Bethnal Green there is little likelihood of being anything else; in Woodford there might perhaps at a later stage be the chance of a council house, but with the sale of such homes the chances are diminishing. Redbridge Council has a declared policy in favour of selling council homes. But most of the Woodford families were anyway home-owners, which meant that most lived in houses.

The council estates

In Bethnal Green the skyline signals the change from the 1950s in the townscape below. Many streets have vanished. In their place are Mrs Gedge's 'blocks and blocks and blocks of flats' arranged in a variety of ways round courtyards of different shapes and sizes or flanking stretches of more or less open space. Only one of the estates lived in by the families had been completed since 1978. By far the highest proportion dated from one of the three decades following the end of the Second World War.

Visiting a family in one such estate, the interviewer wrote that she was amazed to hear from them that the blocks were only twenty years old. She commented on the lack of maintenance of what were pleasant structures. At least one pipe on each eight-flat block was overflowing and each overflow pipe caused, at ground level, a green slimy growth with ferns to mark its existence. Paint was peeling from windows, the walls were covered with stains, and it was smelly. A patch of grass between each pair of blocks was forbidden to children, and the asphalt was crumbling. Another, just predating the year 1900, showed little sign that the transfer of its ownership from the original charitable trust to the GLC could ever have encouraged its tenants to hope for improvements in its drab treeless exterior, unwelcoming staircases and ill-planned interiors. Vivienne Stokes described the place as being in 'a filthy state. I don't like inviting people up here. The people downstairs have got dogs and they mess all over the place. You feel ashamed really. I'm not happy.' In Woodford all the estate-dwellers, with the exception of the MacEwans, were concentrated in that unprepossessing slab concrete estate, already referred to, which I shall call 'Fairfield'.

Housing estates, even though they may consist of flats and maisonettes, do not automatically exclude streets. But in the estates on which the families lived none of the front doors opened on to the ground. To all intents and purposes the street as an extension of the home no longer existed. In Bethnal Green of the 1950s the street had essentially been such an extension. In Woodford today the street-dwellers were nearly all buffered from their public surroundings by their private gardens; they had an 'outside' of their own. The estate-dwellers in both areas had to rely for their outside on the communal space around their block of flats. No wonder then that there was distress like that of Mrs Stokes where the general condition was so wretched and the upkeep and maintenance so poor. Just on two-fifths of the mothers could think of nothing good to say about their estate. The fathers tended to express hostility towards their surroundings in stronger terms, and nearly half could find nothing good to say.

All the estates had caretakers, only one of whom was non-resident. There was a lack of consistency in views about how they carried out their duties on any particular estate. Roughly one-third of the mothers seemed to think of their caretakers as reasonably adequate – 'he sweeps, cleans, does the usual.' An indignant minority who felt they were 'no good' described their activities in much the same terms – 'he just sweeps and sits around. He has no control over the children.' Clearly there are different expectations. A small group of mothers were very satisfied.

But caretakers can do nothing about design and planning which, whatever their intrinsic merits or faults, can be quite inappropriate for young families. A number of the estate-dwellers were severely critical. There were references to 'concrete jungles', particularly by the Fairfield tenants, and to the iniquities of tower blocks. Here are two fathers at Fairfield. First Pat O'Kelly:

'I don't like tower blocks. They're just modern slums built purposely to throw people in. They'll suit anybody, so they thought. Some people are stuck here for years. To me it's terrible to be stuck in a tower block.'

And Tom Peters:

'It's the design of the estates. The people that actually design it say, "We're going to put a tower here." Well, that's fine. Put tower blocks wherever you can, you know, if you're going to give a lot of people homes to live in, but don't build a tower block where you can't actually look out of the window. We can't look out of our bedroom window without someone else being able to see into it. No privacy at all, except in the passage and the bathroom.'

For some council tenants the gravest disadvantage of their accommodation was the floor upon which they were living. Some aspect of this was mentioned by well over a quarter of the mothers and fathers. All three local authorities have a policy about how high up they should place families with children. With the London Borough of Tower Hamlets, families with children under eleven are not to be housed above the fourth floor and in Redbridge at the time of the interviews, they were 'trying to reduce the number of children above the seventh floor'. In fact, for five families in Bethnal Green and four in Woodford the policy had not been strictly observed. For the Farleys in Bethnal Green, living on the fifth floor was one of the chief complaints. Mrs Hill's Bethnal Green flat was on the eleventh floor and she told me that, at the time of seeking a flat, she had said she'd 'go up to twenty floors as long as I had a home. At least, I thought, it'll be my own place. But it's too high.' The lifts came in for heavy criticism – not only of their condition but for the frequency with which they were out of order. What Bob Reagan in Woodford disliked was 'just being stuck up so high; if this flat were somewhere else I'd like it – it's not squashy or anything.'

It was not, however, only tower blocks that were condemned. Most of the blocks of flats housing the families had fewer than six floors. Living on the fourth – or even second or third – floor of an old block with no lift, awkward stairs and nowhere to keep the pram could be just as trying. Part of Vivienne Stokes's distress at having to live in her shabby, depressing old building was because of the stairs. She told me that she had had a miscarriage because of them: 'I love to get out, say like once a day. I can get out but I can't get back in. I have to depend on my sister or wait round at my mum's until my husband's finished work. It's ridiculous.' Mrs Gregg – on the third floor – found that 'now with the baby the stairs are a bother. I can't do it all in one go – so I have to bring up what I can and then run downstairs and bring up another lot.' And Mrs Poulter found living on the fourth floor very different now she had a baby. For one thing there was nowhere to dry washing. She was one of the very few who commented on the lack of general washing facilities: 'Downstairs there used to be a drying cabin, etc. They were only there two years. Then they came and boarded them up. Children broke in to get the money.'

Many mothers were already considering the quality of the immediate environment – its hazards and dangers, its atmosphere and condition, the amenities it afforded, the people – very much in relation to their child's future. Not surprisingly they minded particularly about playspace. Most of the Bethnal Green mothers and fathers living on council estates either deplored its non-existence or non-availability or ridiculed the token offering of 'facilities', normally in the shape of one or two pieces of fixed equipment. Many, like Mrs Price, referred to the dangers:

'I don't think I'd let him play out there myself because it's too dangerous. There is a playing field but it's across the main road, so I'd have to take him there. There's a notice that says it's open at such and such a time but it never is, so the kids just throw in bricks because they can't get in.'

Mrs Tanner, talking of a different Bethnal Green estate, put it as a high priority that 'they should get somewhere for children to play or let them on the grass.' Alice Trent described the 'play area' on another estate as 'a sort of shed at the front with a pit – with steps going down to it. It was meant to be a sandpit, but it's just an empty square pit.'

At Fairfield one could not fail to notice from the equipment that a stretch of space was intended for use by children. But five mothers thought it was not enough. And here is a father's view:

'I'd hate to be here when baby's a few years older – there's nowhere for him to play. He obviously for safety reasons can't play on the veranda. There's no area in the flat and I wouldn't want him to play where the lifts are, it's freezing cold out there. He can't go downstairs, he'd have no supervision and there's dog mess on the only bits of grass. When I was a child we lived by the forest and I was up trees like children should be. There's no play of that sort round here. That's why there's the vandalism there is.'

Not so obvious perhaps were other kinds of more imaginative schemes on this estate. There was a day nursery, for instance, and organised holiday activities for school-age children. Many mothers did not know they existed. This ignorance could only be due to a failure on the part of the providers (the Borough social services department and a charitable trust) to publicise what they had to offer.

As with the neighbourhood in general (see chapter 1), so with the estates. Criticism of fellow residents was the single subject that called forth the largest number of the mothers' unfavourable replies. A fair proportion showed racial prejudice – focused exclusively on the Asian community. Mr and Mrs Lopez – originally from South America and Scotland – and with a checkered housing history – were prominent among this group. Mr Lopez thought it was 'obvious' that he would 'dislike the Indians and Pakistanis'. He talked about 'binloads of rubbish' falling on their heads, tipped out of the windows from the flats. He went on:

> 'There's the smell of rubbish, they just pile it out on the streets. And other things go on in the streets, mainly with Pakistanis. It's happened a few times. A car passes along the street and pulls up and they try to pick girls up. They think any white girl around is a prostitute. The sewing machines are going all night; not in this block but you hear them when you walk past.'

He commented further, 'I could say send them back to their own country but that's none of my business. They could say send me back to where I come from, but they can't do that, I was born here.' Mrs Langley had problems about smells of another sort:

> 'There's a lot of Pakistanis and in the summer when you like

the door and windows open, the smell of their cooking used to come in, so we had to keep the door shut and then it was a sweatbox in here. The smell gets in here and you could cut it with a knife, it was vile and really terrible. It's a health hazard, I reckon!'

It was, however, by no means only the Asian families that were the villains – young vandals, 'nutters', problem families, irrespective of skin colour, were more often to blame. Here is a disabled father talking about Fairfield:

'A lot of people living here are classed as problem families. Too many people around break windows and instead of using the rubbish chutes or taking it down to the basement some people throw it out of the windows or leave it in the lift. I've been standing out on the balcony on a summer evening and all of a sudden a great white thing comes whisking past the window and when it's landed you see it's a washing machine. That's disgusting. This is the kind of thing going on and the other day I tried to come in a different way and found there was no slope. Now, I can't use steps if I'm pushing a pram so I had to go back the other way and found the whole pavement was covered in broken bottles that someone had thrown out of the window. Those people would be complaining if people did things to their scruffy old motor-bikes. The trouble is in a tight-knit community like this you all get tarred with the same brush. My car was in a reasonable state when we moved here. Now it's got dents all over it. By choice I wouldn't be living here. Socially it's disgusting and from that point of view tower blocks are out. Living up here is like a prison. This is a bit of a black spot. I feel embarrassed at having to tell people I live here. A friend the other day said – God, that's a rat hole.'

And on the same estate Mr Peters, with whom racial prejudice is notably absent, said he disliked the attitude of people living there:

'Everyone seems to have problems. Everyone seems to be worse off than you are. My personal opinion of living on an estate like this is you're put in a category. I was brought up in a multi-race society over the other side of London in the sense there was lots of blacks, Indians, Pakistanis. The attitude of the people on this estate is that they dislike blacks – period. And I'm not being biased by saying that; my sister is married to a coloured guy. Well, to me black, green, yellow, pink, it doesn't matter what colour. If that person is happy it doesn't bother me. But it's just their childish attitude. Why in hell's name have they got it? Well, if you pull your finger out you can get it as well. Asking around and finding out what your rights are and whatever. And I dunno, I talk to people on this estate and they just say about that guy and this guy's got that and they're talking about black people as such. And they say it's because they know their rights. This is the last resort – people who apply to Redbridge Council for housing.'

Eileen Scott, Tom Peters's partner, held a similar view:

'It's a slum. A lot of nutters on it. So far away from everything, no nice shops. Children that don't even live on the estate wreck it. And the glue sniffers around. They make a terrible noise in the night. When you say you're living here they turn their noses up. They think you're as bad as everyone else. I don't like people to think that.'

Lorna Field blamed the council as well as the vandals:

'When I first moved here 14 years ago it was a lovely estate. It was really nice. But the council haven't done much to keep it that way. We had people coming round about joining a club, but we never heard no more about that. And the underground car parks – they were going to make into discos and things but nothing happened. So the estate's got into a state because the kids have got nothing to do but vandalise it. The lifts are never working.'

And it can be the same story in Bethnal Green. Mrs Brogan could find 'nothing at all' to say in favour of her estate:

'It's disgusting. Really dirty out there. They told us it wasn't a difficult-to-let place but I think it is. It used to be all right. My uncle has been here for 20 years but they had to move the whole block out because they had rats and mice and I don't know what. And after they cleared it out they put a load of problem families in. I mean we haven't got no problems or anything. We tried to rent a telly from Radio Rentals but they wouldn't let us have one when they heard where we lived. They said the block was blacklisted. I mean we've never been in debt or anything. So we had to go out and buy one. I couldn't let Tracy play out there, I just couldn't.'

Noise was another frequent cause of complaint for the mothers and fathers. Mr Tomlinson described it:

'You lay in bed of a night and you can sit up hours listening to noises. Cars, people slamming doors, tin cans, putting rubbish down chutes at two or three in the morning. They – the other families – row among themselves. You just sit up and listen.'

Mrs Clark did not complain about her fellow residents. Her chief grumble was the invasion from outside:

'We got the two doors smashed in two nights running. It's the boys from the school, they come in and smoke and eat downstairs. They wet down there as well, it's dreadful. They're terrors. They get abusive if you say something to them. They're villains.'

She and her husband were otherwise satisfied with their estate, and with good reason. The gardens were well kept, each balcony had a window-box, some with flowers, the balcony wood had been recently stained and there was a general air of good upkeep. Even a broken pane of glass and a dead light-bulb had been replaced by the second visit. And they were by no means the only ones who found good things to say.

There was a small group of mothers and fathers who expressed no unfavourable views at all and, apart from the completely dissatisfied few, the rest found at least something to praise. Mrs Hill, for instance, approved of the upkeep. 'It's a very clean block. The lifts are always kept in good condition. They're cleaned out with bleach and disinfectant.' Mrs Shelley also thought her estate was 'really clean'.

After upkeep, favourable comments to do with convenience were next in frequency, followed by friendliness and the design and appearance of the estate. Alice Trent liked her part of the estate because 'it's not in courtyards, like the old estates which have this courtyard affair with no trees in them.' And Mrs Ryder was happy with hers:

106

'Funnily enough, when I first came here I didn't regard this
as an estate because you've got so many different buildings.
That's nice, it adds variety to the area. It's a very good
community. You know everyone. I definitely prefer it like this
to one of the newer estates. This wasn't all built at once like
the newer ones.'

Even the much-censured Fairfield received some praise. In fact
only one estate containing more than one sample family was
condemned by all who lived there. None, on the other hand,
received total approval.

If tenants were to have a share in the management of the estate,
would this improve things? The great majority of mothers and
fathers thought that it would but, when pressed, came up with few
ideas on how this could be achieved and what they should do.
Most, in fact, saw little prospect of such a shift in the control of
council estates and virtually all were ignorant of schemes of this
kind which had already started. I shall come back to such schemes
in chapter 8.

What can be made of all this? First, it shows a dislike of council
estate flats by people at the first stage of family formation.
Secondly, it shows that such families are on the whole willing to
recognise any good features about the estates which undoubtedly
exist, or are ready to make the best of things. Thirdly, it suggests
that the deterioration of estates is not necessarily caused by defici-
ences in the original design but arises more through their social
conditions.[1] Dunhill and Macclesfield, for neither of which a good
word was said, illustrate the point. The former was built at the end
of the 1950s, designed as 'a bold attempt to combine high living,
visually and socially, with the terraces of small Victorian houses it
displaced . . . the maisonettes are quiet (sharing only one party
wall), roomy and well laid out.'[2] I wonder how that same architect
would feel if he were to visit his 'bold attempt' today to find it
dilapidated, dirty, classified as 'difficult-to-let', repudiated by its
inhabitants and the subject, I was told, of a recent meeting of
housing department officials to discuss whether or not it should be
demolished.

Macclesfield, in itself a handsome building, was built at the
turn of the century and represents, unlike the Boundary Street
development referred to in chapter 1, the typical tenement building

of that time. So from the point of view of design and layout these two estates were entirely different. What they do have in common is their condition and atmosphere – neglect, disrepair, squalor and an utterly depressing sense of dejection. But why they have become like this is very hard to discover. The problems and how they may be tackled are discussed in chapter 8.

The streets

Only nine Bethnal Green families lived in houses on streets, the majority converted into flats without benefit of a garden or their own front door. Only the three home-owners had a house to themselves. One was a typical Bethnal Green 'cottage', the other two three-storey terrace houses. Only four Bethnal Greeners had a garden.

In Woodford the ratio of street to local authority estate dwellers was more or less reversed – roughly three to fourteen in Bethnal Green; ten to three in Woodford. The eight families living in privately owned or housing association flats – nearly all purpose built – could enjoy an 'outside' of quite a different order from those living on council estates – well-kept gardens, plenty of grass and other amenities, though not all were satisfied with the quality and amount of playspace. The Bakers had the sole use of a large wild garden. More of the families lived in terraced than in semi-detached houses, which was to be expected.[3] It was also no surprise that none were in detached houses, considering the price of these and the stage the families were at.

Street-dwellers were often critical of their immediate surroundings, but their remarks were usually much milder in tone than those of their counterparts on council estates, and the balance of favourable to unfavourable comment was considerably higher. Traffic and parking were their main vexations. Mrs Bates lived in a pretty side road with trees and a grass verge which was used by traffic as a short cut. 'We get quite a lot of heavy lorries and you get parking both sides so that only one car can drive through. We've had our car hit three times since we've been here when it's been parked.'

The remaining street-dwellers' replies covered various complaints. Maintenance of the street was one – 'pot-holes everywhere'. Mary Clifford felt herself isolated partly by her distance from the shops but mainly because nobody else around had a baby. One or two had found their neighbours not particularly friendly or 'too nosey'. But for nearly every minus there was a plus. They praised the 'greenness' of their street and its friendliness. It was 'quiet, convenient and well kept'. Mrs Bell commented:

'I love it. Lots of trees and open spaces and all different houses, very friendly. A very close community, nobody left out. People get their shopping for them. A little corner shop that sells absolutely everything and that's marvellous. Still got a couple of snobs but everybody chats to each other in the street. You've got to be a friendly type to get on.'

Mrs Green's 'plus' far outweighed her small grumble about traffic:

'In summer it looks quite nice with the trees when the sun's shining. I know a few of the neighbours and that makes it quite nice. At the Royal Wedding we had a street party and at the moment we're organising to have a dance for Christmas that's just for people in the street, at one of the local school halls. It's just nice, to get to know people because at the moment, having always been out to work, I didn't really know people other than my immediate neighbours and not having always lived in London, I haven't got that many friends in London, so now being in a position where I'm at home, things like that are very good because I'd like to get to know people. Otherwise you can get a bit lonely and cheesed-off with your own company.'

Inside

Outside the home is one thing, inside quite another. Here you are mistress or master of your environment, and the sample mothers and fathers found more good things to say about their accommodation than about their estates or streets.[4] Even so 16 per cent of all the mothers, and a slightly smaller proportion of fathers, could find nothing good to say. A similar proportion could think of nothing to criticise. Wholesale dissatisfaction was more prevalent among those forced to share their accommodation, while complete satisfaction more among those who had bought their homes.

Change from the 1950s was perhaps nowhere more apparent than in the interior amenities and appearance of the home. In 1961, for instance, only 48 per cent of Bethnal Green households had sole use of a bath,[5] compared with 94 per cent in 1981.[6] Only the Carlyles, as private tenants, were without a bath or inside WC, though all the fifteen families living with relatives or friends had to share them – and the kitchen too.

Another big difference was in the amount of overcrowding. Going back even earlier, Burnett suggests that towards the end of the nineteenth century 'the big jump – the first step . . . towards social distancing' in the housing of the urban working classes was 'the transition from one room to two . . . Two rooms were the irreducible minimum of respectability, the difference between a home and a mere shelter; with two rooms one could begin to take pride, to cook and clean, furnish and decorate, comfort and cherish the family.'[7] Now in the 1980s there were among the sample only a few two-parent families who had not yet been able to take this step because they shared the living space with their parents or friends, as did the ten sharing single mothers. Six of these had to share a bedroom.

In the earlier Bethnal Green study the authors traced the fall in the proportion of shared dwellings from 1911 to 1951 and also in the number of persons per room. Taking as their criterion of overcrowding more than two persons per room, it seems that by 1951 only three in a hundred homes were overcrowded.[8] By the currently accepted higher standard overcrowding begins at over 1.5 persons per room. None of the non-sharing families was over-crowded – though 3 per cent of all residents in Bethnal Green private households were.[9] Some of the sharing families in the sample would figure among these. For one such – three children and four adults living in a three-roomed flat – the density per room was 2.33 persons. This was the highest, but four others would be classed as overcrowded by present-day standards.[10, 11] In Woodford, reflecting the general level, apart from the Reads in their half-way house none of the families – sharing or not – was living in overcrowded conditions, nor were any without a bath or inside WC.

Or take the telephone. In 1954 there were only thirteen per thousand residential subscribers in Bethnal Green; at 'Greenleigh', the new outlying housing estate, at the same period, there were eighty-eight per thousand – nearly seven times as many.[12] I was not able to obtain precise comparable figures for Bethnal Green from British Telecom but was told that today 600 residential subscribers per thousand would be a reasonable estimate. In Woodford it would be more like 800 or 900. Of the total present sample of fifty Bethnal Green families, twenty-nine had their own telephone or the shared use of one, compared with forty-one out of fifty in Woodford, in close agreement with the British Telecom estimates. Comparing the two main tenures, only two of the thirty-eight home-owners but over half the council tenants were without a telephone.

Hospitality was universal, alike in the 1950s and 1980s. But then the interviewers were offered tea; for my colleagues and me it was usually coffee presented in attractive pottery mugs, except for the elegant cups of sweet tea made for us by the Asian mothers. Avant-garde innovations of some years earlier are eventually adopted, in suburb and inner city alike. Such movement with the times, which was noted in the 1950s, was again evident today, but some of it takes effect slowly. *Art deco* was at the earlier period out of fashion with those in the know, but lingered in suburban homes. Now, with the few, it is back, but there was no sign of that yet in the homes we visited. Matching Laura Ashley curtains and wallpaper, brown corduroy or Dralon-covered sofas, glass-topped occasional tables, thick close carpeting, wall-units – these are what you would now expect to find and what we did find in Bethnal Green council flats as well as Woodford owned houses. Bethnal Green in the 1980s was catching up Woodford more quickly than in the 1950s. Witness the cool immaculate, uncluttered home of the Hills, as described by the interviewer, with its Habitat-style furniture, old-fashioned plates on the wall, a few books around. Or the Masons' reproduction tables with leather tops crafted by Mr Mason himself, the Tooleys' collection of porcelain figures and the Brogans' well-equipped kitchen. All these were in Bethnal Green and all were interiors of council flats. Not so different from the Enrights' careful colour co-ordination in Woodford, the top-quality kitchen of the Evanses, the Reeves's Berber carpet or the Shadwells' pine tables, Sanderson linen curtains and matching three-piece suite.

Sometimes there were unmistakable signs of poverty and a generally depressed standard of living in the condition of the home and its furnishings. The interview with the Bakalis took place in a tiny bedroom filled by an unmade double bed, the baby's cot, a small table, one chair and a villainous oil stove. Clothes and bits and pieces were hung over a string along the wall. Something passing for a curtain was tied in a knot over the window. This room was used rather than the sitting-room, as it was easier to heat, but glimpses through into the kitchen suggested that the equipment, furnishing and condition elsewhere were as wretched.

Kathy Garnett – sixteen years old and single – lived in an equally cheerless home, which reflected the general squalor of the block. She was interviewed in one of her brothers' bedrooms. There was no heating, but Kathy, despite her goose-pimples, denied that she was cold. No bedlinen, mattresses piled up against the walls, the pram in the corner and everywhere dirty rubbish and old bits of carpet.

More usual among those with low incomes was the home of another of the very young single mothers – Tina Sydney – which was as clean as it was shabby. Though five people slept in Tina's bedroom where the carpet was threadbare, it was all tidy, the blankets on the baby's cot were neatly folded and clothes were kept in plastic bags. May Riley's home, also in Bethnal Green, was similar. She could 'not afford' any but minimal furnishings. The largest room was empty and the bedroom was furnished only with two single beds, a cheap cupboard, a TV and the baby's cot. She and her friends, however, had themselves repapered the walls and had put up toning curtains. In Woodford some of the council flats were furnished only very basically, and one privately owned home was shabby and sparsely furnished with worn and peeling linoleum.

May was, of course, not alone in having repapered her walls. Practically every home provided evidence of such activity. The response to a comment on fresh-looking paint, was on the lines of 'Oh yes, we did that last month' or 'a little while ago'. Sometimes the decoration was in progress. Newly-built cupboards were pointed out with pride or self-deprecation. Conversions and extensions in owned homes had often been done by the husbands. My predecessors commented on the beginning of DIY in the 1950s and all that it implied:[13]

> the process of removing functions from the domestic to the general economy has been halted. It is surely plain enough that technology has in its later phases reintroduced jobs into the home – ice cream manufacture has come back with the

refrigerator and laundering with the washing machine and entertainment with television. These affect women and children even more than men. But what struck us most was the way in which the wealth which advancing technology yields is being increasingly used to support the new cult of the amateur handyman. He is as busy keeping up with the rapidly changing fashions of interior decoration and design as his wife is kept absorbed in conforming to rising and ever-changing standards of child-care, cookery and dress. More money is used for the house, more leisure used for work. The husbandman of England is back in a new form as horticulturist rather than agriculturist, as builder rather than cattleman, as improver not of a strip of arable land but of the semi-detached family estate at 33 Ellesmere Road.

But now it would not only be the owners of 33 Ellesmere Road who regarded decorations and repairs as their responsibility or their prerogative. Council and other tenants also appeared to take DIY for granted, at least as far as decoration was concerned; so did the three housing departments, though their policies differed slightly.

The GLC re-decorated on a quinquennial cycle but only a room at a time. The tenants could opt to decorate themselves and then receive a grant of £80 for a bedroom or £114 for a living-room. Tower Hamlets expected tenants to carry out their own decorations, making an allowance in two parts of from £63 to £106. These are small sums by present-day costs. All the authorities undertook to put the property in reasonable condition for incoming tenants, an undertaking, as already indicated, that was not, it seems, always carried out. Then there was the possibility of an improvement grant or allowance to outgoing tenants for any improvements made, such as double glazing. Permission had to be asked but, according to the officials, it was not withheld unreasonably. It was, however, according to some of the tenants.

Councils seemed to be sluggish in paying up or informing tenants of their rights. Here are three Bethnal Green tenants of the GLC.

'We done the whole place – we done everything except the kitchen, and then we got a letter to say we was entitled to some decoration! But my Dad's a painter and decorator, so he done it all for us.'

113

'Yes, we did everything because when you move in it's a condition that they don't do anything, you have to do all of it. I think they give you two weeks rent free to do it. Every five years they used to come round and do it, but now they send you the money, not all of it, so much. They come round and have a look first then send you the money.'

'They offered to decorate the living-room for us but I can just imagine the state of it – the left-over wallpapers they've got.'

And Mr Steel in Woodford:

'Yes, we done it twice, because we put Polytex on these walls and they made us take it off, because you're not allowed to put Polytex on council walls! They said they'd give us £80 to decorate, and they gave us £40 half-way through, but haven't given us the other £40 yet.'

It was hard to imagine from the spick and span appearance of the Brogans' Bethnal Green maisonette – beautifully decorated and fitted – that, according to Mrs Brogan, when they had come there it had been quite simply 'disgusting'. And the same could be said of the Reagans' Fairfield flat, about which Bob Reagan said, 'It's all right now – but when we come here it was derelict. It smelt and everything. There was nests out on the balcony. Squatters were here for months. It was in a terrible state this was. I've got quite a bit of it done already, but it takes time.'

There seemed to be even more confusion about obligations and responsibilities for repairs and, according to many of the sample council tenants, inordinate delays on the part of the local authorities in carrying out necessary ones. Mrs Mason reckoned that all the 'decorating and improvements' they had made to their flat – installing a new fireplace, replacing the old kitchen units, and so on – was something they had had to do themselves to get it to their 'way of liking'. When 'a great lump of plaster came out in the kitchen', she thought otherwise. 'We had to pay to get that done, though it was down to them, but we'd have had to wait for a year or so.' Like most of the families when discussing this question, the Masons seemed unaware that in common law they possessed 'a right to repair' and a right to recover the full cost if, through council negligence, they had been obliged to do the job themselves.[14]

Faulty construction and poor maintenance were criticised. Mr Farley complained of 'the leaks and all that. The windows – you can't open them. They're all rotting. The kitchen one you can't open at all – the glass is more or less hanging off. The wood is rotten and the handles are all broken. We've reported that.' Mr Tooley said that he had done 'so many repairs it's unbelievable. I've done more than what the council have done in a year – fixing the sink myself. I ended up mending the electricity box myself.' When asked if he was happy about doing repairs, he replied, 'obviously not, because I'm paying for repairs in my rent – maintenance and services comes through the council, so they're stealing off me again.'

It would, however, be misleading to suggest that this was the prevalent attitude among the sample council tenants in either area. Only one-third had in fact done any repairs. Over half of these were minor and there was little grumbling about doing them. I talked to a housing manager in Tower Hamlets. He complained that caretakers were called on unnecessarily by some tenants to do trivial repairs and maintenance jobs. Some of the mothers praised them for doing just this.

One or two of the non-council tenants similarly criticised the role of their landlords. Mrs Mitchell in Bethnal Green thought that the Crown were 'very amateurish' about repairs – 'It's just that they employ one-man bands to do the lot.' And Hannah Baker in Woodford blamed the 'curious half-and-half' arrangement of their tenancy. They were housing association tenants but the council actually owned the property. She thought this accounted for the sad neglect of the building, which was being 'left to rot away'. The others were reasonably satisfied and expected to do the decorating and minor repairs themselves. Mrs Sadler was very satisfied with her housing association:

'They do it all – it's all covered. In the living-room a joist fell through in the ceiling; they came and repaired it. If the hot water or the heating goes, they come and do it. Any improvements are up to you. We ripped out the kitchen, put in cupboards, put in a shower in the bathroom. We're on our second go now.'

From nearly all, the general impression was the same. 'Inside,' as Tom Peters said of his Woodford Council flat, 'you make it the way you want it to be.' Mrs Lopez, when asked if there was anything she particularly disliked about her accommodation in a dilapidated old GLC block, replied, 'Nothing I can think of. I'll like it when it's all finished and decorated. It's not the flat I want but at least it will be home.' Lorna Field thought the inside of her flat was

'a lot better than some of the places round here. A lot of people say, "Oh I don't want Fairfield", when they want a council place, but compared to some of the other council estates the flats – the one-bedroom flats – are bigger and have more light in them. I like the light.'

But she went on:

'When we first got it we was so pleased to get somewhere I was pleased with it, but it seems to have shrunk, it's so small. There's no room to put any stuff in it. Not even enough room for your clothes. I would like bigger rooms. I'd prefer another room.'

Lorna was in the minority along with one-third of the mothers in her dissatisfaction with the number of rooms and their size. In fact space was more often commented on favourably by council tenants and home-owners alike than any other feature. But with contentment or complaints account needs to be taken of the differences generally between most of the houses and council flats of the sample families. Satisfaction with the size and number of rooms voiced by a home-owning mother living in a six-roomed house with a garden implies a different standard from that expressed by Alice Trent, when she said of the space in her council flat, 'Well yes, we've got enough. We've got a spare bedroom which Rob's got all his tools in.' Or compare Lorna Field's growing dissatisfaction with their one-bedroom council flat with Mrs Perry's about her five-roomed semi: 'My only complaint is that the kitchen isn't as big as the house!'

The kitchen is a case in point. The preparation and consumption of food influences design almost as much as does sleep. In manner of life there has been some convergence between the classes. Improvements in space or other housing standards have also reduced differences between the two main tenure groups. But they have not gone. Space in the council flats could mostly be seen as a series of boxes; the kitchens on the whole were small, though some families contrived to eat in them. The kitchens in the houses varied greatly in size. Probably most had been designed originally as working kitchens. The old custom of middle-class suburbia was for cooking and eating to be separated, as they had been when there were still servants. Now separate dining-rooms, where homes were large enough for them, have given way to 'through living-rooms, or to expanded kitchens with 'dividers' and breakfast bars and the like and to the occasional open plan comprising both living-room and kitchen. Several of the home-owners were in the process of altering the layout of their homes to suit this mode of living or had already done so. Some of the council tenants referred to the desirability of such schemes and the frustration of not being able to achieve them. All these things cost money and quite substantial sums had been laid out. Though a few council tenants had spent several hundreds of pounds on installing cupboards or building a new fireplace or refitting the kitchen, it was among the home-owners that this kind of expenditure was most evident. But then their housing costs generally were inevitably much higher.

Costs

It was quite beyond the scope of this enquiry to obtain the kind of detailed information that would have afforded a sophisticated analysis of comparative tenure costs. Home-owners were asked how much they had paid for their home. Otherwise the questions on housing costs centred on what the families spent regularly over a given period – their running costs. So in what follows I have relied on the replies to simple questions on the amounts actually paid out, just as their income was assessed on the amounts they said they actually received.

Housing costs make a major and an inflexible inroad into family income. Across the board there is less of a correlation between housing payments and the quality of accommodation than might be expected.[15] But there are differences, of course, according to tenure. A crucial one between the two main tenures – home-ownership and local authority renting – is in the initial outlay the home-owners have to make (none had obtained a 100 per cent mortgage). Obviously in any calculation a family will take this initial outlay into account, not only that it must be found and paid over as a lump sum but also that it bears a direct relation to the amount payable on the remaining sum of the loan. The higher the deposit the smaller the total mortgage repayment, and *vice versa*. There are, of course, various ways of raising this money. One or both partners may have saved for it before or after marriage or will already have savings that can be used. Eight of the twelve second-time buyers said that they had used proceeds from the sale of their previous home; seven had received loans or gifts or both from their families.

For the Greys and the Wakefields this help had taken the form of a legacy, and both had been large enough sums to pay for the whole deposits of £1,500 and £2,400 respectively. The Wakefields had bought their house three years before on their marriage, she in her early and he in his mid-twenties, and told the interviewer that they had savings of between £1,000 and £2,500. Their previous joint take-home pay, before Mrs Wakefield had given up work, had been in the region of £175 per week. So though the legacy had clearly been a great help it seems likely that they would – after perhaps a wait – have been able to find the deposit money from their own savings.

The stories of the other lucky recipients of family cash help for their homes were not dissimilar. It too seems to have made possible the purchase of a home at the particular time but not to have made the difference between buying or never buying. The Benthams, for instance, had paid the deposit on their Bethnal Green 'cottage' with the help of a gift of £2,000 from a member of Mrs Bentham's family, using also £400 from the sale of their car and £1,000 of their own savings. This had been a year previously but they had, it seems, still at the time of the interview about £3,000 in savings, and between them they brought home £200 per week from their respective jobs. With the Winthrops it seems altogether to have been a bonus. They had recently paid their deposit with gifts received from both sets of parents – £300 from each – on top of £2,800 from the sale of a previous home. They had, at the time of the interview, over £4,000 in savings and Mr Winthrop's earnings were over £150 per week.

Only the Shadwells had been able to buy their house in Wood-ford without benefit of a loan of any kind, paying £18,500 in 1978.

Rob Shadwell had come into the marriage already the possessor of a flat. Proceeds from the sale of this and accumulated savings had made it possible to purchase their present one outright – fortunately, as he was out of work by the time of the interviews. Otherwise all had taken out mortgages or loans ranging from £8,250[16] to £35,250. Repayment of the loan and the interest was of course the main constituent of the home-owners' housing costs. By far the greatest number had been obtained through a building society. There were only two local authority mortgages, though one or two had been unsuccessfully applied for. Two fathers worked for insurance firms and they had obtained a very favourable rate of interest from their own firms. Another, whose mortgage was with a building society, was being subsidised by his employers, who were paying the difference between the initial and current interest rates.

These mortgage loans and the consequent monthly repayments varied according to the stretch of time over which they were being repayed. The Rosens, for instance, who had bought a home in 1981 for £49,000, had been able to put down a deposit of £26,000 with proceeds from the sale of a previous home augmented by savings with a building society. They were still paying a substantial £293 a month on repayments. The three Bethnal Green home-owners illustrate the extensive range in the mortgage repayments. One family was paying £67 per month, the other two £237 and £327 for houses between £25,000 and £29,000, each bought the year before.

For the home-owners the second major housing cost is rates. At the time of the interview the Tower Hamlets domestic rate in the £ was 167.5 per cent, and that of Redbridge 116 per cent. The actual rates paid by the home-owners varied according to the gross value fixed for their homes and also whether a rebate had been allowed, which was the case for only one couple. Another had applied.

The third more or less unavoidable payment about which they were asked was house insurance – unavoidable since building societies and other home-loan-giving bodies insist on the property being insured. Finally there are repairs and maintenance. These are essential but different from the inflexibility of mortgage and rate payments in that the home-owner can within limits himself or herself determine how much to spend. Some of the families, especially those who had only just acquired their homes, found this item of expenditure – actual or potential – difficult to quantify. Among those who did, the range was considerable. Thus for a five-roomed £14,000 house, bought in 1978, one couple reckoned to allow £100 per year; another, by contrast, for a similar sized house which cost £22,500 in 1979, £300 per year.

The two major regular outgoings for council tenants are rent and rates. Over the country these vary considerably.[17] In the two study areas there were differences, but not very wide. Tenants need not budget for insurance, other than for the contents of their home which is an option with any tenure. Some, as indicated earlier, referred to money paid out for repairs and decoration.

The financial liabilities of tenants of private landlords may in some instances be more akin to those of home-owners, with or without equivalent benefits. With one exception, however, the six non-council tenants were involved in the same sorts of essential payments as their local authority counterparts. The exceptions were the Sadlers, whose housing association was a co-operative and whose outgoings were relatively high, £43 per week 'rent' and rates. The rewards, in their view, made it all worth it. Mrs Sadler explained it as follows:

'It's private. You pay the deposit of £800. When you come in the flat's valued, say £13,000, and you stay for five years and whatever the flat's gone up, say it's gone up £10,000 in five years, you get a percentage of the flat back when you move. You pay your rates and all that separately and your rent goes up and down with the mortgage rate just as though we were buying it, but it's co-ownership. You don't have such a big deposit at the beginning, like, whereas buying you'd have to put thousands down.'

Common to all three tenure groups, but of a slightly different order from those I have mentioned, are fuel costs. They are different in the sense that you can decide, within reason, how much fuel you burn. Candlelight and arctic temperatures were both absent in the homes of my sample, but the amount used obviously depended on a number of factors, including the size of the home, the kind of fuel, the efficiency of the insulation and the need for economy or propensity for extravagance.

Leaving aside fuel costs, how did the outgoings for their housing compare between the home-owners and the tenants?[18] While home-owners, with a fairly even distribution, spanned the whole range of categorised expenditure – from under £21 a week to £89, the council tenants clustered mainly within the £21 to £30 bracket, with just over one in six paying less than £21 per week (see appendix 2, table 2.11). Best off in these costs were the housing association and Crown tenants. With the exception of the Sadlers, none of these was paying more than £16 per week in rent and rates at the time of the interview. But the single most important difference is that, at this stage of forming their families, the home-owners, with a few exceptions, had to find considerably more money to meet their housing costs than local authority or other tenants. More than half were spending over £50 a week just on the basics. I return to these differences as they relate to income in chapter 6.

To sum up. In the interiors of their homes, Bethnal Green and Woodford have come closer together since the 1950s. Standards of space and amenities are altogether higher, and appreciated as such in both places. With some exceptions, the interiors look much more alike and are more comfortable. But differences persist and these are to a great extent contingent upon tenure. They have to do with how free you are to do what you want and also, of course, with how much you can afford. There were signs of acute poverty in a few of the homes. The tenure difference really bites, however, in the exteriors and in the immediate surroundings. Always allowing for exceptions, there are two equations. Council tenant = flat dweller = dependence on public space and facilities of often poor, sometimes atrocious quality. Home-owner = house = garden = street, sometimes traffic-ridden but often quiet and green. Satisfactions and dissatisfactions, occasionally taking the form of a bitter sense of shame, are not hard to fit to these equations nor is it hard to allot them to the two study areas.

6

WAYS OF LIFE

To what extent was the families' way of life affected by the differences in their housing circumstances? What did home mean to them? How contented were they and how vulnerable or secure? And what of change? The homes and neighbourhoods in Bethnal Green and Woodford had changed since the 1950s. In what ways was family life different from that time? How was it remembered?

Memories

The same sort of nostalgia that was evident when the mothers and fathers talked about the neighbourhoods and homes of their youth was apparent also in their recollections of their childhood generally. 77 per cent had been 'happy' or 'very happy' as children. Here is Vernon French recalling his Woodford childhood in the early 1960s:

'It was a very happy home. A very tight family. As near perfect as the average family is. The upbringing I'd like to give my children. No bricks through windows or anything like that. We weren't a rich family, only had a car when I was ill. We only ever once went on a proper holiday, and I paid for that when I was about 18. We even made our own tent and went camping and we thoroughly enjoyed it. This is the trouble with today's society – they don't know how to enjoy themselves with nothing. You've got to be able to put money in the slot to enjoy yourself. We were better off then – despite wages being very poor. I lived on the first floor of a two-floor council flat and I was more into what was happening in the community. I saw more, I heard more – doors banging, taps running, children crying and shouting, wives having a good old ding-dong and husbands having a go. You could hear all that – children playing on the grass right outside your back door. But here there's nothing like that.'

Jacob Henry, now a Woodford home-owner, remembered his East London childhood as a 'lovely childhood':

'A lot of good friends who I've still got today. It was a very exciting time to grow up in. When I was 10 years old – it was 1963 – the Beatles had just come to fame. Things were beginning to change. Young people were beginning to get recognition. There were clothes specially designed for them. There was a lot of optimism which I don't think today's children have got. I think they're under more pressure. More violence imposed upon them. Children today think that strength is shown in violence. But in those days when I was 10 to 16 years old it was fabulous. It's a lot more difficult to live happily now than then. Things are more expensive. People are not so nice and are more stereotyped now. The corner shop's gone. The whole world's got less interesting.'

Marion Henry also described an East End childhood:

'It was always a very happy home. It was a nice flat. The only thing was the bath was in the kitchen, a bit inconvenient but it didn't worry us. School was just across the road. Mother worked in the school I went to. The head mistress asked in assembly if any of our mothers would be interested in the job. I told my mum. She'd done cleaning before, in a factory. She used to go out at five in the morning. But this was not so early, half past six to quarter to nine and then she'd finish off getting me ready for school and then she went back in the evenings till seven. She was there right until five years ago.'

And here is a description by Tom Peters of life twenty-five years ago in another part of London:

'You could leave your street door open and people used to sit on the steps, talk and that. I was even brought up – I was very young then – when the Notting Hill riots were on. But people then, their attitude was they'd rather help, you know. I suppose as the years go on people are not the same any more. I can remember my mother going down to the public

123

baths. We never could afford a washing machine or anything like that. My mother has told me when I was born I didn't have a cot, I was in the bottom drawer of the chest of drawers. I had it hard, yes, but I look back now and I think it was fantastic. You know, the way people are now, they're rushing around . . . people haven't got time to actually talk to you and find out how you really are. In them days if you went down to the doctor's there'd be a great big discussion, "Let's think now, perhaps it was that food you had", or whatever.

You know, the women kept together and the men kept together and if it was like Sunday dinner time my father used to go to the pub and came back drunk with about six other guys. My mother used to be standing there, it was a routine, I suppose. He used to go to sleep, wake up about six have his tea, my mother used to get ready and they'd spend the evening out. Now it's very unusual if my parents go out of an evening. But you can never bring back what really happened in them days. I used to be put out in the pram when they used to be tarring the road, putting down the little pebbles. The whole street would be out, all the kids, all the babies because the tar is supposed to be good for you. That's how I was brought up, on the old traditional things. Not so much, "Oh I'll take an Aspro because I've got a headache", or because you're tensed up. I was brought up to have some milk or cocoa. All those sorts of things, they've gone now. We're not living in the 19th century as such, we are living in the 20th century. The space-age sort of stuff. Why get up, why not just press the button. So I'm a bit of a hypocrite with my telly control. This is something we all seem to be programmed into. I used to remember boiling water on the gas stove to have a bath – the old tin bath used to come off the wall. And in and out every Sunday night. We didn't have an inside toilet and in the cold weather you'd think that's a bit too much going outside, so you'd have a pot underneath the bed. I'd go back to all that any day of the week. I don't like this system – it's making people too lazy. Children's brains are not being used at all nowadays with all these computerised gadgets, calculators and all.

I'm worse off now. When I was a child whatever food was dished to you I could eat. The food that is sometimes dished up now – I can't stand it. Having grandparents that had a fruit and vegetable stall I've always been used to fresh fruit and veg daily. All right, my mother probably had to go out and get the cheapest meat – breast of lamb or whatever – and that'd go into the stew. But there was none of this, "Oh let's open a tin of carrots", it was *actually* carrots. The sort of food now is not good for anyone, though if you looked in our cupboards you wouldn't see many tins, but the food then . . . You don't talk now about children having bread and jam. But in them days you couldn't afford bread and jam. It was tea then – not tea-bags. There's no whistle of a kettle and things like that, it's all electric kettles. It's all so easy now.'

A substantial minority of the mothers and fathers took a more dispassionate view. Their childhood had been 'a normal one', 'quite happy in spite of various problems' or it was 'hard to say'. When Hannah Baker looked back, what she remembered was being happy. But 'in reality', she did not think it was: 'It was pretty fraught.' Only a tiny minority had been 'unhappy' or 'very unhappy'. For one mother, things had improved:

'When I was about nine they put me in a home. When my mum married my step-dad I never got on with him. He never accepted me and my brother and they thought it would be best like if we didn't stay with them. They tried us in a home. But that didn't work very well so when I was about 11 me and my brother were sent to a council boarding school in the country. Yes, I really did like it there.'

Bob Reagan had also had unhappy experiences of a broken home:

'I was never very happy as a kid. I was always in trouble. It's only now I've started to calm down. A lot of problems. It was a broken home. It started to break up when we were young and then it finally broke up a few years ago. But I was just like a yoyo. If I had a row with my dad I'd go to my mum and if I had a row with my mum I'd go back to my dad. There was only my football. I used to be a good footballer.'

Despite the general nostalgia when comparing past and present, Tom Peters was among the exceptions. More favoured the present. This was particularly evident when asked about their economic

Ways of Life

circumstances. Though many found it difficult to compare – 'after all, £10 then could buy you as much as what £100 does today' – the majority were in no doubt that they were better off financially today. Mrs Winthrop, a Woodford home-owner, daughter of Bethnal Green council tenants was one: 'Obviously we're better off than my parents were at the time. As a kid one didn't appreciate the problems, but then people weren't earning the sort of money they're earning now. Living standards have risen.' Mr Clark, a council tenant aged forty-nine, still lived in Bethnal Green as his parents did before him.

> 'I'm better off than my family was when I was a child. At that time it was a penny in the gas and we'd known a time when we didn't have a penny for the gas and weeks someone might call at the door and it might be the fellow for the rent, and my mother was telling the kids to keep quiet and let him take it out on the knocker, not because she didn't want to pay, she just didn't have it. Father was in the shoe trade then but there wasn't many jobs, they worked up till eight o'clock at night. I used to go home and in practically no time at all I was in bed because my mum would be working till eight and the woman would be looking after me till then.'

These pre-war and war-time days were remembered clearly by some of the grandmothers also. Mrs Cohen now lived on the Debden estate. She thought her daughter and son-in-law were lucky, and that there were 'terrific differences':

> 'We were stuck in this one room with no facilities. They have got a nice house; no problems. They're both well off. She's more educated than we were, she's got a better job. When you were out of work you had nothing except labour money. Conditions were much worse. We had difficulty getting the rent together. No one today seems to have that trouble. You couldn't compare it at all, no way. You couldn't compare homes years ago to what homes are like now, not even this. We couldn't have had a home like this years ago, things were very tight. We were just pushed out to work. We didn't have the time for education.'

Or, once again, Mrs Macintosh about her furnished room in war-time Perth:

'There's no comparison. An outside toilet . . . It's true I'd been used to that in my childhood but then I went into married quarters with all mod cons. So to go back to that knowing I would have to be there for some time . . .

Now all my children have their own houses and one has a lovely council flat. And I think of having to carry that pail of slops down the stairs and to go into the wash house to do my nappies with a cold water tap . . . Well, we don't want them to go back to that, do we?'

And so it goes on. Times were hard – Mrs Shaw had had 'very much less to spend' than her daughter. At one stage, she remembered, she managed on 'about two shillings a day'. Going back to the days of his childhood, Mr Cohen thought there was no comparison between then and now – it was 'struggle, struggle, struggle':

'The money was so scarce. My father died in 1927. I was 10. We'd no money at all. Mother earned a couple of bob doing scrubbing. We were on relief. No money – but tickets; and you collected rice and stuff. Terrible. My mother worked very hard. She just scraped and scraped. There were six in the family and one boy they'd adopted.'

Times were hard, but they were good. Mrs Cohen said of the time when her first baby was born – 'we didn't have a lot. We struggled but I enjoyed it. Everyone was the same.' Or Mrs Gedge of the same period but before her marriage:

'It was good. I mean you made your own enjoyment then. We didn't have no box [TV]. We had a piano and a suite of furniture in the back room. You could open it up for parties. You only had the piano but you had a damn good time. And we had the dance halls too and the picture houses, and you could go for a hop for a tanner. And then if you found a bloke who was quite comfortable he took you to a café and you had egg and chips. My dad kept me and I had about a couple of bob a week pocket money. We used to have these clubs – you put in a shilling or two every week – and dad would put in £5 at Christmas and then you'd buy your whole rigout. And then there were the American shoe shops. Very cheap those were. The popular shoe was the high black satin court –

6/11 a pair. Stockings was a bob a pair, hats about 4/11. We never went short of shoe leather or good meals.'

Just after the war, when her daughter was born, she said, they never had washing machines:

'We had mangles and washing hanging on the line, we didn't have no laundrettes. They're far, far better off than we were in the washing facilities. For the accommodation I think I was lucky. Jane always had her own bedroom. Living today I think is far better for the kids. I mean you've got the freezers. If you can afford to buy in bulk it saves money in the end. Jane and I share her big freezer.'

Nowadays there is the Welfare State, appreciated by some more than others. Mrs Cohen, for instance, thought that you get 'more help these days. You couldn't go for a rent rebate or anything like that then . . . Things cost more today but we are pensioners and do get help.' But 'the children's allowance' was a 'sore spot' for Mrs Gedge – 'I don't think all the foreigners should have it. I don't think I'm prejudiced, but when I think of all those six quids it do get me down.'

Mrs Hammer, comparing with a later period (1952), thought that

'in terms of hard cash, my daughter's probably better off than we were, but what we would call luxuries, they take for granted as essentials – the beer, the odd types of food. Even when we came here we would have had a meal of baked beans on toast or spaghetti on toast, which we wouldn't dream of having now. Possibly they have better standards, though they are as hard up as we ever were.'

There was, however, the difference that neither of their lots of parents was in a position to help them when their son was born, whereas they can help their daughter and son-in-law and 'do so readily'. Mrs Stubbs commented on the modern habit of eating out. 'What we had we worked for – fridges, washing machines and all that, but we never had any meals out like they do now.'

Universal change

These kinds of memories were shared by people in Bethnal Green and Woodford living in all tenures and by the better and the less well off. Only six of the poorer mothers and fathers – all with less than £80 per week net income – actually thought of themselves as worse off now financially than they had been in their childhood. The majority had the kinds of household possessions referred to by Mrs Gedge. Take TV sets. In 1955 the number of sets per 100 households in Bethnal Green was 32; in Greenleigh it was 65.[1] In 1981, among the sample of fifty families, only two households were without one. Thus, in Greenleigh in 1955 there were twice as many television sets per household as there were in Bethnal Green at the same time, and in Bethnal Green today there are three times as many per household as there were in 1955. Nearly everyone had a record-player. There were video-recorders in Bethnal Green as well as Woodford. All the households had vacuum cleaners. But there were differences. Though the majority of families in both the main tenures had washing machines, it was a bigger majority among the home-owners than among the council tenants. More than half the home-owners compared with fewer than one-sixth of the council tenants had a freezer. Seventy-nine of the families owned a car. Only fifteen of these lived in Bethnal Green.[2]

The extent to which life was lived outside the home had, earlier, been a major point of difference between Woodford and Bethnal Green. Are people still 'vigorously at home in the streets'?[3] The answer must be no, or not in such numbers and so generally. It is not only that it is difficult to be at home at ground level when you live far about it. There have been so many other changes. More mothers – and grandmothers[4] – go out to work. Television and DIY[5] keep people indoors. There are fewer reasons to 'pop out' often; disappearing corner shops and changing shopping habits, for example. For another thing, more people step from their front door into a car. In the age of the car those who do not have one are doubly deprived. They cannot move about but, because others do, their neighbourhood is less convivial.

Use of the home

The mothers were asked a number of questions about where and how they spent their time and what their preferences were. Understandably, nearly all, because of the new baby, spent more time in the home than outside it but not by any means did they all prefer it that way. Just over half in Bethnal Green and two-fifths in Woodford would rather have been more out than in. Mary Clifford, on the point of returning to her management job, 'didn't like the idea of being stuck in the house all the time. The people here don't like to go away on holiday. They really love their homes and their gardens. To me that isn't life at all. There's far more than just this.' Except for those few already back in paid work their daily round was inevitably focused on the baby and domestic chores. Mrs Green's account of the preceding day was typical, give or take a different time span or a 'visit to mum and dad':

'I got up about 10 o'clock. Then I had breakfast, fed and changed the baby. I got out of the house by 11.30. I came back and then I fed her and did some hoovering and tidying up till 3.00. She then woke. I saw to her, fed and changed her, played with her. At 4.30 I started to prepare dinner. I bathed her at about 6ish. My husband came home at 7 and we ate at 9. We watched TV. The baby's awake all evening – her last feed is at midnight and she goes down about an hour after that.'

Though the mothers, irrespective of area, spent more time in their home than outside it, when it came to leisure nearly twice as many Woodford as Bethnal Green mothers mentioned activities in the home, whether it was reading, some form of creative work or simply cooking or knitting.[6] There was no difference between the two places in the proportion of replies referring to activities outside the home, but there was variation in the types of activity. Relatively more Bethnal Green than Woodford mothers, for instance, liked going out for a drink or to discos. The reverse was true for various forms of sporting activity. Both were probably reflections of the age differences between the families in the two areas and also to some extent to social class differences,[7] though this influence is less strong than it was.

A substantial proportion of the fathers' activities was also in their home (again more, relatively, in Woodford than Bethnal Green), but more of them than of their wives spent free time outside the home, especially on sport. A few were football enthusiasts. According to Samuel,[8] there should have been boxing buffs in

Bethnal Green, but they did not surface among the sample. Other hobbies were snooker, gambling, photography, travel and playing the guitar.

As already indicated in chapter 5, space in the home, for hobbies or just living, was used in conventional ways. Bedrooms were unmistakably bedrooms though whether the cot was in the parents' bedroom or in a lavishly fitted out baby's room it was very noticeable how much a part of the parents' waking life the baby was. I can remember only one interview where the baby had been put to sleep in her separate bedroom upstairs and, despite vociferous protest, was kept there for the entire period. Usually they were in the same room, often bouncing themselves up and down in the ubiquitous baby bouncer or being nursed or fed or played with.

There were also among the non-sharing families few signs of separate spaces for husband and wife except for those few families where one or other spouse used a room for work. It was usually the extra bedroom that was put to use or potential use for work. This formed the only exception in the strict apportionment of adult sleeping and waking space. Otherwise it was 'just a glory-hole for the moment' or was accommodating a granny or a stepson or was used for guests.

Not many mothers had any intention of working for pay in or from their homes or of wanting space for that purpose. Three were actually using their home for their paid jobs – for a physiotherapy practice, for part-time teaching and for book illustrating. A few were either already, like the school teachers, bringing some of their work home, or envisaged at some future date doing that or working directly from home – typing, for instance. In Bethnal Green only four mothers talked of the possibility of home-based paid work.

Even fewer fathers were involved in this way. Just over one-sixth did in fact say that they used their homes for some sort of paid work, but mostly it was a question among the professionals and technicians of bringing work home. Only two Bethnal Green fathers thought they might like to have space in the home for work as craftsmen.

Wives and husbands

It was evident in chapter 2 from the comments on the mothers' return to paid work that traditional attitudes about the husband/

wife relationship were still very much present among the sample families, though light was breaking through and was most evident among the professional and managerial group. There were authoritarian husbands but there were egalitarian ones, too. Wives' expectations on the sharing of tasks were often rather low. 'He's very good around the house. He does lots of things husbands don't usually do.' Not much advance there on the authors' comment on domestic roles in Woodford of the 1950s. 'Some husbands, as well as doing much of the heavy work in the home, carrying coals and emptying rubbish, act as assistants to their wives for at least part of their day',[9] though that was a considerable advance on yet earlier times, particularly in Bethnal Green. Only Jill Reagan among the mothers with paid jobs had to carry the full burden of three jobs (baby, housework and part-time employment) with no more help from her husband than the proverbial 'bit of washing up'. But for others it was 'he does much more than he did', or 'he's always done his share' or 'we've always divided the tasks straight down the middle. If anything, he does more than me.'[10]

As with household tasks, so with baby care. According to the mothers about one-third of their husbands did little more than 'play with the baby'. Mr Stokes

> 'plays with him, sits with him while I eat my tea. No, he's never changed him. I think he'd put the napkin on his head! Feeding, I think he's tried but I don't think he likes feeding him. No, I don't really want him to do more. He works hard. Yes, he would help more when I go back to work.'

Ann Oakley found with her very middle-class sample of first-child families that the 'most favoured paternal task' was playing with the baby and the 'least favoured' changing a dirty nappy.[11] Mrs Macintosh found it all

> 'very interesting because it only takes one person to look after the baby at any one time and until just now I was breast feeding him, there was nothing positive that Alex could do. The baby needed me so I changed him and so on. And he did all the other things – make the meals, wash the dishes, paint and make the house more habitable. It's only in the last few weeks that he's started – that he will change the baby and feed him and get up to do these things for him if the baby wakes

early. Though when the baby was younger he was quite happy to pace the floor with him and get him to sleep. When I get back to work it will be a genuine sharing. He's always done his real share. Though I may resent the time taken away from me being with the baby!'

I wonder how many Bethnal Green and Woodford fathers in the 1950s changed their babies' nappies? Certainly not as many as the two-fifths of my sample who apparently did so. Fred Dixon, from Newcastle, having joked that 'the North was a bastion of male chauvinism', then said that he 'would do anything for the baby, including changing him. I don't want him to grow up with this false stereotype of the male as a cool detached figure. So the more the man becomes involved it will humanise this stereotype.'

The one father of twins recounted how they managed:

'We're fairly lucky inasmuch as we would always help each other. I'll do the cooking or hoovering. The babies I'll feed and change and this sort of thing. With the two, you haven't got a lot of option. But before the babies if I was home before the wife I'd always cook the dinner.'

And Mr Aslam from Bangladesh, living with friends, and merry in the face of adversity. 'Everybody knows how to do things but doesn't do them – but not me. I even help these ladies [the other resident wives] with their babies.'

But, whether they took an active part or not, fathers seemed well pleased with their new role. The enthusiasm of quite a number knew no bounds – Tom Peters was 'over the moon at being a dad. I would hang for her. I would go out and thieve for her, if it ever got to the point. She's everything I've ever dreamed of.' But there were problems:

'It's just a question of getting the right place. I don't like to be on the dole. To me it just lowers me. When I was young I suppose I jet-setted around. Now I've got a family and responsibilities it's totally different. My whole life has completely changed. If I could move to West London I would not be in this situation at all. I'd know where to go, who to ask to get work.'

Dick Reeves, who had had little family life himself as a child, found it had made 'a dramatic difference' to his life:

'In the first couple of months I thought what have we done? Now he's giving a tremendous amount of pleasure. All I want for him is us to give him pleasure. A bit of give and take I suppose. There used to be problems but no more. We both like going out but now have a regular babysitter, so now we can go out one evening a week which I think is essential.'

Jack White took it all more calmly:

'It's all right, I don't feel any different really. I don't feel as if I'm under any enormous strain but that's mainly because Ann takes it all. The first two weeks I did muck in quite a lot then – but it's slowly tailed off. Now Ann's going back to work. This will be a telling time, won't it? This'll be the test. I won't have any choice. I'm going to have to pull my socks up and do some work, aren't I?'

So it can be seen that for most family life was focused on the home. This was further corroborated in reply to a question the mothers and fathers were asked on what their home meant to them.[12]

The meaning of home

The home as a 'centre of moral goodness, inculcating Christian lore, truth and obedience and preserving the social and sexual respectability associated with such virtues'[13] belongs more to the nineteenth century than to our largely secular age. But in so far as the family as an institution is still very much alive the home can bathe in that reflected glory. The majority of the mothers and fathers thought of their home as 'somewhere to be on their own'. The concept of privacy came through strongly. It made no difference whether they lived in Bethnal Green or Woodford nor, with exceptions, what their form of tenure was. Sadly just over one in three of the sharers thought of their home mainly as 'a place to get away from', though for a slightly smaller proportion it was seen mainly as 'somewhere for family and friends to come to'.

This last came second (though a long way behind) as the most important side of home for the sample as a whole. Nearly two-thirds of the home-owning mothers felt that the value of their home as a future investment was important. But very few gave it first priority. A somewhat higher proportion of fathers in the homes they owned saw them as an investment. One further point that emerged is that, apart from several of the sharers, the meaning they attached to home did not appear to be affected by the standard of their accommodation nor how they regarded this.

Contentment, vulnerability

The picture of home-centred couples devoted to their new baby and pleased with their new way of life was rounded out by replies to another set of questions on what they thought were the most important things for a good life and which of those they reckoned they had. Their criteria for a good life ranged from that of 'happiness' in general to more specific requirements such as 'a good job', though surprisingly few mothers or fathers mentioned this, or 'watching the baby grow up'. There was a clear distinction in their minds between the importance of a physical home and a home which embodied family life. This last interpretation, or equivalent ideas, figured very high in their needs. In fact, it took its place along with happiness, health and enough money and security among the top most important things. It was the same with the fathers.

These ideas for a good life and the order of importance are not surprising, but what I did find surprising, even allowing for the special time in their lives, was how many said they had what was needed to make life good. Ninety-seven mothers found over 250 suggestions to make and, of these suggestions, 82 per cent were felt to be things which were already contributing to a good life for them. As many as 64 per cent of the mothers thought they had all the things they mentioned. The response from the fathers was only slightly less impressive.

Even among those who said they did not have everything, only six mothers and two fathers could think of no balancing assets. These last two, both unemployed, had specified enough money and a job. Of the mothers, three were single. April Lang said a husband was necessary; Carrie Nichols talked of a home of her own and a job, and May Riley of enough money. The necessities for a good life of the other three mothers were also particular and limited rather than general. Sandra Russell wanted a home (she was sharing at the time with her in-laws); and two Bethnal Green council tenants specified money. Of the necessities people thought they did *not* have, 'enough money' was in fact mentioned most often, five times as often as by those who said they had enough.[14] There were more home-owners than people in other tenures among this last group. Not all the suggestions were equally serious – the necessities, for instance, that Mrs Enright found lacking: 'comforts, drink and cigarettes'. Of the nine mothers who mentioned a home or the home of their choice as a necessity of which they were deprived, four were council tenants, one – Betty Read – was still technically homeless and four were in shared households.

Social class differences in all this were not apparent, with one exception. A small group of the mothers made some reference to their own attributes. It was, for instance, necessary for a good life to 'have a sense of humour', to 'be able to relate to other people'. Among this group those whose jobs were or had been professional or managerial predominated. 'As well as a loving husband,' said one, 'it is also necessary to have the ability to enjoy what you have.'

This high level of contentment was maintained when I tested it by grouping the answers to several questions and calculating a score (see appendix 2). There were some, particularly among the non-home-owners, whose dissatisfaction with their housing, or whose problems of another kind lowered their score so that they could be described as only reasonably contented rather than very contented. These two groups were in fact of similar proportions. But there were very few (only about one-sixth) whose sum of responses added up to discontent.

There is a seemingly obvious equation between security and contentment, with its obverse of vulnerability and discontent. This I also tested using for the security/vulnerability scale such variables as marital status, income level and certain indicators of housing conditions (see appendix 3). As might be expected with a group of people with new family responsibilities, there was no really high contentment for those with low security. Nor were any discontented who seemed to have everything going for them. There was the sad little group, familiar by now, all either single mothers, sharers or both, who scored low on both counts. There were also a few who were less contented than might have been expected from their position on the security scale. But other reasons made this less surprising. One father, for instance, told me that he and his wife had serious trouble hanging over them, all caused, he said by his temper.

'Yes, I've done a Borstal – DC, YP, prison. Done it all. Learnt the hard way. If you've got to do it, I'm glad I did it when I was young. I'm grown up now. I've got my daughter. She keeps me out of trouble. It's always been for fighting – quick temper. Not actually thieving or breaking into people's homes. I don't do things like that. It's just I've got a quick temper and I just go a bit mad like. I'm waiting to go up now to the Crown Court. I don't reckon I'll get away with it but I hope so. I should do now with the baby and that. I've pleaded not guilty anyway.'

Generally, however, people are higher up on the contentment scale than their level of security might seem to warrant. It is moreover noteworthy that though it is the home-owners who cluster at the highest levels of both scales there are six couples in council tenancies who are very contented and only three who are discontented.

An important element in the families' level of security was the amount of financial support they had from their parents and other relatives (see appendix 3). This obviously affected their way of life. So too did the relationship generally that they had with members of the extended family, and in particular between mother and daughter. In a modest way some comparison may be made about this with the earlier studies.

Extended family

A comparison can be made between the 1950s Bethnal Green marriage sample of forty-five couples and the present sample of fifty Bethnal Green families (see appendix 2, tables 2.12 and 2.13), for the extent of the change in the numbers who actually lived close to relatives. In the earlier study the authors found that, between them, the forty-five couples had a total of 1,691 relatives excluding parents, cousins and remote kin,[15] while the present sample of fifty families (for not all of whom there is full information) had 1,145 between them. Only four of the 1950s families had no Bethnal Green relatives. Nearly half the couples had ten or more. Allowing for differences in the composition of the two samples,[16] it is striking how much higher today is the number of families who have no relatives other than parents living in Bethnal Green. Comparing the couples, roughly one in eleven had none in the 1950s whereas now it is getting on for half. Only one mother had more than twenty Bethnal-Green-based relatives, compared with twelve couples in the earlier study. Not surprisingly, proportionately even more Woodford than present-day Bethnal Green families had no relatives living in the same neighbourhood.

Furthermore, it seems the bonds have loosened. The traditional family gatherings have remained – the weddings, funerals, christenings, bar mitzvahs and so on – which bring together a varying number of relatives at irregular intervals. But only a handful of mothers mentioned regular occasions at which a collection of relatives assembled, such as Sunday lunch at the grandparents', or an annual party given by a great-aunt which had originated in celebration of her seventieth birthday. And with substantial numbers of uncles, aunts and cousins, all contact had been lost. This applied to just over half the Bethnal Green mothers and, incidentally, to considerably over half of those in Woodford. These were most likely to be overseas or far off in the UK.

The telephone was much used by the mothers and fathers, particularly in Woodford, to maintain contact with their parents. This had been so in the 1950s in Woodford,[17] and was true too of the newly-arrived families in 'Greenleigh', in contrast to Bethnal Green at that time.[18] Mr Grey, a Woodford home-owner, whose parents lived in a neighbouring district, in answer to the question whether he *saw* his parents as often as he would like, replied, 'Yes, because I phone her every day to see that things are OK.' But where the parents were within reasonable distance, contact was maintained by visiting, supplemented perhaps by telephone calls. The great majority of the Bethnal Green mothers had parents living in the East End, either in Bethnal Green itself – over half – or in other parts. With the Woodford mothers, although nearly three-quarters had parents living somewhere in East London, they were more distant than those of the Bethnal Green families. Only something over one-quarter had parents in Woodford. This inevitably affected the frequency of contact. Nearly all the Bethnal Green mothers whose parents were alive and resident in the UK saw both or one or other of them at least once a week, often three or four times.

Naturally, if you are living in the same house as your parents, you will see them every day. Most of these were the single mothers who had bonds of a different kind, being still dependent on their parents practically as well as quite often emotionally. Apart from these, eight daughters saw their parents, or possibly only their mother, every day. And no Bethnal Green, or for that matter Woodford, daughters with parents living in the same neighbourhood saw them less often than once a week. But was there something special about the mother/daughter relationship as there had been in Bethnal Green of the 1950s?

Mothers and daughters

A whole chapter of *Family and Kinship in East London* was devoted to mothers and daughters. The authors concluded that, for the daughters, 'even if they resent her interference, she is a presence in their lives'.[19] In the present study, contact between mother and daughter was frequent. Some daughters talked about their mothers and what went on when they met in the same way that the earlier Bethnal Green daughters had done – in both places. Eileen Scott told me that she 'ran to her mum for everything'. Occasionally the baby's grandmother was visiting at the time of the interview and a comfortable intimate relationship between mother and daughter was apparent. Sometimes there were difficulties. Mrs Gregg had 'cried her eyes out' when she had left her parents to get married some years previously and had succeeded in getting a transfer back to Bethnal Green from Bromley-by-Bow so as to be near them. She now found her mother's disability a problem:

> 'Yes, it's different if I could just go up there for the sake of going up there, but it's like I've got to go up there. There's things I could be doing and I'm sitting there thinking I could be getting on with the ironing, or whatever. Instead I'm just sitting there watching the telly. It's become more boring really since I've had the baby because she gets bored and we've got to keep her occupied. If I say to her, "I'm going now, mum, I've got something to do", she doesn't say anything, but she doesn't like being up there on her own. "Oh you haven't been up here five minutes, and you want to go already." It's like a duty, because she's ill.'

This was exceptional. Generally their mothers – and fathers – were not regarded as a burden. It was nevertheless possible to detect a loosening of the bond. When asked to name the member of their family they felt closest to, two-thirds of the Woodford mothers named their mothers. In Bethnal Green it was just under half. For them it was more often their father, a sister or a brother. Then there was the fact that many fewer had started their married life in the parental home (see chapter 3).

The loosening of the bond was also apparent in the replies to the questions on help and advice. As the *first* source of advice on the baby, by no means all followed Eileen Scott's example of running to mum. Only about one-third in Bethnal Green or Woodford turned to their mothers. Most of the eight grandmothers interviewed admired the way their daughter was managing with the new baby, though paid work was deplored and one or two disapproved of modern methods. 'Interference' was on the whole taboo in the grandmother's eyes, though some of these daughters did turn to their mother. Occasionally, it seems, advice was given more than it was sought.

'I've old-fashioned ways but sometimes they say, "Oh yes, we should have done what you said", but . . . I think, well, let them find out for themselves. The feeding would *not* come out of a packet if I had my way. She used to bring *packets* of stuff . . . One day I cooked dinner there and baby had already had this powdered stuff and he was showing off, playing up in his high chair, so I gave him a little bit of potato and gravy. Well he loved it! Even my son-in-law said, "Here, didn't he half enjoy that!" I said, "That baby should have solids, if you don't mind me telling you. That *packet* is not solids to me, it goes in one end and out the other, that's all it's doing."'

In Bethnal Green husbands were mentioned as helpers and advisers as often as mothers. In Woodford husbands took top place for over half the wives. Specialist advice, from health visitors, doctors, the clinic and so on, was fairly low down on the list. When they returned from hospital after having had their baby the majority relied on their husband's help, sometimes in tandem with that of their mother, mother-in-law, sister, and so on. A number of husbands took time off from work – none, be it said, as formal paternity leave. On the other hand, for those mothers who at three

140

months or thereabouts after the baby's birth were already going out in the evenings, the maternal grandmother or grandparents were the ones who mostly did the babysitting.

As one measure of family get-togetherness the families were asked about Christmas or the equivalent for people of other religions. Roughly one-third of the families had spent the previous Christmas in their own home, just over one-quarter in the home of the mother's parents and the remainder in that of the father's parents or with other relatives or friends. The majority shared Christmas with either or both sets of parents and often with grand-parents, brothers and sisters and other relatives. It was usually with the mother's side of the family.

Questions were also asked about who would look after the parents in the future. The replies from wives and husbands suggested that this is seen as the daughter's role rather than the son's. Many of the young daughters in both areas had 'never thought' about the possibility of either of their parents needing care or were not prepared to commit themselves before the need arose. They were echoing what was said by the parents themselves. Talk to any parent about their approaching old age, and the phrase 'I don't want to be a burden' will soon make its way into the conversation. Daisy Gedge, Mrs Mitchell's mother, said it all: 'No way would I expect Jane and her husband to look after me – I don't think it's fair. Yes [great laughter], of course I would have looked after my father. Anyway, she's got no accommodation here. I wouldn't want her to have the burden.'

What is, perhaps, surprising is the number of daughters in both areas, regardless of their often inadequate accommodation, who said they would be glad to have their parents living with them. In all, just on two-thirds of those in Bethnal Green and over three-quarters in Woodford were prepared to look after their parents in their own homes either 'willingly,' 'if the worse came to the worst', or sharing with brothers and sisters.

Friends and neighbours

The general impression in Bethnal Green was of a greater isolation from the surrounding community than had been found in the earlier study, though it has to be allowed that many were newcomers to their estate. An important element is probably the fact that all but four of the Bethnal Green sample were flat-dwellers. They were asked how well they knew their neighbours on either side or opposite. As many as fourteen (not including the recently arrived families from Bangladesh) did not know either one or the other at all. And among the majority who did, it was mostly 'just to say hello to' or 'quite well'. Only a handful knew them 'very well'; a minority regarded them as friends. As for other people in the block or on the estate, the majority knew fewer than ten people. Only two mothers made the splendid claim of knowing 'everybody', and as many as one in six said they knew no one other than their immediate neighbours. Relatively few were said to be friends. So what about friends as opposed to immediate or near neighbours? How many, roughly, did they have? Mostly between one and five or six, and mostly living in Bethnal Green or other parts of the East End. Very few had a large circle. Bob Brett[20] told me that all his same-generation friends had left the borough.

This does not add up to the kind of network of relationships found in the earlier study. The change accords with a recent opinion poll finding where a majority said they had less contact with their neighbours than their parents' generation.[21] If anything, good neighbourly relations, already apparent in Woodford in the 1950s, were a little more in evidence in present-day Woodford than in present-day Bethnal Green. More immediate neighbours were known 'very well' and fewer were not known at all, and though there was not the universal kind of relationship with people in the locality evident in Bethnal Green in the 1950s, they were, in the main, not strangers in their streets. There were no very marked social class differences in the numbers of friends that people had or the frequency of contact with them. In general it cannot be said that the Woodford 'suburban housewives' were conforming to the kind of minority group attitudes suggested by Popenoe,[22] though some were already showing signs of house-bound, baby-bound blues and there was some criticism of neighbourhood facilities. Nevertheless, a few of the council tenants who would certainly qualify as the 'suburban poor' did feel themselves isolated.

The first conclusion is that at this stage of their lives the family unit of mother, father and first child is a thriving one and it thrives as a unit centred on its own home. Husbands returned home straight from work and, on the whole, remained there. At weekends, rather than join their mates at the football stadium, they stayed at home for DIY or television. The mothers, in the main, spent more time in the home than out of it; relatively few were already back at work and those who were planning a return were for the most part hoping it would be part time.

Secondly, this home-centredness seems to be partially at the expense of the wider family. In Bethnal Green fewer lived near by than had been the case in the 1950s. The mother/daughter bond had loosened, even though daughters in both neighbourhoods saw their parents regularly. Thirdly, their present way of life gives rise to a signal contentment despite, for many, dissatisfaction with their housing or a general lack of security and the rumblings of a sense of isolation. The exceptions were either particularly vulnerable or had acute housing difficulties or intractable problems of a different kind.

Fourthly, the universal and well-charted changes that have occurred since the 1950s have to a limited extent accelerated the process, already observed in 1960, of bringing Bethnal Green and Woodford closer together, cutting across social class boundaries. The rise in real incomes and consequent increase in material possessions and changing leisure habits seem to have had more effect than the increase in feminine consciousness and consequent changing roles of women and men within the domestic sphere. We shall see in the next chapter if the mothers' and fathers' housing aspirations reflect this partial coming together, or if so many of the differences described in earlier chapters, sharpened by the prevailing tenure patterns, are a stronger influence.

7

HOUSING ASPIRATIONS

Whatever the sphere, aspirations range from the possibly attainable to the probably unattainable. Strung out along the route from the immediate goal to the distant ideal are a host of options which may be approached with varying speed at different stages of an individual's or a family's life. They may be discarded, modified or leapfrogged as circumstances dictate. For a few the distant ideal may be achieved sooner than they had dared to hope; for some it will never be realisable; for others even the immediate goal proves impracticable. In their housing, some of the sample families would not have expected to have reached their (possibly attainable) immediate goal by the time we met them; others, with varying degrees of pleasure, resignation or dejection, judged their present home to be the best they could hope for; a very few reckoned it had everything that they could want, even when set against their distant goal – their ideal home. For in the questioning about future aspirations I distinguished between these two goals; on the one hand, their plans to move or hopes for the next five years; on the other, how they perceived their ideal home and what chances they thought they had of getting it.

But, first, what were their priorities in home seeking as told to the interviewer? How important for them was tenure and did they think of themselves as in the home of their choice?

Priorities

The mothers and fathers had been asked to give reasons why they were in their present home (see chapter 3). They were also asked two questions specifically about tenure. One concerned the tenure of their own home: what they particularly liked and disliked about being a home-owner, a council tenant, a private tenant, living in a shared household, and what the problems were. The other asked how they saw the differences between owning and renting. There was no doubt from the replies to both questions that home-owner-ship was highly popular. Among the mothers, irrespective of tenure or area, 72 per cent gave views that were solely in favour of owning. Only 10 per cent were solely in favour of renting. The remainder found something good in each or could find virtually no difference between them. An even higher proportion of fathers (78 per cent) were unable to find anything favourable to say about renting compared with owning.

In their retrospective reasons for becoming home-owners, financial considerations had been predominant. But, once established as home-owners, independence, being your own boss, freedom to do what you want and freedom of choice became what mattered most. Here is Mrs Bell:

'If you want to live in a road like this you can, or in a cottage in the country, or up in London in a tower block, you can. It's the freedom of choice. You can sit in your own home and know that if you want to you can get up and knock down every wall in the house; you can shout and scream. It's your own home and you haven't got to answer to other people.'

And Mrs Rush:

'We can choose where we want to live. As a council tenant you can't, you have to live where you're put, you're stuck there for life. As a home-owner you can pick where you want to live and not where people say you must live.'

Mr Selby, as a Bethnal Green home-owner, appreciated, if only as a joke, an added advantage that ownership brought in choice of dwelling type:

'If I want to knock my old lady about I can, and no one'll hear, like in a flat! Well, you feel more at ease. It's your own place, so you can do what you like. There's no one can tell you not to.'

Often, of course, they saw more than one advantage.

But more generally there was the widely-held view about the 'naturalness' of home-ownership. This was summed up by Clarice Berman: 'Every human being like every animal has got their own

145

little bit of territory. So that everybody must want their own little bit of seclusion.' There were problems, too. Here is Mrs Bell again:

'When I think about it now, I would never have it any other way. As long as you can make that first break then you're laughing. It's very hard for young couples today and it's still hard for us, but once you've done it – perhaps it's the sense of freedom – you know that it's your own home and you can live where you want as long as it's within your means. If it ever came to it that this place had to go then I'd go back to work. I'm not a snob or anything like that because I've grown up in a council flat all my life and so did my husband. But once you've done it you must keep on, must pay the mortgage and the rates. And you just hope that in years to come it won't seem so much. After all my mum pays £20 per week for a three-bed flat. That's a lot of money.'

Isobel Turner, an exception in many ways, was less sure what she thought about being a home-owner. She and her husband had lived previously in a council flat 'very simply out of choice, not because we couldn't afford to own'.

'I find it a bit embarrassing. I'm not very practical about these things. As long as we're comfortable and happy I don't mind. But the worst would be to have to live in somebody else's house. Council property's OK. I worry about the morality of home ownership, though I feel justified in moving because of the size of our flat. This piece of ground is ours but does it go into a V at the centre of the earth? And also the fact that when you own anything you do have a lot of advantages that people who can't afford it don't. The fact that the property appreciates is irrelevant because once you've got a house and want another they all go up at the same rate. But it's the status that society gives you if you own a house that I don't like, and the lack of it if you don't own a house, which I dislike even more.'

Not only did she have moral qualms, but she betrayed a scepticism over the alleged financial advantages of owning. Neither did she believe in the 'naturalness' of property ownership.

Nearly one-third of the home-owners could think of no problems. Responsibility for repairs and maintenance was raised most

often. Mrs Green voiced her worries about 'something going dread-
fully wrong. The roof caves in or whatever. You have to maintain
the house and keep it in a reasonable state of repair. If you rent
somewhere, the landlord sees to that.' It was nevertheless a
problem, having taken the plunge, they were clearly prepared to
live with.

For a few of those in tenancies it was a reason for not taking the
plunge. Mrs Gregg felt that if you owned – 'You'd be everlastingly
with your hand in your pocket. To me it would be a worry whereas
with these places, if things go wrong, you can get somebody down
to it – or attempt to. I just couldn't stand the worry of owning. I
have to pay my bills on time and that.' But delays and difficulties
over repairs were regarded as a problem by just over one-third of
those who rented. So what for one form of tenure is declared a
disadvantage may be seen as an advantage for another but may, at
the same time, be a drawback.

Council tenants were altogether more inclined to view their own
tenure with disfavour than favour. Well over half the thirty-three
mothers replying could think of no advantages. Mrs Reagan in
Woodford resented that fact that 'once they give you a place, that's
your lot', and Mrs Brogan in Bethnal Green had 'nothing at all
good to say', complaining about the expense of her unnecessarily
big flat:

'There's a lovely new estate over there. Why couldn't they
have put me in there? I mean they've put me in a three-
bedroom place with one baby. I'm paying £29 a week. It says
in the rent book this is for seven and a half people.'

Mr Tooley thought it was unfair that, though you owned nothing,
you were paying rent for 'something that is actually your own
because it belongs to the people'.

When it came to preferences for ownership, the council tenants
were as orthodox as the home-owners. Thus Mrs Hill:

'With owning, what you do to the place you're doing it
because you know it's going to be your own. With renting,
you can't do much to it – you can't knock a wall down, you
wouldn't be allowed to.'

And many others:

147

'With renting you're forever paying out the money and not really achieving anything. At least with owning you've got something stable behind you. You can always sell it and move on. With renting you've got to wait for something to come up.'

'With owning, if your money ever gets better you can always sell up and get something better, or worse, as the case may be. It's a good investment.'

'The difference? Buying your own home you get tax relief. With the council you buy it over and over again. It just goes up and up and up.'

Did they therefore support the sale of council homes? Three-quarters of the mothers and fathers believed unequivocally that it was 'a good thing'. There was however a marked difference in the proportions holding this view between families in the two main tenures, the larger numbers predictably being among the home-owners. Many of the familiar arguments on either side were advanced. Mrs Poulter thought that 'when people have been paying rent for years and years it's their only chance to buy'. She went on:

'If you've got a place you like and you want to buy it then you should be able to. Yes, I think if this flat was on the ground floor and in better surroundings I would definitely buy it because I like the size of it. I'd get rid of all these cupboards. I could make it into a lovely flat like I want it to be.'

Several referred to the fact that their parents had bought their council homes and how satisfactory that had been. But some, like Mrs Ryder, could see both sides.

'From a personal point of view I would like one because it's cheaper and as nearly all homes in Bethnal Green are council owned and this is the area we choose to live in, the house of our choice would be a council sale. For other people I suppose it is a bit unfair really, but then – I suppose it's a bit conservative of me – if you can afford it I don't see why you shouldn't. It's quite good because it gives people a sense of security, moneywise. I don't really mind because I've been quite happy as a council tenant.'

Then there were those who felt strongly that it was a bad idea. Mr Grainger, a home-owner, thought that 'if you sell council property it condemns the people who can't afford their own homes to live in even worse conditions than they are actually living in.' Mr Bentham, also a home-owner, was quite clear that it was 'wrong'.

'You're depleting your housing stock for no good purpose. It will make council housing even worse. They only sell off the best ones. Who's going to buy the others – the tower blocks? It's wrong. It'll take years to catch up. It's just going to make the waiting lists worse. Decent housing is a right. I felt a bit guilty because we've gained it as a privilege.'

Another home-owning father in Woodford 'disagreed in principle with the sale of council property'. He did however think that

'in a borough like this I'm not sure I'd find it too much of a problem to be in favour because if the host community is not prepared to accept those in council property as an acceptable part of the community then by selling council property you're not going to change that. It's therefore not a solution to the problem. In some areas, like Liverpool, they have too many council homes and then it's not only an economic necessity but it also provides opportunities for families they wouldn't otherwise have.'

In another question they were asked to say which of all the things in seeking a home that they had mentioned was the most important. In particular they were asked to decide between tenure, dwelling type and neighbourhood. If, for instance, they wanted to own, to have a house rather than a flat, or to move to a different neighbourhood, but could only have one of these possibilities, which would they choose?

My object in asking this question was to try to divorce the fact of ownership from all those advantages which I had assumed would be attached to it and which, in the event, as my examples above have shown, were by so many of the mothers and fathers. In fact, when obliged to sort out the three main components of housing – tenure, dwelling type and neighbourhood – they came up with a somewhat different viewpoint. Several found the question difficult to answer. For others it was easy. Taking the sample of mothers as a whole, although ownership just commanded the single highest proportion of votes – 30 per cent – it did so only because of its relatively high priority among the home-owners (see appendix 2, table 2.14).

Mrs Bentham had reservations like those of Mrs Turner and Mrs Macintosh, and only just came down on the side of owning:

> 'If I could rent this house in the area I'd be almost as happy, but I think it's more stable to own. Though you've got to find the money you haven't got someone else who can sell the place. I've got mixed feelings about mortgages. I don't like the feeling that we owe somebody a lot of money. I think small collectives work quite well and housing associations. In an ideal world housing would be centrally owned and everybody would have what they needed, but it's too big a concern. I don't know.'

Fathers once again set a greater premium on home-ownership compared with mothers, particularly where, like Mr Dixon or Mr Henry, they were already home-owners. 'Very important to get your foot in the property market. It's a vicious world out there. Things are measured by success, by money. I never started it. I just became part of it. Losers get left behind.' Mr Rush found it 'a very hard question'. 'In the beginning I might say, well, I'd rather have the area, but if you're going to look into the future then it's best to start with owning because if you've got something to sell you can choose your area.'

Second in importance for mothers was the desire for a house. For those in council tenancies it was most often given top priority. Lorna Field, for instance:

> 'I'd like a better place for the baby, and a garden and a better area for him when he grows up. I wouldn't mind at all still being a council tenant, or even this area, if we could have a house because they're not so strict with you. You can do things to it.'

Of the three choices offered, for mothers the neighbourhood came third, though still given top priority by a substantial minority.

For fathers it was the second most important of the priorities. Jean Macintosh was quite sure:

'Without a doubt the area is the most important. If it were a council house in a fishing village on the west coast or the east coast of Scotland or a Yorkshire dale, that would be splendid.'

For Mrs Poulter the neighbourhood took precedence because of the recent changes in her family.

'Somewhere for children. Better facilities. I would prefer something better for my daughter. To get away. I'm thinking more of her now. Now we've got a child I just don't want her brought up in Bethnal Green.'

For Mrs O'Kelly, by contrast, it took precedence because of her attachment to her present area, Woodford. 'I'd rather stay in this flat than move out of the area.'

Whether it was owned or rented, a house or a flat, or in a particular neighbourhood was immaterial to most of the mothers in shared households. Janet Tate expressed the general feeling. 'To have a home of my own so I can bring up the baby my way. We've got too many people interfering here. While I live here I'm not my own person.'

This was a hypothetical question. But they were asked another question about their present home which I hoped would also throw light on their housing aspirations. *Do you think of this present home as the home of your choice?* In the answers was perhaps the most revealing difference between the tenures. Taking mothers and fathers together, 76 per cent of the home-owners regarded their present home as the home of their choice or had so regarded it in the past. This was so, however, for only 18 per cent of the council tenants, and 1 out of the 22 mothers and fathers in shared accommodation (see appendix 2, table 2.15). For mothers and fathers, irrespective of tenure, the chief barrier to obtaining it was insufficient money. The home-owners, most of whom were anyway already in the home of their choice, regarded money as an obstacle to moving on, expanding, and so on. They did not for the most part see it as one that would necessarily last. When the council tenants mentioned a lack of money as a difficulty, which nearly two-thirds did, it was as one that was likely to remain. So what of their future plans?

Plans to move

The majority – 67 – of all the 100 families hoped to move within the next five years. Of those, eight – seven in Woodford and one in Bethnal Green – had already set about it. This seems a lot of people with itchy feet, particularly in comparison with general data which showed that 'in 1980, just under one in six private households in Great Britain was currently thinking of moving'.[1] But in my sample there was a relatively high proportion of sharing families. Furthermore, the whole sample was special for its stage in the family cycle. For most these were hopes, not plans. Though the basis for comparison is somewhat tenuous, the proportions in my sample approximated to those of the Madge and Brown sample families who were hoping to move within the next five years.[2] Proportionately more Bethnal Green families (over three-quarters) than Woodford families (over one-half) were hoping to move. This difference was once again largely associated with housing tenure, and when this sample is compared with others on the basis of tenure there are marked similarities. Among households in general, 28 per cent of potential movers were in owner occupation with mortgage and 39 per cent rented from a local authority or new town corporation,[3] compared with 25 per cent and 39 per cent respectively in the present sample.

The sharers simply wanted a home of their own. All but one – single and two-parent families alike – 'hoped to move' within the next five years. Geraldine Herbert, at sixteen years old, considered herself still too young to contemplate a move. One year later seven of these families had moved (see chapter 4). Of those in other tenures, the desire for privacy and to be self-contained or to have a garden was given as the main reason for wanting to move by the three Bethnal Green 'private' tenants and, from their tied flat, by Mrs Michalios. None had moved a year later, nor had the Farrows, who were planning to buy their own pub. Of the three housing association tenants in Woodford, one year after the interviews the Bakers had succeeded in their wish to leave London, and the Blacks, against their expectations, in exchanging their flat for a larger one in the same block. Only the Sadlers in their co-operative had no plans or desires to move within the next five years.

And what of the two main tenures? Among the seventeen home-owners with definite plans or hopes of moving, the wish for more

152

space was given as a reason by over half the mothers. The great majority of these potential movers – in all tenures – not surprisingly envisaged their future home as larger. Thus, nearly half the council tenants also referred to the need for more space, more bedrooms and so on, a minority specifying a house *and* garden. The fact that not more than just under one-quarter mentioned a garden does not mean that most of the others did not want one; the replies to other questions made that clear. They were just being realistic about their chances of getting one. But, among the council tenants, marginally the highest number of replies were about the need to get away from their present place as soon as possible rather than what they hoped for from anything new.

Altogether thirteen mothers gave – either as their sole reason or one among others – the desire or the need to move to another district. There was no marked difference between the areas. In both places some of these families, along with all the ones who had gone before, were hoping to move 'a bit further out'. The husband's job was likely to bring about moves for two of the Woodford home-owners. The Greens hoped to return to the North of England. The Macintoshes wanted to move to the country to change their 'way of life'.

But the majority of the mothers (and fathers) seemed content to stay in their locality, either expressing this as a preference in a proposed move or because they were not planning to move at all. Minorities in Bethnal Green and Woodford, when asked how they felt about the neighbourhood in general, had viewed it with disfavour (see chapter 1). Voting with your feet is another way of showing dissatisfaction. But this minority and the other did not always coincide. What seemed to be more important for those wishing to stay was whether or not they had been brought up in the neighbourhood. Only two mothers with roots in Bethnal Green hoped to leave it; in Woodford also only two with a similar anchorage were probably moving away because of their husbands' work.

One year later these last two families had in fact moved. Four other Woodford home-owning couples had also moved, realising their ambition for more space. Three had exchanged flats for houses; one had bought a larger house. But all the council tenants were still in the same place. What were their chances from then on?

153

Opportunities

Only one of the council tenant mothers in Bethnal Green had mentioned the possibility of an eventual move out of the borough as a council tenant, confident of a transfer to Harlow, if she and her husband wanted one. What were the possibilities generally of extra-borough moves within the local authority sector? For moves to places outside Greater London there is now the National Mobility Scheme which started in 1981.[4] After a slow start, things began to pick up. By the end of the first year over four thousand moves had been accomplished or were under way.[5] But now it seems that cuts, red tape and delays are halting its development, and would-be movers from London within the public sector are as restricted as ever they were.[6]

The means by which council tenants can move from borough to borough within Greater London have inevitably been affected by the handover of housing responsibilities from the GLC to the boroughs, which is still in its transition phase. First, under the statutory Greater London Mobility Scheme launched in 1980, those authorities to which GLC stock has been transferred are required to contribute up to 50 per cent of new vacancies in this stock to a mobility pool. Secondly, in the voluntary Inter-Borough Nomination Scheme (IBNS) started by the London Boroughs Association (LBA) in 1978, the boroughs originally agreed to contribute a standard 15 per cent of net vacancies to the mobility pool. But this was never attempted, nor has the 10 per cent later agreed on yet been achieved.[7] Redbridge moreover has never joined the IBNS Scheme. It is early days to assess the likely success of the new arrangements, but it seems that through the IBNS scheme the proportion of new and outstanding nominees actually housed has risen,[8] and it is predicted that the number of lettings under the Greater London Mobility Scheme will rise.[9] The numbers nevertheless are small and, as already indicated (see ch. 3, note 21), movement to the outer boroughs from council tenancy to council tenancy is very limited. Furthermore, GLC officials with whom I talked, referring to their own scheme, were unhappy with it. One complained that there was no longer any 'freedom of movement'; there were no 'patchwork bits and pieces available'. Another said that the complicated 'pooling arrangements succeeded only in reducing the potential vacancies'.

Within the borough, which was after all where most wanted to stay, the chances of a move in the near future were bleak. There is the Transfer List and the Mutual Exchange Bureau – both beset by restrictions – and there are the informal means of exchange, word-of-mouth information passed to and fro through kinship and other networks, or notices on newsagents' boards, such as this one seen recently:

COUNCIL EXCHANGE

2-bedroom flat in Bethnal Green or Bow
for 1-bedroom flat in Stepney

If initial contacts are successful, then the exchange must be formalised after investigation through the District Office. This is necessary, I was told, 'in order to sort out the rogues'. In Woodford there is a qualifying period of two years before registration on the Transfer List is allowed. But the Borough housing department, in principle anyway, will waive the rule on medical grounds. It is the same in Tower Hamlets. GPs and consultants in inner-city areas are kept busy with demands for such medical certificates. The housing departments of Tower Hamlets and the GLC are also sensitive to the need to make 'positive transfers' because of racial and other harassment, though local groups think not enough.[10] On the whole it seems that if 'race' can be singled out as a factor divorced from poverty, unemployment and so on, discrimination resides more in the *quality* of the council housing offered than in access to it.[11]

Six council tenants aspired to home-ownership. Perhaps one or two will achieve it, but the chances for most, as discussed in chapter 3, are slim. Such ambitions occasionally merged with those centred on their ideal home. Four mothers and two fathers – all home-owners – said they were already living in their ideal home. But for the most part this last was something quite distinct in the mothers' and fathers' minds from their immediate prospects.

Ideal homes

Their ideal was modest. They did not go for villas on Capri. The overwhelming majority talked of a house, or sometimes a cottage, which would be of such and such a size, would usually have a garden or 'a bit of land' and for well over half the mothers and fathers would be in some particular neighbourhood of their choosing. The 'country' was often preferred. Mrs Poulter lived in Bethnal Green and her ideal was in a place like Woodford:

'A nice little house, council or my own. Waltham Abbey, Epping Forest. I'd rather be near a big park where you can have a stroll. Somewhere I know I can take the children out to on nice days or in the evenings. Living in the East End all you can do is take a stroll down the road and look in the shop windows. I'd rather live near a park where you could have a stroll every evening, or on Sundays in particular.'

Mrs Patel, hailing from India and at present sharing her in-laws' home, wanted 'a small house – full of calm – where I can be relaxed and can manage everything and where I can do everything I want.' The ideal home for another Woodford mother – Mrs Reeves – was a grander version of her present one: 'a detached or semi-detached house with a larger garden, four beds, separate lounge and dining-room, a larger kitchen, a downstairs toilet if possible, and working room or conservatory, within this area.' And for Mrs Perry, also a home-owner, it was to be 'a four-bedroom detached doll's house, with black and white gables, leaded windows with a large garden and a very large kitchen'.

A few were more ambitious. Mrs Benson, a Bethnal Green council tenant, wanted a 'big house with tennis courts, like my mum's eldest brother's got'. Janet Tate wanted 'a mobile home'; Denise Fox, another single mother, simply wanted to live next door to her parents. Some envisaged changing their life style. Mr Selby spoke of a 'farm, a cottage, a bit of land, a pond in the back with ducks and swans on it, trees all around and wildlife – roses growing there – you could come and visit us.'

Hannah Baker's Christian values permeated many of her replies:

'I'd like a huge old Vicarage. We'd live in one part and convert the rest and fill it with people from hostels where they could have their own homes but still be with other people. A nice big garden where we could grow vegetables, in a friendly little town. My husband and I are both Christians and we've both come from very different backgrounds, but we've both always had a dream for that sort of home. We just meet so many people whose main problem is just that they're alone . . . and we have people here . . . that's fine in a way but obviously we can't go any further. When I was at university four of us shared a house and we had "open house". We kept a visitors' book – by the end of the year we'd had 150 people through. They just took us at our word – they just came. It was difficult and yet I've never felt so sure that we were living in the right way. It was good.'

On the whole, both actual plans or hopes for moving and the ideal home reflected the present financial, social, employment and housing circumstances of the families. And the same was true for their replies to a question they were asked about their chances of achieving their ideal home. Three-quarters of the Woodford mothers, but only two-fifths of the Bethnal Green, were reasonably optimistic. The fathers were altogether more hopeful. Much depended, of course, on how realistic their ideal was and on other things, such as support from parents, and certainly on temperament. Rob Tooley envisaged a simple house, 'with a nice front garden and a nice back garden, couple of bedrooms, nice kitchen, a little garage. A nice little house in the country near Beaconsfield.' But he had set his sights on a change of tenure (from council tenancy to home-ownership) as well as a move to the country. He thought his chances were 'very good. If everything works out, I should imagine we'll do it.' 'Everything' seems a very great deal for an electrician unemployed for some time because of a badly broken arm, with a net income of less than £100 per week, no savings and a partner who was, at the time of the interview, planning only to work part time when the baby was a bit older. A closer look, however, at the circumstances makes it all seem possible. He was awaiting an operation to 'rectify' the break. Meanwhile he did 'jobs on the side' and labelled himself 'a tax invader'. His parents owned their house, were comfortably off, had already lent and given Rob money and seemed good for further loans or gifts. He had a close relationship with Alice's parents and hoped also to involve them in any future moves. At twenty-three years of age, with a 'college' education behind him – he had done a Building Management Course at a technical college – his confident, amused, sceptical approach to life coupled with parental backing seemed likely to get him what he wanted.

By contrast, neither young Dan Sutton's parents nor his in-laws were in any position to help him. Unemployed, unskilled, hoping for 'six or more kids', his ideal home though modest would, like Rob Tooley's, also be bought. He too was optimistic:

> 'Get a job, see how much the money is. Save up, use our loaf and when the baby's old enough and is at school and Julie goes to work and we both pull our weight, I think we've got a good chance.'

Neither Rob nor Dan had got jobs by the time of the follow-up interview.

Mrs Selby had an even more modest goal – 'just an ordinary little house in Kent'. But she thought she had 'no chance at the moment', unless by means of the often-invoked football pools. And yet the Selbys already owned their home, and Mr Selby was in seemingly reliable employment. It is true that their income after their housing costs had been taken into account was very low (around £50 per week). Nevertheless, Mrs Selby had managed to save as much as £100 or so.

There are three main conclusions from all this. First, that on the whole newly-formed families living in Bethnal Green or in council tenancies in either area had very few opportunities to acquire the home of their choice either now or in the future. Secondly, such families take a rational approach to their housing future. The home-owners are anyway more fortunate and can afford – in both senses – either to be more ambitious in their future plans or to stay where they are. Very few of the tenants or those in shared households, though preferring home-ownership to renting in the abstract, talked of buying. Furthermore, despite the high priority given to a house and garden, most anticipated with apparent equanimity moving to a flat. So tenure differences *are* reflected in housing aspirations.

Thirdly, it is evident that home-ownership was important more for the advantages it brought, whether these were financial or to do with freedom of control or mobility, than for any virtue intrinsic to owning. Pride of ownership was not at all dominant as a sentiment.

8

THE MAIN ISSUES DISCUSSED

What stood out among the 100 families of this study, wherever they lived, was the home-centredness of their lives and their high general contentment. This was true both of mothers and fathers. Knowingly or unknowingly some of the families were confused about the direction in which they were heading,[1] particularly in the case of the twelve single mothers, mostly very young. Among the rest a very few were determined to pursue their careers; patriarchal attitudes were less in evidence than in the earlier studies; 11 per cent had been married before; 10 per cent had not troubled to legalise their present partnership. But the majority could be described as 'conventional families',[2] behaving in the way that families with new first children have behaved for a long time, tagging along comfortably in the wake of demographic, social and technological changes or quietly converting them to their own ends.[3] How they will behave in five or ten years' time, how these changes and others of deeper consequence will affect their lives, is another matter. For many, the auguries are not good and circumstances may defeat their present buoyant optimism. Others are likely to be more attuned to the changes. Some may benefit from them. A few may become innovators, in their housing and family circumstances no less than in their working lives.

In this study the families are cast in a sociological mould, but I like to think of the mould as having transparent sides. Clarice Berman is still a friendly, intelligent, questing young woman, whether or not she has been a part of the 'slow march' or of 'centrifugal population movement', and Kathy Garnett, sixteen years old, poor, ill-educated, is still a tender mother, whether or not she is a statistic as a black one-parent family. And yet Clarice and Kathy are poles apart. One, with her husband, owns her attractive Woodford house. The other lives with her parents in a grim block of council flats in Bethnal Green. In their way of life there is virtually no meeting point.

As originally stated, the central question of this study was whether housing changes in Bethnal Green and Woodford since the 1950s had held the two places apart or contributed to their convergence. The answer has been that though some changes have brought them closer together, their housing has separated them further. In the 1980s, families in Woodford who have just had their first child on the whole fare well in their housing and the equivalent families in Bethnal Green fare less well, and home-owners fare better than council tenants, no matter which of the two districts they live in. They fare better because initially they had been able to choose the kind of home they wanted where they wanted, because they could do what they liked with it and to it inside and outside, because they could move elsewhere when they wanted with comparative ease and because, though their present running costs were high, they had in their home an inflation-proof investment and something to leave to their children. These are undoubted advantages enjoyed by none of the Bethnal Green or Woodford families in council tenancies. Furthermore, the council estates in their quality and standard compared badly with the owned homes. These are matters of fact. They are matters too of public policy, for in recent years central government has consistently encouraged and financially supported home-ownership and discouraged and de-funded public housing. Small wonder then that home-ownership has gained the ascendancy in people's minds.

Home and status

There is moreover the association of the two tenures with social status. The connection between status and owner occupation was remarked on in the earlier Woodford study.[4] In the present study, two grandmothers talked about this. Among the younger generation, though it was implicit in the remarks of some of the Woodford home-owners, nobody made any overt reference to it. But where so many put themselves one class down,[5] this was not surprising.[6] Status is of course far too subtle and complex a concept to be recognisable simply on the basis of whether or not an actual reference to it has been made. After all, in so many ways the status acquired by a removal from Bethnal Green to Woodford – the

160

migratory link was still very much in evidence – is implicit in the consequent changed circumstances. The new status is all around them, in the street they live in, the type of house they have bought, the very fact that they have bought their home, and in the people they are likely to frequent. These will not, as I learned from one home-owning mother, include the neighbouring council tenants, one of whom deliberately withdrew from proposed further contact after a chance encounter at a baby clinic.

Status works both ways. Council tenants are labelled as of low status. Inequalities of status, Runciman has argued, can be justified only on a single maxim: 'free inequality of praise, no inequality of respect'.[7] Today, self-respect and respect for others among council tenants is under a two-pronged attack. It is being undermined by the premium set on ownership and at the same time by the conditions under which some are obliged to live. In both areas there was evidence that such conditions resulted in the refusal of services. Taxi-drivers would not come to certain estates, firms would not rent TV sets; even GPs were said to discriminate in the matter of home visits.

Poverty and security

What is happening in the two study areas in many ways reflects what is now common knowledge – a 'polarisation' of the 'haves' and the 'have-nots'. The poor and the vulnerable – the relatively deprived – are being pushed further down the scale into the worst housing. By worst I do not mean council housing as such, but poor quality or neglected council housing, 'sink estates'; or that they will still be without any home of their own. Meanwhile, the well off, the secure – the relatively advantaged – are climbing further up the scale into better housing. And here, 'better housing' is likely to be synonymous with owner occupation, for the proportion of families belonging to the professional and managerial class in council housing in my sample was negligible.

There are counteracting tendencies. Apart from housing, a range of differences between Bethnal Green and Woodford families, notably in patterns of consumption, was already disappearing in the 1950s.[8] This middle ground is still common to home-owners and council tenants, embracing a mixture of skilled manual and non-manual occupations often in the same family or the same area, often indistinguishable leisure activities, a similarity of attitudes and so on. All these are unifying elements. They might, if other circumstances were favourable, bring council tenants and home-owners together but, as things are, their housing pulls them apart.[9]

The divide, moreover, is likely to widen and deepen on economic and political grounds though, as Forrest and Murie suggest, 'basic class divisions may be finding new forms of expression rather than being fundamentally transformed in the restructuring of housing tenure'.[10] The occupational structure of the country is undergoing radical change. Temporary unemployment figures will soon have to be re-interpreted as permanent non-employment figures. The nation is becoming less and less dependent on its army of unskilled and semi-skilled workers. These, whether in or out of work, along with other minorities, will be the marginal group of the future, undifferentiated because all alike are disadvantaged. They will be thought fit only, in government eyes, for welfare aid and for 'residual housing' which, with the continuing decline of private renting, will be synonymous with public housing. They may be a marginal minority group, but they nevertheless make up two-thirds of the five million households in council dwellings.[11] This is a lot of people.

There is ample evidence that segregation by tenure is made worse by the sale of council housing where there are no compensating measures. The council homes purchased, according to Forrest and Murie, are typically small semi-detached houses.[12] With the decline of new building at one end of the council chain and the loss of houses at the other, it is to be expected that there will be fewer chances of transfer for tenants of high-rise and other unacceptable flats. Fewer than 5 per cent of the council homes sold in London by March 1982 were flats.[13] The purchasers are likely to be skilled manual workers in their mid- to later forties with grown-up families.[14] In social status this is the 'middle ground' of my sample families, while the age is that of their parents.

So home-ownership is now the mass tenure and with this has come a change in its nature and meaning. First there are the impli-cations for government and democracy. Malcolm Harrison has put forward the idea that in the move towards owner occupation privatisation is not quite what it seems. Government intervention is still very much present, but now is hidden and indirect.[15]

When central government moves policy away from direct local authority responsibility towards indirect aid through financial institutions it comes to depend on a private bureaucracy securely isolated from popular pressures . . . Selected organisations now have *privileged access* to Whitehall. When house builders and building societies become agents for government they participate in determining planning and housing policy. Housing welfare groups stand largely ignored outside the charmed circle of decision-makers.

Secondly there are the implications for tenure relations, for social mobility and the redistribution of wealth. Already in 1973 dwellings accounted for nearly two-fifths of total net wealth, and the proportion of personal wealth between 1960 and 1973, and of course subsequently, reflected 'the rise in the number of owner-occupied houses and, to a greater extent, an increase in the relative value of dwellings'.[16]

As more and more people join the ranks of owner occupation, depleting the common middle ground, they will become increasingly stratified. The main concern of those who have arrived will be to hold on to their position and do nothing that might jeopardize it. With its expansion the image of home ownership 'as a positional high status good [will be] progressively undermined'.[17] At the same time, as the *majority* of the workforce, they must be propitiated, negotiated with, listened to. Those left in public housing have little economic power and, as Forrest and Murie suggest,[18]

in terms of housing needs there is considerable logic in minimising costs associated with direct housing provision. Increased rents and means testing, council house sales, reductions in public expenditure and subsidy in the housing market are logical reactions to a situation where those affected are unable to respond to increases in costs with wage demands or political action.

The logic as far as financial costs are concerned, as appears below, may not be so straightforward. The *social* costs – destructive and divisive – are all too clear. But even these, as the 1982 riots illustrated, may have repercussions to disturb the equanimity of government.

In all this the social fact of rented communal housing on a large

scale emerges as a kind of constraint, a mere consequence of war-
time destruction. But it too was once seen as an opportunity – to
correct the evil legacies of the past with their industrial slums. It
too has its ideals – of comradeship and modern communal living.
Nor is it even now the case that everyone would be a home-owner
if they could. This study and others[19] have shown that there is still
an important minority which does not want to own, or at any rate
not now, or not throughout their lives. The ideology of home-
ownership is a matter more for politicians. Home seekers view it
as a practical choice. A young couple without capital have above
all to ask themselves whether their job prospects are good enough
to secure the mortgage payments. If not, ownership may be rejected
or remain a long-term objective to be saved for.

Neither does history suggest that ownership, in this country and
elsewhere, has been the main issue. To the pre-industrial agricultural and the post-industrial urban poor, security of tenure has
been of far greater significance. Over the last sixty years there has
been a major redistribution of property rights and it is this, as
Lansley has pointed out, that has 'transformed the lives of most
households'.[20] Security of tenure has always been paramount in the
battles fought in and over the private rental sector. Imperfect as
the provisions are, it is at the heart of legislation for the homeless.
Local authority tenants now have security of tenure, though for
some this may have a hollow ring.[21] So do people who own their
homes outright. But mortgagees – the majority of home-owners –
do not, as more and more are discovering. The number of repos-
session orders against defaulting mortgagees almost doubled
between the first half of 1981 and the first half of 1983, and since
1979 the number of people in serious difficulties with their mortgages trebled.[22] How can those already struggling desperately to
hang on to their TV sets and their bits of furniture manage to hang
on to their home?[23]

The problem of security of tenure cannot in the long run be
separated from poverty, and, in many societies, the vulnerability
of homes to poverty and debt has been a worse problem than
landlords. Here and now, moreover, there is the additional problem
that thousands and thousands of homes are so undesirable that
nobody would want to own them.[24] Miracles I know can happen,
as with the Edinburgh tower block that was taken over – at enormous cost – by a property developer and transformed from a

warren of appalling council rented slum dwellings into a collection of 'desirable residences' for sale. But such exceptions, and there have been others, only prove the rule. Flats thus renewed are taken right out of reach of the poor and the not so poor in the first stage of family formation.

So the outlook for a substantial minority of the population, particularly those living in the type of inner-city area which has figured in this study, is an unhappy one. Whether people live in such districts against their inclination or, as with so many of the Bethnal Green sample families, because they prefer them to more remote, low-density ones, they are locked into a particular form of housing. There is moreover the minority group of council tenants in just such a low-density district – Woodford – whose housing problems, though they reflect the different nature of the environment and different goals of the council in control, are like enough to those in Bethnal Green in their immediate impact. Present trends are not conciliatory. As declared government policy, the war of attrition on public housing is being intensified. The Environment Secretary, Patrick Jenkin, has explicitly stated that the era of councils building homes for rent to meet general needs is almost at an end.

Yet, given this policy, given the fact that housing problems can respond to treatment in isolation only up to a certain point, there are some practicable measures suggested by the housing experiences of many of the sample families which would produce an improvement in their prospects and which even the present administration might adopt.

Funding

But, first there *must* be investment. Sometimes, as suggested earlier, governments get a scare which causes them to see their policies as damaging. Such was the reaction to Toxteth and Brixton with a consequent injection of funds. But even if this necessity were to be recognised elsewhere before similar outbreaks of violence occurred, we must expect that grant-giving will continue to be patchy and meagre. Even if special grants for special purposes were still to be forthcoming, like the Priority Estates Project funded by the DOE, the fact must be faced that the latest Housing Investment Programme for 1984/5 heralds further cuts.[25]

The complexities of housing finance are beyond the scope of this study, but some points of controversy must be mentioned. There is first of all the 'Catch 22' of underspend and overspend in which the local councils seem invariably to come out the losers. Cuts force local authorities to use their accumulated capital receipts. This means they are liable to overspend against the government's annual cash limit. But if those capital receipts are larger than expected and cannot quickly be converted into capital expenditure then councils are accused of underspending. They are penalised either way.

Secondly it is forcefully argued on the one hand[26] that the balance of cost in national housing policies is not, as is often thought, in favour of home-ownership but that council housing in fact costs the nation considerably less.[27] Though this has been challenged, there is no doubt about the enormous hidden subsidy to home-owners in the form of tax relief on mortgage payments. It is also incontrovertible that, as the average subsidy for council dwellings has fallen, so that for owned homes has risen.[28] The question of who is subsidising whom comes up again with the latest round of council rent increases. According to Nick Fielding, 'the decision to increase rents, and thereby boost Housing Revenue Account (HRA) surpluses and remove all subsidy' has in effect made tenants 'responsible for all council housing finance and some other costs as well', to the extent that they are now, in some parts of the country, subsidising ratepayers.[29] The rent increases have brought rents almost up to the level of mortgage payments in many places. This fact has undoubtedly contributed to the success of the sales policy, though it is important to remember that it is not by any means always a question of cash in hand. Fifty-nine per cent of council homes were sold with a council mortgage in Greater London between 1980 and 1983, and that proportion is thought likely to increase.[30]

It must be said that bureaucratic finances are as susceptible to mismanagement as other parts of the machinery. But the limit to streamlining and redeployment has in most cases probably been reached. Central government is not prepared to foot the bill, and housing finance has been a frequent victim of the struggle between central and local government over the raising of local government revenues. In the foreseeable future, therefore, it seems that programmes for improvement of council estates must depend increasingly on private enterprise.

There is of course a long tradition of development licences to private firms in return for the inclusion of public housing provision in their schemes. Whether or not this has been to the ultimate benefit of the public sector, there is no doubt how well the private sector has done out of it, and at least the mechanics of co-operation are there. There are other possibilities. On the edge of Bethnal Green, twenty-four two-bedroomed houses have been funded by a building society and constructed by a national building firm for 'cost sale' and 'cost rent' under the provision of the 1980 Housing Act.[31] Design standards are poor, purchase price is low (£24,000), rents not so low (£33 per week), and, of course, in two years' time the tenants may join the ranks of the home-owners if the building society is willing to sell. In the meantime it has enabled a very few families to exchange a flat in a tower block for a house. Such schemes are proliferating but are not likely on a large scale, even though the government is forcing councils to sell off their 'land banks', land they are keeping for future development. Assuredly council development of vacant land could and should be speeded up, as many councils are themselves only too aware.[32] They do however have to contend with the uncertain needs of other statutory bodies[33] and changes in demand, as well as with the pressures of budgetary control.

Then there are the experiments with calling in the private sector on a grand scale such as with the Merseyside council estate where millions were put into an improvement scheme by a building society and a bank, with participation also by the Housing Corporation and a national firm of builders. Though many tenants have already benefited from this particular scheme and many more will undoubtedly do so, here as elsewhere it seems to favour those wishing to buy, or at any rate to debar certain groups of tenants from enjoying its success.[34]

The physical environment

Whether by private or public investment, there is not much room left for new buildings in high-density areas like Bethnal Green without pulling down those already there. There will always be some natural wastage, liable now to increase at an alarming rate. The present deplorable deterioration of buildings is due in part to lack of funding for maintenance and repair but also to serious design and construction faults in the mass-produced housing of the 1960s and 1970s.[35] Scores of these, including those dismal tower blocks, will have to go. Some already have. Yet wholesale demolition and replacement is scarcely feasible. Where are the necessary millions to come from?[36] There would furthermore be a grave risk that haste and untested methods would produce the same kind of disaster as that generated by the post-war boom. Equally important, large-scale clearance, as was seen in those post-war years, carries with it severe social problems. The evidence from this study suggests that Bethnal Green still suffers in its community life from the devastation that occurred there during the years following the earlier studies. So the goal must be to improve existing stock while steadily replacing it with the kinds of homes that people want.

People's tastes and requirements change. Architects and planners have a bad time of it. On the one hand they are accused of ignoring the social needs of their clients and the community at large and on the other of designing their schemes so as to 'secure the social ends which their idealism leads them to desire'.[37] Nor, as critics of a recent experiment in urban villages allege, do their schemes always achieve these social ends,[38] even where the scheme is based on such a widely accepted concept as 'defensible space', which proposes that the fewer the number of people who share a common entrance to their private dwelling the safer it will be.[39]

Then, demographic trends are unpredictable. Who knows how many children per family there will be twenty-five years hence, or what advances in geriatric and life-lengthening medicine will be made? Should homes be designed for one-child, two-child or three-child families, or for communal families? How many sheltered homes should there be? How can durable buildings anticipate these social and demographic changes? What is the influence, for instance, on neighbourliness of public and private space? Bethnal Greeners in the 1950s had no private outside space. Today, still with no private space but with a different kind of public space, they are a lot less neighbourly. The migrants to the new housing estate of Greenleigh in the 1950s also had no private outside space, but they were not particularly friendly. The home-owners of Woodford who, then as now, had their private gardens, surprised Young and Willmott in the 1950s by their friendliness, which if anything has increased in the intervening years. So the connection between the immediate surroundings of the home and the quality of the neighbourhood relationships must be much more complex than a simple correspondence of public ownership with sociability and private ownership with exclusiveness. It is not only that in Bethnal Green of the 1950s front doors opened on streets, or that Woodford, despite its private gardens, is primarily a neighbourhood of streets or that the public open space surrounding the Greenleigh and many present-day estates is so hostile and ill designed. Inner-city streets of the 1980s are very different places from those of the 1950s because people lead different lives. And it is not only the lives of street-dwellers that change. More than one of the sample mothers and fathers recalled a happy childhood spent on one of the less popular sample estates where they had known 'everyone'. But though this space was certainly no more beautiful in the 1950s, cars and pollution have taken their toll. True, if car parks are provided, as was seen on the Woodford estate, they are vandalised. But that is another side to the problem, which I shall come to later.

Going back to what people *want* rather than what observers think may affect their wants or their behaviour, the present trend is for private gardens, and it is not new. High-density *houses* and gardens should eventually replace the blocks of flats. This longing for a garden is recognised by Tower Hamlets planners.[40] People also want safe play areas for children; more grass and trees, less concrete in the communal spaces, greater ease and safety of access for adults, however this may be achieved – through the use of defensible space or some other principle of design. Much of this could be done for relatively little outlay. Parts of the communal space could be fenced off. Even a part of the pavement can be appropriated, as I see has been done on one new Bethnal Green estate. Though the resulting private bits are very small, they meet a need, especially where there are no balconies. I have already mentioned the objections to large-scale clearance, but piecemeal demolition, as indeed is already taking place on one of the sample estates, would provide the initial space without too much disturbance. Most of the demolished flats on this particular estate have been empty for a long time, so the existing numbers of available dwellings would not be affected.

Management

Hand in hand with environmental regeneration must come the much needed and widely demanded improvement in the management of estates. This was mentioned or implied over and over again by the mothers and fathers in this study. It is probably the main and continuing source of failure. Turner has suggested that there are three basic principles of housing which form a 'law of dweller control . . . When people have no control over, nor responsibility for, key decisions, housing becomes a barrier to personal fulfilment and a burden on the economy; deficiencies in your housing are infinitely more tolerable if they are your responsibility; the important thing about housing is not what it *is* but what it *does* in people's lives.'[41] For people living on council estates it is the outside as much as the inside of their homes which makes them feel the lack of such control. It would also promote that sense of responsibility among themselves which is so often lacking in face of large-scale bureaucratic management.

Management problems on big estates – and smaller ones – will differ in kind and scope from area to area, but above all they will differ from those in the past. As the Housing Research Group notes, housing management is not only dealing with 'a wider variety of stock and tenants than ever before', but the stock 'is deteriorating more rapidly, and an increasing minority of council tenants require some form of special response'.[42]

'Intensive management' is what this group prescribes for the worst estates.[43] It draws on the experiences of the DOE Priority Estates Project (PEP)[44] and other experiments in housing management which have helped to make this kind of approach feasible. Additional resources are certainly needed, but there are many lessons still to be learned about their development from the PEP and other schemes which would be applicable to Bethnal Green, Woodford and elsewhere. Decentralised management, what Power calls the 'corner shop' rather than the 'supermarket' approach,[45] and tenant involvement seem to be the crucial elements. But such things depend on confidence. The mothers and fathers of my sample were slow to respond to suggestions about tenant participation and democracy. If their apathy is to be overcome, the more difficult task of building up their own confidence in themselves must first be attempted. Community workers, housing managers, other outsiders who try to bring some autonomy into the lives of those dependent on public services for much of their daily living, must all contend with this problem.

Fellow residents are often a difficulty. One of the central questions facing the managers of council estates is how far, as a matter of ordinary policy, families should be mixed with those whose social behaviour is often intrusive and objectionable by any standards – the vandals, the violent, the creators of noise, nuisance, dirt and mess. Yet it cannot be expected that improved housing conditions would automatically or at once transform all types of anti-social behaviour. Until such time as this malaise is grappled with, people who seem totally resistant to the influence of environmental improvements or changes in management should perhaps be isolated. Anne Power in a private discussion suggested that housing departments should use any 'street properties' they might have for this purpose. Since these properties are likely to be few and far between, such a temporary measure would avoid the risks attendant on concentrating too many dissident and angry people together.

But sometimes grievances seem simply to be due to one set of neighbours considering the others inferior. And in Bethnal Green the 'inferior' for many local families included people from Bangladesh and elsewhere whose behaviour, almost never intrusive, offended merely by the colour of their skin or their different cultural habits.[46] Sometimes, too, when material conditions were bad and proper standards of maintenance neglected, bad relations and cultural differences between neighbours were blamed for a deterioration of administrative origin. John Rex believes that the failure 'to deal with the racial discrimination inherent in our housing and planning policy [produces] ghettoes that will provide the terrain in which all the problems of our society burst out into violence.'[47] He pleads for 'an overall urban policy' and puts great faith in the efficacy of the appointment of 'a senior race relations officer in all the inner city partnerships who would bring a new perspective to all decisions that are being made'.[48]

Bob Brett, a worker in the social field and a local council tenant himself,[49] was understanding when I talked to him about the resistance by tenants on 'good' estates to the entry of groups they considered inferior, for whatever reasons. Brett did not preach tolerance; he offered 'no easy solutions'. His approach was pragmatic. He pointed to the difficulties inherent in creating a *social* organisation, which was how he defined tenants' associations, from a heterogeneous group with different interests and backgrounds. He contrasted an estate made up of such a group with one from an earlier period which might, for instance, have consisted almost exclusively of dockers and their families who had known each other all their lives. But tolerance, he suggested, would come if it could be seen that 'inferior groups' brought with them extra resources to benefit *everybody*. He also equated good human relations with good management. There are good, very good, estates throughout the country. The formula for these has to be rediscovered.

Administration

Good human relations are not only a matter for estate managers. Bureaucracy begins further up. It was very noticeable in the present study that practically none of the concerned attitudes of senior housing officials which I came across had filtered down to the level of young families just embarking on their housing careers. And, despite efforts at public consultation, the same applied to proposals by the planning department for improving the environment, though it is true that at the time most of these had not been implemented.

Going further up the chain, a current example reaching tragic proportions, not only of bureaucratic muddle but also of non-comprehension by the law-makers of how things actually work, is the housing benefit scheme, which has been described as the 'housing nightmare scheme'.[50] Introduced with the intention of simplifying procedures and avowedly making housing assistance fairer, it has achieved the exact opposite. It is unbelievably complex. An endless series of regulations issued since the original Act of 1982 have made it ever more incomprehensible to the officials who must administer it, let alone to the claimants. Hundreds of thousands of people have lost benefit altogether and about three million households will be worse off than they were before.[51] But it is impossible to estimate the numbers who through no fault of their own have suffered hardship, fear and anxiety. Threats of eviction, disconnection of service supplies, seizure of goods, have for some become realities because of impossibly delayed payments. Some of the young families in the present sample would have been vulnerable to such disasters.

Most of all, the failure in communication showed itself in the initial search for a home. The public has become too inured to the infinitely discouraging and humiliating experience of housing by rationing, of waiting lists, queues, 'points' and the like. None of the sample mothers deliberately started a baby in order to get a flat, but equally most would not have got one if they had not. In Bethnal Green, taking GLC and Borough properties together, I was told by a GLC official that there were, at the time of the field work, enough dwellings to match the number of actual and potential households. Why then was there a waiting list of 10,000?[52]

Well, first, by the principal housing officer's own admission, the list was in need of overhaul. It contained at least 2,000 dwellings too many – out-of-date paper entries. Secondly, a proportion of the available properties was classified as 'difficult to let'.[53] Some of these, and for different reasons some others too, stood empty. Thirdly, the figures became much less relevant to first-child families when broken down into the various categories of size. More than one-third, for instance, were bedsitters and over one-quarter were flats with three or more bedrooms. Undoubtedly there should be much more careful matching of these categories of need and what they represent with the available dwellings.[54] And for it to be effective the applicants should be involved from the start, and continuously, rather than being presented with a *fait accompli*. True, applicants do not have to take the first flat they are offered,[55] but sometimes the offers are a pure waste of time. All in all, the whole process could be more effective and a lot less painful. Most of the special lists and ballots (for engaged couples, for example) have been discontinued. Why? And surely there could be more imaginative use of temporary accommodation, though not if its temporary nature is then conveniently forgotten.

Of course, if properties are improved, opportunities for transfer to bigger and 'better' flats will be increasingly jeopardised by the right to buy. Also, the better smaller flats, suitable for the families of my sample and their equivalents, may be snapped up by older couples whose children have left home. But at least a possible compensation may be that the purchase of some flats on an estate may help to improve the quality of the environment, though the finances and management of this kind of dual tenure will be formidable. Those young families who cannot afford or do not want to buy, who already hold a council tenancy, and who are satisfied with the size of their present flat, can sit tight and reap the benefit. In areas such as Bethnal Green, because of the present high proportion of council dwellings and because of the economic level of many of its residents, the right to buy does not constitute as great a threat as in areas like Woodford. In Bethnal Green, if resources are made available for real improvement, then it is the tenants and would-be tenants who will most benefit. In Woodford, the direction and the pressures are such that anything left in the way of council housing could well become just that – the left-over, the 'rump', welfare housing, with all the stigma those names suggest. The social segregation they already suffer because of their housing will get worse.

Alternatives

A better range of housing possibilities could be offered to first-child families just starting out on their housing careers if they had a wider choice of affordable tenure. The barrier between private and public ownership can be broken down or at any rate lessened in various ways. Local authorities could provide more schemes such as 'homesteading' or 'equity-sharing'. In the former, home seekers pay a low price, in some cases with a waiver of mortgage interest payments in the early stages, for properties in need of renovation and repair. It appeals more to keen do-it-yourselfers or to those with friends or relatives in the building trade.[56] In the latter, ownership is shared between the local authority, usually on a 50/50 basis, and the individual, who progresses in stages towards full purchase. This process, however, may be checkered, and the difficulties faced by poor non-sharing home-owners are no less difficult ultimately than for those who start out on a sharing basis.

Both these schemes and others like them in the long run are simply ways of shifting the barrier between home-owners and tenants to include on the private ownership side more people who could not otherwise afford to be there. But the greatest hope of really breaking it down is through the subsidised voluntary housing movement – housing associations, tenant co-operatives, co-owner-ship schemes – what the authors of the DOE Lambeth Study describe as 'social ownership'.[57]

A switch in emphasis from collective ownership of one kind (local authority) to another (housing associations) will not affect the crude quantity of the total housing stock. But it may provide the opportunity for increase in the number of homes available for renting. First, councils could divert funds (particularly if, rightly or wrongly, they find themselves forced at any time to underspend) to swell the numbers of housing association properties by relinquishing some of their own. These may be safer with charitable housing associations, for the time being anyway,[58] since an attempt to extend the right to buy to tenants of charitable housing associations was defeated in the House of Lords during the government's previous term of office. Secondly, in relatively small organisations the turnover of properties is easier to administer. They too may have waiting lists, and of course a lot of nominations come from the council, but the process seems to be less disagreeable and the goal often achieved more quickly.

But, most important, such a change in emphasis would improve the individual's freedom of choice and alter the balance of tenant control. Councils have proved not very skilled at managing vast congregations in face of modern individualism, though the ideas of decentralisation outlined above have evoked considerable response. The machine is cumbersome and slow-moving. Housing associations have a good record, as the handful operating in my two study areas show. Their importance everywhere, if only in principle, is now generally recognised. But more than goodwill is needed; there must be greater financial support, not less, as for the 1984/5 programmes is now the case.[59] This means a reduction in rehabilitation and conversion work on already acquired properties and in the provision of various schemes for low-cost housing. But here again things could improve with the injection of private loans.

The branch of the voluntary housing movement which could provide the most rewarding alternative to the two main tenures is that of the co-operatives. These also have been hit by the cuts. There will be no do-it-yourself shared ownership schemes in the current programme. At one time there was a special Co-operative Housing Agency.[60] But that was only a brief moment of encouragement. The Agency has been disbanded and now the Housing Corporation itself directly administers the grants and loans. It reports that 'the Housing Co-operatives continue to develop steadily with 195 now on the Co-operative Register'.[61, 62] This is surely a very small number. Colin Ward, one of the movement's most fervent advocates, is more realistic in his recognition that it

175

has 'dwindled to a trickle'.[63] Moreover, members of co-ownership schemes have succumbed in large numbers to the lure of private ownership.[64]

But the co-operative movement in its various guises is just managing to hold its own and with sufficient encouragement could revive, despite the general mood of individualism. For those who cannot or will not afford private home-ownership, it satisfies the widespread desire for the housing freedoms more than most other possibilities. Of course there are practical difficulties in co-operation, major as well as minor. But so there are, without any ideology to oil the wheels, in the innumerable and fast-growing private ownership schemes of flats in converted houses and purpose-built blocks.

One enthusiastic couple in the Woodford sample were members of a co-ownership scheme. No co-operatives were represented in the Bethnal Green sample. But they exist in the neighbourhood, with optimism and to effect.[65] The movement may be small but its impact in places like Bethnal Green can be considerable, as also in Woodford where there will soon be a desperate need for alternatives to private ownership.

A wider choice of tenure for people with a limited income should help towards a greater freedom of mobility. But there are warning signs here which will probably strengthen rather than weaken the barrier between private ownership and renting. The typical sequence of the 1980s is apparent over the latest threat to the Green Belt. Government intervenes to remove controls; private development is encouraged, and this will include private individuals belonging to the mushrooming self-build groups as well as the major house-building firms; opportunities for those wanting to 'move further out' but who cannot afford to buy shrink further; no compensating funds are forthcoming for housing in the inner city.

Housing is central to inner-city population decline and unrest. All governments in recent years have expressed concern about this development. If for no other reason, inner-city council housing must be made more acceptable. It must recover the quality and attractions it once held. If, against all the odds, this were to happen and by these means were to succeed in keeping the more fortunate – the middle ground of the sample – as well as the vulnerable within it, and drawing new home seekers towards it, there would be a double gain, not least for the families in the first stage of family formation. These are the young, the economically active; and if this last has in the 1980s an empty ring, it also points to the thrust of economic regeneration we need. These young families are the junction of the past with the future.

APPENDIX 1

SAMPLE SELECTION AND RESPONSE

Sample selection

I kept strictly to the boundaries of the Borough of Bethnal Green of the earlier study. For this purpose in Bethnal Green the Community Health Services and Hospital Medical and Nursing Staff in the City and East London Area Health Authority allowed me to use the hospital birth register to identify mothers whose addresses were within the Bethnal Green boundary. In the case of Woodford, with the permission of Redbridge and Waltham Forest Area Health Authority, I obtained from the central register of birth notification those addresses falling within the Wanstead and Woodford areas of the earlier study. After consultation I reckoned that I should need from three to four months to achieve the quota. In the event, this estimate was accurate for Woodford. The first baby of the sample was born on 16 March 1981 and the last on 17 June. The Bethnal Green sample took longer to collect (from 12 March to 3 September) for three reasons. First, it is a smaller area with consequently fewer babies being born. Second, on a reciprocal basis, half-way through, I had to give way to another study with whose population mine was liable to overlap. Because of this I 'lost' nine mothers. Third, it appears to be a less stable population than Woodford's. Nine mothers had either moved out of the area by the time of the main interview (or were untraceable) compared with only four in Woodford. To achieve the quota of fifty in Bethnal Green, therefore, it needed sixty-seven mothers to whom surviving first babies had been born (table 1.2). In Woodford it needed sixty-two. There was no evidence to suggest that any of the mothers who had left the area had been placed in the dreaded bed and breakfast accommodation.

The great majority of the Woodford mothers were interviewed first while they were still in hospital. The main reasons for this were to avoid causing annoyance to the mothers through strangers knocking on doors and to save time for the interviewers, and also to eliminate mothers whose babies might not be well babies. After I had started this way in Bethnal Green, the District Ethics Committee expressed concern that there might be a breach of confidentiality or that mothers might be submitted to pressures at an emotional time of their lives, despite, of course, very great care on the part of the interviewers that this should not be so. So, with permission still to use the hospital birth registers, the remainder of the

178

Appendix 1

Bethnal Green first interviews were held in the mothers' homes shortly after their return from hospital. Where in either study area babies were born at hospitals outside the Area Health Authority district, separate permission to contact the mothers at home was sought.

TABLE 1.1 *Who was interviewed (numbers)*

	Bethnal Green	Wanstead and Woodford	Total (numbers)
Married/living together mothers and			
fathers	28	38	66
mothers only	11	11	22
Single mothers	11	1	12
Total families	50	50	100
Total interviews	79	88	167

TABLE 1.2 *Response rate in the two sample areas*

	Bethnal Green		Woodford	
	(nos)	(%)	(nos)	(%)
Number of refusals at 1st or 2nd interview	7		10	
Not interviewed for other reasons[a]	10		2	
Number interviewed	50	75	50	81
Number of first-child families resident/traceable in sample area at time of 2nd interview from whom quota of 50 obtained	67		62	

[a]These included in Bethnal Green the nine 'other study' eliminations and one mother who had decided to have her child adopted, and in Woodford one mother with a spina bifida baby and one for whom I failed to get permission from the hospital to interview.

Questionnaires

Copies of the questionnaire are available from the Institute of Community Studies at photocopying cost.

179

APPENDIX 2

THE SAMPLE FAMILIES: TABLES AND SUPPLEMENTARY INFORMATION

Referred from Introduction

TABLE 2.1 *Housing tenure of the sample families (numbers)*

	Bethnal Green	Woodford	Total (nos)
Owner occupation	3	35	38
Council tenancy	27	9	36
Living as part of other's household	15	2	17
Other	5[a]	4[b]	9
Total	50	50	100

[a]Two Crown rentals, one private rental, two tied homes. All, except one of the tied homes, unfurnished.
[b]Two housing association rentals, one co-ownership, one local authority hostel accommodation.

Referred from ch. 1, note 16

TABLE 2.2 *Place of birth: mothers and fathers*

(*a*) Bethnal Green sample (numbers)

	Bethnal Green	Other inner East London	Outer London	Other GLC /other UK	Non-UK
Mothers	13	13	4	11	9
Fathers[a]	16	3	1	8	7
Total	29	16	5	19	16

[a]Four not known.

Appendix 2

(b) Woodford sample (numbers)

	Inner East London	Wanstead and Woodford	Other outer East London	Other GLC /other UK	Non-UK
Mothers	9	5	9	21	6
Fathers[a]	12	5	8	16	7
Total	21	10	17	37	13

[a]One not known.

Referred from ch. 1, note 22, and ch. 2.

TABLE 2.3 *Mother's age in the sample areas*

Mother's age	Bethnal Green (nos)	Woodford (nos)	Total (%)
Under 21	23	7	30
21 < 25	11	12	23
25 < 31	11	22	33
31 and over	5	9	14
Total	50	50	100

Referred from ch. 2

TABLE 2.4 *Approximate total net weekly family income according to its main source and marital status*[a, b]

	Main source(s) of income (numbers)				
	Married/living together				
Approx. total weekly income	Joint take-home pay	Father's take-home pay only	Other sources only	Single mothers' other sources	Total
Bethnal Green sample:					
£60 or less	–	2	3	11	16 ⎱ 30
£61 to £80	–	10	4	–	14 ⎰
£81 to £100	–	6	1	–	7
£101 to £120	–	1	1	–	2
£121 to £140	1	2	–	–	3 ⎱ 7
£141 or more	1	3	–	–	4 ⎰
Total[c]	2	24	9	11	46

181

Woodford sample:

£60 or less	–	–	1	1	2} 8
£61 to 80	–	2^d	4	–	6}
£81 to £100	–	5	–	–	5
£101 to £120	–	4	–	–	4
£121 to £140	1	3	–	–	4} 26
£141 or more	9	13	–	–	22}
Total^c	10	27	5	1	43

[a]Current at the time of the interview, not counting savings but including housing subsidies; all amounts include weekly child benefit, except where it has been deducted from supplementary benefit payments.

[b]On the three sources of money income there was information on earnings and on 'transfers' or what are more commonly known as statutory or social benefits. Only very few of our families had capital assets which brought in an income of any size. Such dividends as were mentioned by one or two were so small as not to merit a separate category and have therefore been included in income from the main source. Secondly, during the earlier part of the interviewing a number of mothers had been unable to claim their child benefit because of a strike (the same thing applied in one or two other instances with other benefits). Since there would be back payment for these and for a few instances where application had not yet been made the delay was discounted. Three-quarters of the way through the interviewing the amount per week was raised from £4.75 per child to £5.25. As the income estimates are only approximate it seemed reasonable to iron this difference out and call it £5 for all the families.

[c]Excluding no replies.

[d]In one instance the mother was earning and the father was not.

A χ^2 test of significance was carried out on the family net income differences between the two areas (table 2.4), which were found to be highly significant (P < 1%).

TABLE 2.5 *Family's social class according to father's occupation*[a]

Family's social class by father's occupation		Bethnal Green (nos)	Woodford (nos)	Total (%)
Professional etc.	I	–	7	7
Intermediate	II	5	14	19
Skilled non-manual	IIIN	8	9	17
Skilled manual	IIIM	14	13	27
Partly skilled	IV	16	5	21
Unskilled	V	7	2	9
Total		50	50	100

[a]According to the Registrar-General's six-fold classification.

Appendix 2

TABLE 2.6 *Family's social class according to mother's occupation*[a, b]

Family's social class by mother's occupation		Bethnal Green (nos)	Woodford (nos)	Total (%)
Professional, etc.	I	1	2	3
Intermediate	II	3	16	21
Skilled non-manual	IIIN	19	26	50
Skilled manual	IIIM	4	2	7
Partly skilled	IV	11	1	13
Unskilled	V	4	1	6
Total		42[c]	48[d]	100

[a]According to the Registrar-General's six-fold classification.
[b]According to the mother's present or, if not employed, previous occupation.
[c]Excluding eight mothers who have never worked.
[d]Excluding two mothers who have never worked.

TABLE 2.7 *The two main tenures according to fathers' and mothers' social class (numbers)*

	Service Class		Intermediate Class		Working Class	
	Fathers	Mothers	Fathers	Mothers	Fathers	Mothers
Owner occupation	22	21	15	17	1	–
Council tenancy	2	2	18	17[a]	14	17
Total	24	23	33	34[a]	15	17

[a]Two council tenancies are held by single mothers.

Referred from ch. 4

TABLE 2.8 *Mother's age at marriage and tenure: two-parent families and main tenures only (numbers)*

		Age at marriage	
	Under 21	21 < 25	25 and over
Owner occupiers	6	21	11
Council tenants	19	11	5
Total	25	32	16

A χ^2 test of significance was carried out on the relative ages of mothers at marriage (table 2.8) among owner occupiers and council tenants. The differences were found to be highly significant ($P < 1\%$).

183

TABLE 2.9 *Period between start of marriage[a] and birth of baby according to present tenure: two-parent families in owner occupation and council tenancies only (numbers)*

Period between start of marriage[a] and birth of baby	Owner occupiers	Council tenants	Total
Less than 2 years	4	24	28
2 years < 6 years	23	7	30
6 years or more	11	2	13
Total[b]	38	33	71

[a]Or cohabitation, whichever the longer.
[b]Excluding no replies.

A χ^2 test of significance was carried out on the relative periods between start of marriage and birth of baby (table 2.9) among owner occupiers and council tenants. The differences were found to be highly significant (P < 1%).

TABLE 2.10 *Family planning decisions regarding present baby according to tenure: two-parent families in owner occupation and council tenancies only (numbers)*

Decisions	Owner occupiers	Council tenants
Baby: planned	34	19
not planned	4	15
Total	38	34

Referred from ch. 5

TABLE 2.11 *Regular basic housing costs[a] according to tenure: owner occupiers, council and other tenants only (numbers)*

Total weekly sum	Owner occupiers (mortgage payments, rates, insurance, maintenance and repairs)[b]	Council tenants (rent & rates)	Other tenants (rent & rates)
Under £21	1[c]	6	5
£21 to £30	4	28	–
£31 to £40	4	–	–
£41 to £50	5	–	1
£51 to £60	6	–	–

Appendix 2

£61 to £70	5	–	–
£71 to £80	2	–	–
£81 to £90	5	–	–
Total[d]	32	34	6

[a]Excluding rent and rate rebates which have been added in to income. The water rate is not included but it should be noted that for Bethnal Green council tenants it is not charged additionally.

[b]Under housing expenses, it was found that a number of respondents had been unable to give any figures for repairs and maintenance. The number of failures was greater than the number of responses. But as the weekly repairs and maintenance figures were small compared with the values of the houses, a series of notional figures was constructed as follows:

1 A 'present value' of each house was calculated as purchase price accumulated at compound interest of 5 per cent per annum (i.e. since the year of purchase, a modest estimate of inflation) (cf. Kemeny, *The Myth of Home Ownership*, 1981, p. 23).

2 Each actual repairs and maintenance return was represented as a percentage of the respective 'present value'. This series of percentages, from 0.0031 to 0.0893 was found to be not too badly askew, with median 0.0144, arithmetic mean 0.022, and standard deviation 0.025 per cent.

3 This arithmetic mean was therefore used to complete table 2.11 with 20 notional values each 0.022 per cent of the respective 'present value'. Some council tenants also referred to money paid out for maintenance and decoration – but here a notional sum is more difficult to calculate, partly because of the grant entitlement and partly because of some uncertainty as to the regularity of the sum. Nothing, therefore, is shown on table 2.11 for council tenants on this item.

[c]Including the one outright owner who was paying only rates.

[d]Excluding no replies.

Referred from ch. 6

TABLE 2.12 *Numbers of relatives other than parents living in Bethnal Green: 1950s study*

Marriage sample – 45 couples with 1,891 relatives[a]

	Number of relatives, excluding parents, in Bethnal Green					
	None	1–4	5–9	10–19	20–9	30 and over
Number of couples	4	8	12	9	7	5

[a]Relatives include siblings, siblings' spouses, uncles and aunts, nephews and nieces, and grandparents, but no cousins or more remote kin.

185

Appendix 2

TABLE 2.13 *Numbers of relatives other than parents living in Bethnal Green: present study*

Bethnal Green sample, 78 informants with approximately 1,145 relatives[a]

Number of mothers & fathers	Number of relatives, excluding parents, in Bethnal Green						
	None	1–4	5–9	10–19	20–9	30 and over	Total
Couples	13	7	5	3	1	–	29
Mothers only (no fathers or no information on father's family)	8	8	4	1	–	–	21
Total families	21	15	9	4	1	–	50

[a]Relatives include siblings, uncles, aunts and their spouses and grandparents.

A χ^2 test of significance was carried out on a comparison of the 1950s record of relatives living in Bethnal Green and that in the present study (tables 2.12 and 2.13). There were 90 individuals (45 couples in the earlier sample and 78 (27 couples 21 mothers only) in the present. The differences were found to be highly significant (P < 1%).

Referred from ch. 7

TABLE 2.14 *Mothers' priorities in home seeking according to tenure*

Priorities	Owner occupiers (nos)	Council tenants (nos)	Living as part of other's household (nos)	Other tenures (nos)	Total (%)
To own one's home	21	5	–	1	30
To have a (larger) house	11	11	2	1	28
The neighbourhood – home can be owned or rented	9	9	1	2	23
To have a home of one's own/to get away from parental home	–	7	9	2	12

Somewhere to live is all that matters, home can be owned or rented	3	6	–	2	12
Other, including a self-contained (council) flat, or garden, to be near mother/family	–	4	2	1	8
Total informants[a, b]	37	32	13	8	90

[a]Excluding no replies.
[b]Multiple replies: total no. 90 = 100.

TABLE 2.15 *Whether or not home is of their choice according to tenure: mothers and fathers (numbers)*

Home of their choice	Owner occupiers		Council tenants		Other tenants	Living in others' household & other
Yes	19		6		4	–
Yes, for the time being	22	76%	4	18%	–	1
Was, but no longer	7		–		2	–
No	15	24%	47	82%	5	24
Total[a]	63		57		11	25

[a]Excluding no replies.

A χ^2 test of significance was carried out on the yeses and noes of mothers to the home of their choice question among the three groups of owner occupiers, council tenants and others. The above findings (table 2.15) were found to be highly significant (P < 1%).

187

APPENDIX 3

SUPPLEMENTARY INFORMATION TO CHAPTER 6

Contentment/dissatisfaction; vulnerability/security

My choice of variables to denote a continuation of circumstances from vulnerable to secure and of attitudes from dissatisfied to satisfied was to some extent arbitrary. I wished to avoid too much complexity for such a small sample and then it was necessary to maximise the chances of completed replies. I finally chose for circumstances: marital status; employment status; net income level; savings; family financial support; health and, as indicators of home conditions, overcrowding and the possession of a telephone. For attitudes I chose answers to questions concerned with the following: home of choice; possession of things thought necessary for a good life; incidence of problems; comparison of problems; perceptions of need; views on accommodation; views on immediate surroundings. All of these were allotted scores of from 0 to 3. The minimum and maximum numbers possible for circumstances were 0 to 26 respectively; and for attitudes 0 to 15 respectively. In the event the lowest scores on the circumstances scale was three and the highest 26, and the lowest and highest attitude scores were two and 13 respectively. The two sets of results were then plotted on a chart.

There were complete replies for 70 mothers (37 in Bethnal Green and 33 in Woodford, 70 per cent of the total sample of mothers); 45 fathers (20 in Bethnal Green and 25 in Woodford, 51 per cent of the total sample of fathers).

Material support from the family

Such support can, of course, take many forms. There can be gifts or loans of substantial sums for a special purpose – towards the purchase of a house, as already discussed, or for a car, or there can be small or greater sums given or lent to help meet regular commitments or unexpected demands. The help can also be in kind – furniture, baby equipment and so on or the sort of support received by the families living with their parents (most of the single mothers) at less than cost. And, in fact, of the single mothers only three said they had received a money gift. Of the two-

188

parent families, just one-half had received, according to the mothers, some kind of tangible cash help from their own or their husband's family. A small proportion of these had also had loans from others but mainly in the form of a bank loan. A further fifteen had received loans only from outside the family. I have not included the mortgage loan. So there is quite a substantial minority (one-third) of all the families who said they were and had been independent of all financial support either from their families or outside. When those who had received no family help were asked if they would, if necessary, be willing to go to them for money either as a gift or loan, nearly twice as many said they would as would not, though sometimes only 'at a pinch'. This group of non-recipients covered the full income range and their refusal of help or unwillingness seemed mainly to be matter of independence.

NOTES AND REFERENCES

Introduction

1 I use the same definition for 'East End' as my predecessors, i.e. what were then the boroughs of Stepney, Poplar, Bethnal Green, Hackney and Shoreditch. The present-day London Borough of Hackney now incorporates Shoreditch; Stepney, Poplar and Bethnal Green are now included in the present London Borough of Tower Hamlets.

2 Peter Willmott and Michael Young, *Family and Class in a London Suburb*, Routledge & Kegan Paul, 1960, and the New English Library after, p. 7.

3 Michael Young and Peter Willmott, *Family and Kinship in East London*, Routledge & Kegan Paul, 1957, and Penguin Books after.

4 Willmott and Young, 1960, op. cit., p. 111.

5 Ibid., p. 7.

6 Ibid.

7 Ibid., p. 114.

8 Louis Wirth, 'Urbanism as a Way of Life', *American Journal of Sociology*, vol. 44, July 1938, quoted in Herbert Gans, 'Urbanism and Suburbanism as Ways of Life', *Readings in Urban Sociology*, ed. R. E. Pahl, Pergamon Press, 1968, p. 95.

9 For an exception see David C. Thorns, *Suburbia*, MacGibbon & Kee, 1972.

10 Lewis Mumford, *The City in History*, Secker & Warburg, 1961, p. 486.

11 Ibid.

12 Ibid., p. 494.

13 Paul Oliver, Ian Davis and Ian Bentley, *Dunroamin: the Suburban Semi and its Enemies*, Barrie & Jackson, 1981.

14 David Popenoe, 'Urban Sprawl: Some Neglected Social Considerations', *Sociology and Social Research*, vol. 63, no. 2, January 1974, p. 262.

15 Michael Young and Peter Willmott, *The Symmetrical Family*, Routledge & Kegan Paul, 1973, and Penguin Books after, p. 38.

16 Ibid., p. 41.

17 Ibid., p. 42.

18 Young and Willmott, 1957, op. cit., p. 11.

Notes and References

19 See e.g. W. V. Hole and M. T. Pountney, *Trends in Population, Housing and Occupancy Rates, 1861–1961*, HMSO, 1971; David C. Thorns, *The Role of the Family Life Cycle in Residential Mobility*, Working Paper 69, Centre for Urban and Regional Studies (CURS), University of Birmingham, 1980; Judy and Geoff Payne, 'Housing Pathways and Stratification: a Study of Life Chances in the Housing Market', *Journal of Social Policy*, vol. 6, no. 2, 1979; Bernard Ineichen, 'Housing Factors in the Timing of Weddings and First Pregnancies', from *Sociology of the Family: New Directions for Britain*, Sociological Review Monograph, 28, 1979; Janet Madge and Colin Brown, *First Homes: a Survey of the Housing Circumstances of Young Married Couples*, Policy Studies Institute, 1981.

20 Herbert J. Gans, 'Urbanism and Suburbanism as Ways of Life', *Readings in Urban Sociology*, ed. R. E. Pahl, Pergamon Press, 1968, p. 111.

21 David Donnison, *The Government of Housing*, Penguin, 1967, pp. 216–17.

22 Department of the Environment (DOE), *Fair Deal for Housing*, Cmnd 4728, HMSO, 1971, p. 4.

23 Douglas Hay, 'Property, Authority and the Criminal Law', *Albion's Fatal Tree*, ed. D. Hay, P. Linebaugh, J. G. Rule, E. P. Thompson and C. Winslow, Penguin Books, 1977, p. 19.

24 George Eliot, *Felix Holt*, 1866, Everyman edition, Dent, 1909, p. 192.

25 DOE, *Housing Policy, Technical Volume*, Part 1, HMSO, 1977, para. I.90.

26 Ibid., para. I.93.

27 Tenure proportions are changing rapidly. Figures from the 1981 Census were as follows: owner occupied: 57.8 per cent; council rented and new town: 28.8 per cent; privately rented and other: 13.4 per cent (Housing and Household Table 21). By June 1983 owner occupation in England had increased to almost 62 per cent (*The Government's Expenditure Plans 1984–85 to 1986–87*, vol. 2, HM Treasury, February 1984, p. 51), with a corresponding decrease in the other two main tenures.

28 See note 27. It is also important to note that the proportions for Greater London differ markedly from those of England and Wales. In 1981 these were: owner occupied: 48.6 per cent; council rented and new town: 30.7 per cent; privately rented and other: 20.7 per cent (County Report for Greater London, Table 20).

29 John Burnett, *A Social History of Housing, 1815–1970*, Methuen, 1978, p. 215.

30 Jim Kemeny, *The Myth of Home Ownership*, Routledge & Kegan Paul, 1981, p. 133.

31 Greater London Council, *A Social Review of Greater London*, Review and Studies Series, no. 3, 1980, p. 82.

32 *Housing Corporation Report, 1982–83*, p. 34, and see ch. 8.

33 Hole and Pountney, 1971, op. cit., p. 36.

34 Nevitt suggests that there are two concepts of housing markets. The first emphasises the tangible, physical nature of the housing stock and the dependence for its supply on economic factors – trade cycles and 'their modern equivalent the credit cycle'. In the second, housing is seen as 'a collection of intangible legal rights which give access to land and the buildings, or parts of buildings, thereon . . . The value of the security of a legal right to occupy a piece of land depends upon the income and wealth of each purchaser and the shortages are caused by unequal distribution of incomes.' Nevitt concludes that 'like so many public and academic controversies, these two views on the causes of housing shortages appear on close examination to be like opposite sides of the same coin' (A. A. Nevitt, 'Issues in Housing', *Issues in Urban Society*, ed. Ross Davis and Peter Hall, Penguin Books, 1978, pp. 183–8).

35 The decline in housing starts in recent years, though there is now an upturn, plus a further increase in the number of households because people are living longer, does in fact mean that there is again an absolute shortage.

36 *The Times*, 24 December 1980.

37 *Guardian*, 16 December 1980.

38 *The Times*, 4 November 1982.

39 *New Society*, vol. 62, nos 1049/50, 23/30 December 1982.

40 There is no up-to-date breakdown of the various categories of one-parent families for the area. National figures for 1979–81 on marital status are as follows (per cent):

married couples	88.1	
lone mothers	10.4	
single		2.2
widowed		1.7
divorced		4.1
separated		2.5
lone fathers	1.5	

(*General Household Survey (GHS) 1981*, HMSO, 1983, Table 2.5.)

41 In a few instances it has been possible to test certain differences for significance. Where this has been done it is indicated with the relevant table.

42 For the distribution see appendix 1, table 1.

43 The Crown Estate is an estate in land administered by a Board of Commissioners. Its origins go back at least to the reign of King Edward the Confessor. It includes a wide variety of land and landed property deriving from a number of different sources. Since 1760 the surplus rents and profits (after deducting management expenses) have at the beginning of each reign been surrendered by the Sovereign to Parliament as part of the arrangements for the provision of a Civil

List. The estate itself remains part of the hereditary possessions of the Sovereign in right of the Crown. It is not government property but neither is it part of the private estate of the reigning monarch. The estate holds a small number of 'fair rents' estates which, according to the Commissioners' public relations officer, follow 'the spirit of the Leasehold Reform Act,' but are not bound by it. They are, however, now bound by Part II of the 1980 Housing Act.

44 General Register Office (GRO), *Census 1961, County Report Essex/ London*, Table 15.

45 OPCS (b), *Census 1981: Small Area Statistics, 100 per cent sample*, by courtesy of GLC Research & Intelligence Unit, Table 13.

46 The figures are a close estimate but not exact, as calculations have been made from ward rather than enumeration district data, and two of the Bethnal Green wards are split with other Tower Hamlet districts.

47 London Borough of Tower Hamlets (LBTH), *Census 1981, Information and Analysis, Preliminary Results*, May 1982.

48 OPCS (b), *Census 1981*, Table 13.

49 GRO, *Census 1961*, Table 15, and OPCS (b), *Census 1981*, Table 13.

Chapter 1 The Neighbourhoods

1 A. J. Robinson and D. H. B. Chesshyre, *The Green: a History of the Heart of Bethnal Green and the Legend of the Blind Beggar*, London Borough of Tower Hamlets, 1978, p. 2.

2 Noorthouk's *History of London, 1773*, quoted in Robinson and Chesshyre, op. cit., p. 4.

3 Robinson and Chesshyre, 1978, op. cit., p. 4.

4 Burnett, 1978, op. cit., p. 87.

5 Robinson and Chesshyre, 1978, op. cit., p. 26.

6 Reginald L. Fowkes, *Woodford then and now*, Battle of Britain Prints International, 1981, p. 6.

7 J. E. Tuffs, *The Story of Wanstead and Woodford*, published by the author.

8 Burnett, 1978, op. cit., p. 101.

9 K. J. Dyos, 'The Making and Unmaking of Slums', *The Victorian Poor*, 4th Conference Report of the Victorian Society, 1966, quoted in Burnett, 1978, op. cit., p. 58.

10 Tuffs, op. cit.

11 Burnett, 1978, op. cit., p. 182.

12 Raphael Samuel, 'The Terror of Brick Lane', *Guardian*, 2 May 1981.

13 Wanstead and Woodford were amalgamated in 1934 and became a municipal borough in 1937.

14 Burnett, 1978, op. cit., p. 185.

15 Willmott and Young, 1960, op. cit., p. 13.

16 See appendix 2, table 2.2 for sample families' birthplace, and chapter 3.

Notes and References

17 Peter Willmott, *The Evolution of a Community*, Routledge & Kegan Paul, 1963, p. vii.
18 Ibid.
19 Young and Willmott, 1957, op. cit., p. 89.
20 R. Glass and M. Frenkel, 'A Profile of Bethnal Green', paper given to the Association for Planning and Reconstruction, 1946, quoted in *Planning in West Bethnal Green*, Planning Department, Directorate of Development, London Borough of Tower Hamlets (LBTH), 1978(a), p. 8.
21 Ibid.
22 See chapter 2 and appendix 2, table 2.3 for age distribution of families.
23 Anne Power, Consultant on the Department of the Environment (DOE), Priority Estates Project, 1982, told me that there are 45 kilometres of corrugated iron in Tower Hamlets.
24 LBTH, 1978(a), op. cit., p. 17.
25 LBTH, *Census 1981 Information and Analysis, Preliminary Results*, May 1982.
26 Concentrations vary throughout the borough. The proportion of Bangladeshi-born inhabitants in Bethnal Green is only about 5 per cent (OPCS (b), *Census 1981*, op. cit., Table 4).
27 LBTH, 1978 (a), op. cit., p. 19.
28 LBTH, *Planning in East Bethnal Green*, Planning Department, Directorate of Development, LBTH, 1978(b), p. 65.
29 Gans, 1968, op. cit., p. 106.
30 OPCS (b), *Census 1981*, Table 1 and see Introduction, n. 44.
31 Ibid.
32 London Borough of Redbridge (LBR), *Redbridge Borough Plan: Housing*, LBR Department of Planning and Development, 1976, p. 10.
33 Willmott and Young, 1960, op. cit., p. 105.
34 Gareth Stedman Jones, *Outcast London*, Clarendon Press, Oxford, 1971, p. 152.
35 Colin Jones, 'Population Decline in Cities', *Urban Deprivation: the Inner City*, ed. Colin Jones, Croom Helm, 1979, p. 212.

Chapter 2 The families

1 OPCS, *Population Trends*, 30, HMSO, winter 1982, p. 7.
2 See appendix 1.
3 Assessment of the babies' health was based partly upon the interviewers' subjective evaluation of their appearance and behaviour (it was very rare for a baby not to be present during at least part of the interview) and partly on the mother's own report. No objective criteria were used.
4 No objective criteria were used to assess the parents' physical and mental health; nor were any detailed questions asked.
5 Only two fathers – both Bethnal Greeners – out of the sixty-six

interviewed, described their physical health as 'not very good'. Mr Sharif was recovering from a major operation and Mr Smith had been hospitalised on leaving school with a severe spinal condition and was unemployed owing to 'long-term disability'. The majority said they had never suffered from any nervous troubles. For none of the very few who had sought medical help had the problem apparently been serious, and none were currently affected.

6 An (unpublished) research project carried out by Stephen Wollkind for the Family Research Unit of the London Hospital Medical College, reported by Joy Melville in *New Society*, 63, 1060, 10 March 1983.

7 National data for 1979 showed that 10 per cent of women of all ages, irrespective of whether they have been married before, were said to be cohabiting. Central Statistical Office (CSO), *Social Trends*, 12, HMSO, 1982, Table 2.9.

8 See Madelaine Simms and Christopher Smith, *Teenage Mothers and their Partners*, Institute for Social Studies in Medical Care, 1983.

9 Housing Services Advisory Group, *The Housing of One-Parent Families*, DOE, 1974, para. 2.16; National Council for One Parent Families (NCOPF), Information Sheet no. 5, December 1982.

10 National data show a marked increase over the last ten years in births outside marriage among the under-twenties (*Social Trends*, 12, op. cit., Table 2.18).

11 See n. 10.

12 This was suggested by both Pauline Crabbe, Vice-Chair of the Brook Advisory Centres, and Dr Judy Greenwood, Senior Registrar at the Royal Edinburgh Hospital, at a seminar on Women and Children outside Marriage held by NCOPF, on 20 May 1983.

13 See e.g. Lindsay Mackie, 'My Boyfriend Threw my Pills on the Fire', *Guardian*, 9 June 1982, Pauline Crabbe also referred to this subject (see n. 12).

14 Seven of the single mothers were non-white, all of Caribbean descent, but only two had been born out of this country.

15 Percentages for women with children aged 0–4 (with or without other dependent children) are: 17.1 per cent in Tower Hamlets and 31.4 per cent in Redbridge; 27.2 per cent in Inner London and 29 per cent in Outer London, OPCS (c), *Census 1981, County Report, Greater London*, Part 1, Table 37. Though the actual proportions of mothers back at work are lower in my sample than in the Census figures the relative difference between the areas matches well; more Redbridge than Tower Hamlets mothers are in paid work.

16 See e.g. P. Moss, G. Bollard and R. Foxman, 'Transition to Parenthood Project', Final Report (unpublished) to DHSS, Thomas Coram Research Unit, University of London Institute of Education, 1983.

17 Twenty-six Bethnal Green and thirty-six Woodford mothers had received their maternity allowance (though not all for the full period) before and after pregnancy. Most were receiving the flat-rate allow-

ance (£20.65 per week) which was payable for a maximum of 18 weeks, and a very few who had been earning over £6,000 per year also had the earnings related supplement.

18 Far fewer than others have found. Oakley suggests that at least 40 per cent of her 66 mothers were suffering from the 'monotony' of their routine five weeks after the birth. Ann Oakley, *Becoming a Mother*, Martin Robertson, 1979, p. 253.

19 These were the only two mothers in Woodford who had returned to work a year later. Jill Reagan and her husband had both lost their jobs. In Bethnal Green the total number of 'working mothers' had been increased from two to four.

20 A small proportion of mothers, other than the thirteen already in work, were still technically on maternity leave from the employers they had worked for before having their babies. Three of these were unsure whether or not they would return; the others had decided not to.

21 OPCS (b), *Census 1981*, op. cit., Table 9.

22 For the whole Borough of Tower Hamlets the male unemployment rate was the highest in London – 19.2 per cent – and 11 per cent for women, the second highest (LBTH, May 1982, op. cit.).

23 Only two of the unemployed Bethnal Green fathers and one in Woodford had obtained work a year later, but two others in Bethnal Green and one in Woodford who had been previously employed had lost their jobs by then.

24 The 'poverty line' is usually calculated as below or within 120 or 140 per cent of the current supplementary benefit level. At the time of the interviews, the basic ordinary and long-term rates for a two-parent family with one child under ten were £41.50 and £50.75 respectively.

25 Peter Townsend, *Poverty in the United Kingdom*, Penguin Books, 1979, p. 31.

26 The Royal Commission for the Distribution of Incomes and Wealth (*Report* no. 5, HMSO, 1977), describes income as a 'flow . . . composed of various components' as distinct from wealth, which is a 'stock representing the capitalised value of resource claims at a given point of time.' There are, they suggest, two forms of income – money income and income in kind. Income in kind, which consists of three parts, 'fringe benefits and work on own account, imported rents and welfare and medical benefits', was beyond the scope of my questions except in so far as a little of 'fringe benefits' appears in the answers to certain questions – use of a company car, for example – but as these benefits tend to increase with size of income, there were probably not a great many among our families.

27 See e.g. Jan Pahl, 'Patterns of Money Management within Marriage' *Journal of Social Policy*, vol. 9, no. 3, 1980, p. 317. She quotes evidence from Michael Young, 'Distribution of Income within the Family', *British Journal of Sociology*, 3, 1952; Geoffrey Gorer, *Sex and Marriage in England Today*, Nelson, 1971; A. Hunt, J. Fox and

Notes and References

M. Morgan, *Families and their Needs with Particular Reference to One-Parent Families*, HMSO, 1973.

28 Young and Willmott, 1973, op. cit., p. 82.
29 In a recent study Jan Pahl found that 'most wives these days are aware of how much their husbands earn, though in many cases their knowledge was approximate rather than exact' (expressed in a private communication; the study is awaiting publication by Macmillan).
30 Pahl, 1980 (op. cit.), draws inferences of regional differences from the Hunt *et al.* (op. cit.) findings, pp. 317, 318.
31 There is a third difficulty in conveying a sufficiently full picture of family finances, and that is that how much you 'can afford' depends not only on how much money you have coming in and on the priorities you set or which are set for you by the standards of your group (the relative principle) but also on the flow of money within households, which in turn has everything, as Pahl (op. cit.) suggests, to do with its control and management. There may have been awareness of amounts but control and management may still have been one-sided. This last complexity has unfortunately been denied a place in this investigation for want of interview time.
32 The field work was carried out before the introduction in 1982 of the unified Housing Benefit whereby rent is paid direct to the Housing Department by the DHSS.
33 The median net weekly income can only be approximate, since informants were asked whether their income fell into one of fifteen categories rising by £10 from 'under £20' to 'over £150'. Any sum below £20 was known; anything above £150 was taken as £160 (probably an underestimate); for those categories in between I took the mid-point.
34 See n. 33.
35 Willmott and Young, 1960, op. cit., p. 22.
36 Ibid., p. 22.
37 Young and Willmott, 1957, op. cit., p. 93.
38 OPCS (b), *Census 1981*, op. cit., (10 per cent sample), Table 52.
39 John H. Goldthorpe, *Social Mobility and Class Structure in Modern Britain*, Clarendon Press, Oxford, 1980.
40 The correlation between social class and school attainment level is reasonably predictable: 21, for instance, out of the 22 mothers in the Service Class took A levels; only 1, as far as I know, of the 17 in the Working Class did so. The majority of those in the Intermediate Class stayed on at school, but only one-quarter of these reached A level or beyond. It is the same with income. The highest and the lowest groups were associated more often with the two other classes; the two 'middles' correspond most often. All these differences of course overlap. Thus the social class and neighbourhood disparity between educational standards was also reflected in the distribution of the families between the two main tenures of the sample – council tenancy and owner occupation. Of the total mothers and fathers among council tenants (63) for whom there was information, well over one-half left school as soon as possible without CSEs, O levels or the equivalent,

197

and nearly three-quarters had had no further education or training. Among the 69 mothers and fathers in owner occupation, fewer than one in eight had left school as early as possible with no CSEs or O levels and only just over one-quarter had had no further education.

41　J. Lopreato and L. E. Hazelrigg, *Class, Conflict & Mobility*, Chandler, 1972.

42　Willmott and Young, 1960, op. cit., p. 101.

43　Where people graded themselves as middle class or working class there was in each case a small proportion who qualified their statement. A few either did not know or did not 'believe in all that'.

44　See e.g. Willmott, 1963, op. cit., p. 102; and Townsend, 1979, op. cit., p. 379.

45　Willmott and Young, op. cit.

46　Townsend, 1979, op. cit., pp. 371–412.

47　Ibid., p. 411.

48　See chapter 3.

Chapter 3 Housing history

1　See Madge and Brown, 1981, op. cit.

2　Ibid.

3　Payne and Payne, 1979, op. cit. The Paynes originated the idea of 'tenure pathways'. I do not however use their sample for comparison with mine since their pathways started from and proceeded to different points in the family cycle.

4　Madge and Brown, 1981, op. cit., p. 11.

5　Ibid.

6　Ibid.

7　Young and Willmott, 1957, op. cit., p. 31.

8　Ibid.

9　Two-thirds of the 1957 marriage sample of 45 couples had both themselves been born in the locality (in Bethnal Green or an adjacent borough) and had married spouses within it (Young and Willmott, 1957, op. cit., p. 104).

10　'Regulated tenancy' was introduced under the 1965 Rent Act. It applied to most privately rented unfurnished properties.

11　Full Rent Act protection is in principle enjoyed by tenants of non-resident landlords. Tenants of resident landlords have the 'limited protection under the Rent Acts' of being able to apply to the Rent Tribunal for suspension of a notice to quit and the fixing of a reasonable rent' (Stewart Lansley, *Housing and Public Policy*, Croom Helm, 1979, p. 184).

12　Steve Schifferes and Roger Mathews, *Shelter's Annual Waiting List Survey, 1976–1980*, Shelter, 1980.

13　For registration with the Tower Hamlets housing department, for instance, three preliminary qualifications were necessary: You must already live in Tower Hamlets; you or your partner must have lived for the last year within Tower Hamlets; you must continue to live in Tower Hamlets while you are on the list. Points at the time were allocated as follows:

For each additional room required (i.e. bedroom, living-room or kitchen)	20
For each additional room in excess of requirements	20
Separation of sexes	
(a) Where two unmarried persons of the opposite sex, the youngest being over three years, have to share a bedroom	25
(b) For every child having to share a bedroom with parents	20
Shared accommodation and facilities:	
Living	10
Kitchen	10
Water supply (if not in shared kitchen)	4
WC	4
Bath	3
Lack of facilities:	
No bath	10
No cooker	6
Badly situated facilities:	
Cooker on landing, etc.	3
Water supply on landing, etc.	3
WC outside the dwelling	6

14 Young and Willmott, 1957, op. cit., pp. 41, 42.
15 David Donnison, *The Politics of Poverty*, Martin Robertson, 1982.
16 Young and Willmott, 1973, op. cit., ch. 1.
17 In February 1984 the government responded to pressures to make the whole business of house transfer cheaper and more efficient chiefly by their proposal to end the monopoly of solicitors on conveyancing.
18 See Young and Willmott, 1957, op. cit., p. 31.
19 See e.g. Alan Murie, *The Sale of Council Houses*, CURS, Occasional Paper no. 35, University of Birmingham, 1975, and, more recently, Ray Forrest and Alan Murie, *Right to Buy? Issues of Need & Equity and Polarisation in the sale of Council Houses*, Working Paper 39, School for Advanced Urban Studies, Bristol University, 1984.
20 See Introduction, n. 43.
21 My own sample provides only very limited evidence of these movements and shifts, apart from the striking confirmation of the known decline in private renting at the Bethnal Green end and the continuing move towards owner occupation at the Woodford end. There is a problem in filling out the picture. Despite a great deal of help from GLC research staff, who made available what material they had and advised in its interpretation, from staff of the two Borough Authorities and the GLC at local level, and diligent searching through their files and through census data I drew a blank on much of the information

Notes and References

I was seeking. Data bases vary; area boundaries have changed; statistics were not collected before a certain date or, on a given subject, have not been collected at all.

It, however, is known that, between 1931 and 1955, nearly 1,000 families containing over 40,000 people were re-housed from Bethnal Green on LCC estates (Young and Willmott, 1957, op. cit., p. 124) but not all these moves were to Essex or other parts of outer East London. Census (unpublished) migration tables for 1960–1 and 1970–1, for instance, show an increase of 1,970 over the ten years in the numbers of people leaving Tower Hamlets for Redbridge, Barking and Waltham Forest. It is known that the inner-city population declined over this period. It is still happening, though at a slower rate. The general pattern of GLC lettings across local authority boundaries seems to be that outward moves fell since the peak reached in 1976, while moves in the other direction were maintained (GLC, *Housing Strategy and Investment Programme, 1982–3*, 1981, p. 50 and Table 3.12). From the last major Bethnal Green clearance scheme under the GLC involving 150 families, which took place between 1971 and 1973, only 9 per cent were rehoused on estates in outer East London boroughs. This compares with 15 per cent from a 1965 scheme. The difference is not great and the proportions are small. But it can be seen as a reflection of the success of the policies of the outer suburban authorities throughout the 1960s and 1970s. While welcoming and actively encouraging as they had always done the immigration of prospective house purchasers, the outer boroughs resisted and actively discouraged that of the less affluent local authority tenant. This is shown clearly by Young and Kramer (K. Young and J. Kramer, *Strategy and Conflict in Metropolitan Housing: Suburbia versus the Greater London Council, 1965–1975*, Heinemann, 1978). Any GLC strategies of resistance failed; there is no grand design.

The big Greater London exodus to the New and Expanding Towns had passed its peak by 1971 as had the clearance schemes theirs. Whether the great outlying estates were built in the 1920s or the 1950s or 1960s, they all shared at their inception a common family age structure. The new tenants were largely couples with young children. Willmott describes how this forces the second generation out (Willmott, 1963, op. cit.). It equally inhibits entry. There are clear indications of a decline in outward migration within the last five years (the years for which near comparable figures are available); it is very possible that something of the kind will have been happening in the years before.

So the general conclusion may be drawn of a slowing up of movement *within the local authority sector* from inner city to outer suburb. See also chapter 7.

Notes and References

Chapter 4 Family building and housing

1 Payne and Payne, 1979, op. cit.
2 Ineichen, 1979, op. cit.
3 Bernard Ineichen, 'The Housing Decisions of Young People', *British Journal of Sociology*, vol. 32, no. 2, 1981.
4 Ann Cartwright, *How Many Children?*, Routledge & Kegan Paul, 1976.
5 A speculation which bears no relation to the sophisticated prediction techniques used by Myra Wolf in her study, *Family Intentions*, OPCS Social Survey Division, HMSO, 1971.
6 *Social Trends*, 30, op. cit., Table 2.17.
7 Cartwright, op. cit., ch. 3.
8 Ibid., p. 120.
9 Though, as I suggest in chapter 8, these days mortgagees may have less security of tenure than council tenants.
10 Cartwright, op. cit., p. 115.
11 Ibid., p. 138. Cartwright was of course discussing all forms of tenure.
12 M. J. Murphy and O. Sullivan, *Housing Tenure and Fertility in Post-war Britain*, Centre for Population Studies, London School of Hygiene and Tropical Medicine, University of London, 1983, Table 2.15.
13 Ibid.
14 See e.g. ibid., pp. 26–9.
15 Fifteen per cent of my total sample had started a second child a year after the main interview or in two instances had already had one. But there was no difference to speak of according to tenure.
16 Using 1977 *General Household Survey* (*GHS*) data, Murphy and Sullivan (1983, op. cit., Table 2.10) have estimated that for owner occupiers (whose first conception was post-marital) the average age of the mothers at marriage was 22.1 years, while for those in local authority and new town tenures it was 21.2 years. The average age at marriage (irrespective of the time of the first conception) of the mothers in the two main tenures was 23.1 and 21.5 years respectively.
17 A. E. Holmans, 'Housing Careers of Recently Married Couples', *Population Trends*, 2c, 1981, p. 13, and Table 3.
18 See e.g. Payne and Payne, 1979, op. cit.; Ineichen, 1979, op. cit.; and Murphy and Sullivan, 1983, op. cit.
19 Murphy and Sullivan, 1983, op. cit., p. 46.
20 See e.g. Cartwright, 1976, op. cit.; Payne and Payne, 1979, op. cit.; Ineichen, 1981, op. cit.
21 Payne and Payne, 1979, op. cit.; Ineichen, 1979, op. cit.; and Ineichen, 1981, op. cit.
22 Ineichen, 1981, op. cit., p. 252.
23 Payne and Payne, 1979, op. cit., p. 150.
24 Holmans (op. cit.) and Madge and Brown (op. cit.) were discussing entry in relation to the baby's arrival (66 per cent and 58 per cent respectively) before entry, whereas the Paynes (op. cit.) were looking

at entry over three stages of pregnancy (but it should be noted that nearly 16 per cent of their sample had at least two children by the time they entered the local authority sector).

25 Ineichen, 1979, op. cit., p. 136.

26 Madge and Brown, 1981, op. cit., p. 113.

27 Payne and Payne, 1979, op. cit., p. 149.

28 Ibid.

29 Ineichen, 1979, op. cit., p. 135.

30 The Bangladeshi mothers were very shy and had had little or no formal education. The interpreter had difficulty in explaining to them the difference between family planning and intentions.

31 Ineichen, 1981, op. cit., p. 256; P. Niner, *Local Authority Housing Policy and Practice: a Case Study Approach*, CURS, Birmingham, 1975.

32 Ineichen, 1979, op. cit., p. 132.

33 Ineichen has strong evidence for the deferment of the wedding date for the same reason (ibid., pp. 130, 131).

34 Ineichen (1981, op. cit., p. 255) found links between unstable childhood backgrounds and council tenancy. He also traced a connection between the tenure of the childhood home or the parents' tenure and present tenure of the sample families as did Madge and Brown (op. cit.). But the latter thought that they did not have enough evidence to enable them 'to describe *the way* in which parents' tenure influences the tenure of their children (ibid., p. 108). The evidence from my sample was inconclusive on both these counts.

35 Murphy and Sullivan (op. cit., p. 69) suggest that despite often small sample size and unavailability or unsuitability of the presentation of much research data, findings have been consistent, though they also emphasise 'the problems involved in identifying and distinguishing the effects of tenure on fertility, of fertility on tenure, and the extent of the inter-dependence of the effects.'

36 The fertility/tenure argument is linked to the theory of choice in housing and models of constraint and choice. In the constraints model, competition for housing is 'mediated by various agencies'. These are 'constrained by and are linked to various aspects of the structure of economic and social power. The relative strength of households in competing for housing is affected by this situation' (Alan Murie, *Process and Change in Housing*, Working Paper no. 43, CURS, University of Birmingham, 1976). Thorns has developed this model to include 'individual dimensions' as well as structural (David C. Thorns, *The Role of the Family Life Cycle in Residential Mobility*, Working Paper no. 69, CURS, University of Birmingham, 1980). It has been suggested that there is also a 'choice' model (Payne and Payne, 1979, op. cit., p. 131), but it seems to me that they are not pure alternatives and that a varying degree of choice may operate within the constraints model, depending on the strength of the constraints.

Notes and References

Chapter 5 The homes

1 In their study, Grey and Henderson found that 70 per cent of dissatisfied tenants gave reasons of a social nature (Alexander Grey and Alan Henderson, *Letting the Difficult-to-let: A Report of a Survey of Tenants Obtaining Instant Lettings from the GLC*, Working Note no. 5, Housing Strategy Office, GLC, 1981, p. 7.

2 Michael Webb, *Architecture in Britain Today*, Hamlyn, for Country Life Books, 1969, p. 81.

3 The proportions of terraced and semi-detached houses generally in Redbridge are 48.6 per cent and 21.3 per cent respectively (DOE, *National Dwelling and Housing Survey (NDHS)*, HMSO, 1977, Table 62B).

4 See e.g. Grey and Henderson (1981, op. cit., p. 5). More of Madge and Brown's (op. cit.) sample families were satisfied than dissatisfied with their accommodation but there is no comparison with the immediate environment (p. 79). High proportions of the NDHS (op. cit.) sample were satisfied with their accommodation (Table 82B) and also with 'area' (Table 83B). But 'no guidance was given to the respondent about what was meant by the area and they were left to interpret this themselves, as, for example, the immediate vicinity, the block or the town (p. 17)'. This, in my view, has distorted the findings on satisfactions.

5 GRO, *Census 1961, England and Wales County Report*, Table 22.

6 OPCS (b), *Census 1981*, Table 10.

7 Burnett, 1978, op. cit., p. 67.

8 Young and Willmott, 1957, op. cit., p. 24.

9 OPCS (b), *Census 1981*, Table 10.

10 Another space standard is known as the 'bedroom standard'. This is used in the *General Household Survey* and also by local authority housing departments. It presumes the following: one room for a married couple; one room for each additional person over 21; one room for two children up to the age of 10 irrespective of gender and up to age 20 if the same gender. A separate room for children of different gender from age 10 to 20.

11 The 'Parker Morris Report' (Ministry of Housing and Local Government, *Homes for Today and Tomorrow*, HMSO, 1961) was an important landmark in the matter of space standards. Their recommendations were made mandatory by the Labour Government towards the end of the decade, though only as maximum standards and only for public sector housing. The present government has relaxed the requirements.

12 Young and Willmott, 1957, op. cit., p. 159.

13 Willmott and Young, 1960, op. cit., p. 33.

14 The government's new right to repair scheme in which tenants are entitled to claim 75 per cent of costs will undermine this common law right.

15 Lansley, 1979, op. cit., p. 86.

16   Information is missing on the actual size of the loan for the Selbys' £5,250 house, though the monthly rate at which they were repaying it is known.
17   See e.g. Lansley, 1979, op. cit., pp. 114–15.
18   I have not included those sample families in shared households in·the discussion of comparative housing costs as their financial arrangements were quite different from those in straight tenancies or of home-owners. Moreover, they differed considerably from each other. Some were paying weekly sums for 'board and lodging' which included the cost of food; for some this also included fuel costs, for others not. Some of the single mothers and one couple, paid no regular sums. The highest regular amount paid was £25 per week, the lowest (by a single girl) £5.

Chapter 6 Ways of life

1   Young and Willmott, 1957, op. cit., p. 143.
2   This proportion of non-car-owners in Bethnal Green corresponds almost exactly with that for Tower Hamlets as a whole. The 1981 Census showed that at 32.6 per cent Tower Hamlets had the lowest percentage of car ownership in Inner London. LBTH, 1982, op. cit.
3   Willmott and Young, 1960, op. cit., p. 13.
4   Nearly half the maternal grandmothers of the present sample babies were still in employment.
5   See chapter 5.
6   The actual number of replies referring to activities in the home were 38 by Bethnal Green and 71 by Woodford mothers; and outside the home were 44 and 48 respectively.
7   See *Social Trends*, 12, HMSO, 1982, chart 10.1, p. 173.
8   Raphael Samuel, 'An Exaggerated Death', *Guardian*, 9 October 1982.
9   Willmott and Young, 1960, op. cit., p. 29.
10   There were no examples of genuine job-sharing or role reversal between husband and wife, with the husband either in part-time employment or none at all. Where husbands were not working, this was because they were unable to get work, and they were not notice-ably more active domestically than their employed counterparts.
11   Ann Oakley, 1979, op. cit., p. 214.
12   They were shown a card which had on it some ideas about how people might think of their home. They were first to say if any of them were what they felt about their present home or if they wanted to add anything. They were then asked to say which was the most important, followed by the next two.
13   Burnett, 1978, op. cit., p. 108.
14   The majority of these mothers and fathers in both groups were talking about the importance of money as a means of improving the quality of life. The remainder were referring to money for basic necessities.

Of these, more reckoned they did not have enough than that they did.

15 Young and Willmott, 1957, op. cit., Table 10, p. 87.
16 Eleven of the present sample Bethnal Green families were without fathers and for a further eleven no information about the fathers' families was available. There is also a slight difference in the composition of the relatives in that I have excluded nephews and nieces (because of the relatively young age of the sample) and included the spouses of the aunts and uncles. It must also be said that the number of relatives is probably underestimated, since, where contact had been lost, the informants were rather vague. Nevertheless, when tested (see appendix 1) the difference between the numbers of relatives in the two samples was found to be highly significant.
17 Willmott and Young, 1960, op. cit., p. 73.
18 Young and Willmott, 1957, op. cit., pp. 157–9.
19 Ibid., p. 60.
20 Bob Brett was secretary of the Tower Hamlets Tenants Association. He was an ex-teacher and had been born and brought up in the locality. He still lived there on a council estate.
21 Reported in the *Sunday Times*, 12 December 1982.
22 Popenoe, 1979, op. cit., p. 264, and see Introduction.

Chapter 7 Housing aspirations

1 These figures are for those moving as a complete single unit, as two or more housing groups, or with just some of the present household members 'intending to move'. *General Household Survey (GHS), 1980*, HMSO, 1982, p. 42.
2 These were the families interviewed between 16 and 20 months after marriage. Madge and Brown, 1981, op. cit., Table 15, p. 97.
3 *GHS*, 1982, op. cit., Table 3.40.
4 The scheme was drawn up by the local authority associations in conjunction with the GLC, the National Federation of Housing Associations and the DOE. It aims to facilitate transfer at two levels – county and national – on a matching basis with, at national level, the addition of a one per cent allocation of lettings (these can include families from non-council accommodation). Ninety-eight per cent of the local authorities and new towns of England and Wales take part and finance the scheme.
5 Greater London Council (GLC), *National Mobility Scheme, Report for Year, 1981–82*, GLC, 1982.
6 See 'The Ins and Outs of Internal Migration', *Roof*, vol. 8, no. 6, November/December 1983.
7 GLC, *Housing Strategy and Investment Programme*, 1981, op. cit., p. 51.
8 Ibid.
9 Ibid.

10 According to a *Guardian* report (27 September 1982) the GLC reacted to accusations of discriminatory policies by changing its allocation rules. A GLC official in conversation denied the basis of the allegation.
11 Paul Harrison, 'How Race Affects Council Housing', *New Society*, vol. 67, no. 1103, 12 January 1984.

Chapter 8 The main issues discussed

1   It could be said that they were no longer behaving as if there were 'a single overriding norm of what society should be like' (Robert Rapoport and Rhona Rapoport, 'British Families in Transition', *Families in Britain*, eds. R. N. Rapoport, M. P. Fogarty, and R. Rapoport, Routledge & Kegan Paul, 1982, p. 476).
2   See Ann Oakley, 'Conventional Families', *Families in Britain*, op. cit., pp. 423–37.
3   It has been suggested that 'in the interaction in the course of history between the family and the social structures of which families are a part . . . in general the dynamic of development originates in the latter. Changes in family constitution respond to processes of social change more readily than they initiate or stimulate them' (Michael Mitterauer and Reinhard Sieder, *The European Family* (English translation), Basil Blackwell, Oxford, 1982, p. 5).
4   Willmott and Young, 1960, op. cit., pp. 101, 102.
5   See chapter 2.
6   The apparent lack of interest among families of the present sample in the status aspect of home ownership was evident also among Murie's Birmingham sample of council house purchasers (Murie, 1975, op. cit., p. 135).
7   W. G. Runciman, *Relative Deprivation and Social Justice*, Routledge & Kegan Paul, 1966, p. 275.
8   Willmott and Young, 1960, op. cit., p. 106.
9   Rex and Moore propose that 'there is a class struggle over the use of houses and that this struggle is the central process of the city as a social unit . . . There will therefore be as many potential housing classes in the city as there are kinds of access to the use of housing' (John Rex and Robert Moore, *Race, Community and Conflict*, Oxford University Press, 1967, pp. 273, 274).
10 Ray Forrest and Alan Murie, 'Residualization and Council Housing: Aspects of the Changing Relations of Housing Tenure', *Journal of Social Policy*, vol. 12, no. 4, October 1983, p. 466.
11 David Walker, 'Now We Shall Pay the Rent for the Council House Poor', *The Times*, 2 February 1983.
12 Ray Forrest and Alan Murie, *Right to Buy? Issues of Need, Equity and Polarisation in the Sale of Council Houses*, Working Paper 39, School for Advanced Urban Studies, University of Bristol, 1984, p. 27.
13 Ibid., p. 29.

Notes and References

14 Ibid., p. 33.
15 Malcolm Harrison, 'The Coming Welfare Corporatism', *New Society*, vol. 67, no. 1110, 1 March 1984.
16 Royal Commission on the Distribution of Income and Wealth, *Report* no. 1, Initial Report of the Standing Conference, HMSO, July 1975.
17 Forrest and Murie, 1983, op. cit., p. 465.
18 Ibid., p. 463.
19 Forrest and Murie, 1984, op. cit., p. 47.
20 Lansley, 1979, op. cit., p. 72.
21 Provided by the 1980 Housing Act. But, also under that Act, there are exceptions.
22 The information was contained in confidential papers prepared for the Building Societies Association (reported in *Guardian*, 20 February 1984).
23 Forrest and Murie, 1984, op. cit., p. 46.
24 A recent survey commissioned by the Building Societies Association found that though 45 per cent of council tenants would prefer to own their own homes, only 18 per cent are interested in buying their rented house (reported in *The Times*, 29 June 1983).
25 Brian Bronterre, 'Big Investment Cuts – and More to Come', *Roof*, vol. 9, no. 1, January/February, 1984.
26 See e.g. Lansley, 1979, op. cit.; Bernard Kilroy, *Home Ownership in the 1980s; Financial and Economic Implications*, extract from 1980 Policy Paper 3, SHAC, 1980; Kemeny, 1981, op. cit.; Henry Aughton, *Housing Finance: a Basic Guide*, Shelter, 1981; *Housing and the Economy; a Priority for Reform*, Shelter, May 1982.
27 Much simplified, the argument runs as follows: council housing, built with borrowed money, is paid for over a term of years by rents. This can happen because rents are index-linked and increase yearly with inflation, whereas amortisation of council borrowing is at an annual rate fixed by the original uninflated cost of the buildings. The balance of advantage to the council increases with inflation year by year, rents overtake repayments, and the cost of new housing is effectively amortised within 40 years or so. Private home ownership, however, is mostly paid for by mortgages from building societies. But these are heavily subsidised by tax reliefs. The resulting huge tax loss is borne by the Exchequer; it is the home owners who keep pace with inflation by the steady increase in the money value of their homes. Thus under the present system, council housing is much more economical to the state than private home ownership. The private home owner gains at the state's expense.
28 Forrest and Murie, 1984, op. cit., p. 62.
29 Nick Fielding, 'Who is Subsidising Whom?' *Roof*, vol. 9, no. 2, March/April, 1984.
30 Fifty-nine per cent of council homes were sold with local authority mortgages in Greater London between 1980 and 1983, and that proportion is likely to increase (Forrest and Murie, 1984, op. cit.).
31 Reported in *New Society*, vol. 56, no. 960, 9 April 1981.

Notes and References

32 See e.g. the consultation planning reports for East/West Bethnal Green (LBTH, 1978(a) and (b)).
33 Education departments, for instance, who may find difficulty in deciding if and when to close a school, thereby releasing land.
34 Anne Grosskurth, 'Selling Off the Slums', *Roof*, vol. 9, no. 2, March/April, 1984.
35 As identified in the report of the Association of Metropolitan Authorities (AMA), *Defects in Housing*, AMA, 1984.
36 It has been estimated that £500,000,000 would be necessary (AMA, ibid.).
37 M. Broady, 'Social Theory and the Planners', *New Society*, vol. 9, no. 229, 16 February 1967.
38 As suggested by Julienne Hanson, 'Out of Touch with Front Doors', *Guardian*, 27 July 1983.
39 The idea was first conceived by Oscar Newman in America.
40 LBTH, 1978 (a) and (b), op. cit.
41 See Colin Ward, 'Using Heseltine's Moratorium; *New Society*, vol. 54, no. 942, 4 December 1980; and see also Colin Ward, *Tenants Take Over*, Architectural Press, 1974; Colin Ward, *Housing*, Freedom Press, 1976; and John F. C. Turner, *Housing by People: Towards Autonomy in Building Environments*, Marion Boyars, 1976.
42 Housing Research Group, *Could Local Authorities Be Better Landlords?*, City University, 1981, p. 35.
43 Ibid., p. 191.
44 See Anne Power, *Priority Estates Project, 1982, Improving Problem Council Estates: a Summary of Aims and Progress*, Department of the Environment, 1982.
45 Ibid.
46 Though there was not much evidence of racial harassment from my study, it does come from elsewhere, see e.g. *Racial Harassment on Local Authority Estates*, a report prepared by the London Race and Housing Forum and published by the Commission for Racial Equality, 1981. Also Barbara Powis of the Community Alliance for Police Accountability contends that racially-based assaults are common in Tower Hamlets (reported in *The Observer*, 4 March 1984). Councillor Ashik Ali, however, said that things were better than they had been and The Community Liaison Officer, Patrick Pridige was much less critical of the police than Powis.
47 John Rex, 'Black Marks for a White Paper', *Guardian*, 15 February, 1984.
48 Ibid.
49 See chapter 6, n. 20.
50 Stuart Weir, 'Housing Nightmare', *New Society*, vol. 67, no. 1105, 26 January 1984.
51 Reported in *The Times*, 18 November 1984. Since this date the government has proposed some alleviating measures.
52 Figure for 1982 supplied by the Principal Housing Officer.

53 In 1982 there were 2,835 dwellings in the London Borough of Tower Hamlets classified as difficult-to-let (GLC, *Housing Strategy and Investment Programme: Analysis of 1982 London Borough and GLC Submissions*, GLC, 1983).

54 In an analysis of tenancy offers, one of the main reasons for refusals was felt to be a mismatch between peoples' preferences and needs and the offers made (Roger Mathews, *Offers of Tenancies in London*, Shelter, December 1982, p. 5).

55 It has been calculated that more than half of all new tenants accept the first offer. In contrast, according to a survey carried out by *Which* in November 1978, the average house buyer looks at about eight properties before buying, following, of course, extensive sifting of agents' lists, etc. (Roger Mathews, op. cit., p. 7).

56 GLC, *Housing Strategy and Investment Programme 1981–83*, GLC, 1983, p. 56.

57 Graeme Shankland, Peter Willmott and David Jordan, 'Inner London Policies for Dispersal and Balance', *Inner Area Studies, Liverpool, Birmingham and Lambeth. Summaries of Consultants' Final Reports*, DOE, HMSO, 1977, p. 45.

58 Tenants of the 'industrial provident' associations already have the right to buy.

59 See 'Housing Diary', *Roof*, vol. 9, no. 2, March/April, 1984.

60 The Co-operative Housing Agency was set up under the aegis of the Housing Corporation following the Report of the Working Party on Housing Co-operatives, 1976.

61 *The Housing Corporation Report, 1982–83*, op. cit., p. 6.

62 These are the so-called par-value co-operatives where the equity is retained by the Corporation.

63 Colin Ward, 'Making the Best of a Bad Job', *New Society*, vol. 60, no. 1021, 10 June, 1982.

64 Information supplied by the Housing Corporation.

65 See Solon Co-operative Housing Services Ltd (SCHS), *Annual Report 1982–83*.

BIBLIOGRAPHICAL INDEX

Note: publications are entered by name of author and date of publication. Where an author has several publications an abbreviated title is also given.

Bibliographical Index

GENERAL INDEX

For Product Safety Concerns and Information please contact our EU
representative GPSR@taylorandfrancis.com
Taylor & Francis Verlag GmbH, Kaufingerstraße 24, 80331 München, Germany

www.ingramcontent.com/pod-product-compliance
Lightning Source LLC
Chambersburg PA
CBHW050427280326
41932CB00013BA/2016

*9 7 8 1 0 3 2 5 4 2 3 8 6 *